ART, LITERATURE AND RELIGION IN EARLY MODERN SUSSEX

T0330609

Art, Literature and Religion in Early Modern Sussex

Culture and Conflict

Edited by

MATTHEW DIMMOCK, ANDREW HADFIELD AND PAUL QUINN
University of Sussex, UK

Routledge
Taylor & Francis Group

LONDON AND NEW YORK

First published 2014 by Ashgate Publishing

2 Park Square, Milton Park, Abingdon, Oxfordshire OX14 4RN
711 Third Avenue, New York, NY 10017

Routledge is an imprint of the Taylor & Francis Group, an informa business

First issued in paperback 2018

British Library Cataloguing in Publication Data
A catalogue record for this book is available from the British Library

The Library of Congress has cataloged the printed edition as follows:
Art, literature and religion in early modern Sussex : culture and conflict / edited by Matthew Dimmock, Andrew Hadfield and Paul Quinn.
      pages cm
  Includes bibliographical references and index.
  ISBN 978-1-4094-5703-9 (hardcover)
  1. Sussex (England)–Intellectual life–16th century.
2. Sussex (England)–Intellectual life–17th century. 3. Reformation–England–Sussex. 4. Art, English–England–Sussex–History. 5. English literature–England–Sussex–History. 6. Religion and culture–England–Sussex–History. I. Dimmock, Matthew. II. Hadfield, Andrew.
  III. Quinn, Paul, 1977-

  DA670.S98A723 2014
  942.2'5055–dc23
                                                                        2014005014

  ISBN 978-1-4094-5703-9 (hbk)
  ISBN 978-1-138-37987-9 (pbk)

Contents

Acknowledgements

It has been a great pleasure working on this volume and many people have helped us over a number of years. The book first began as a series of workshops, discussions and research events at Chichester Cathedral, East Sussex Record Office, Petworth House, University of Chichester, University of Sussex and West Sussex Record Office. The conference out of which the book developed was held in Chichester in 2011, jointly funded by the Universities of Chichester and Sussex and organised by the three editors. We would particularly like to thank Anthony Caine, Brian Cummings, Andy Dixon, Nicholas Frayling, Charlotte Hansen, Margaret Healy, Tom Healy, Barbara Kennedy, Andy Loukes, Graham Mayhew, Alison McCann, Suzannah Monta, Catherine Parsons and Christopher Whittick. We would also like to thank our contributors and Beatrice Beaup, Lianne Sherlock and Pam Bertram at Ashgate for being models of courtesy, professionalism and patience, and for being such a pleasure to work with.

We'd also like to thank Caroline Adams, Karen Coke, Nigel Llewellyn and Daniel Starza Smith for providing the fine images included in their papers. The editors would like to Cambridge University Library for permission to reproduce the map of Sussex on the cover; Daniel Starza Smith would like to thank the British Library and Chichester Cathedral Library for permission to reproduce the images featured in his chapter.

List of Figures

List of Contributors

Caroline Adams has been Senior Archivist at West Sussex Record Office for just under twenty years, specialising in outreach and partnership working. Her work has involved local community projects and archives, and producing a number of publications, including the Local History Mini-Guide series, based on places and topics in West Sussex. In 2012, she completed a doctoral thesis on Elizabeth I's progresses in the south-east and their impact on gentry society at the time. She continues to research sixteenth-century gentry, particularly in Sussex.

Karen Coke is an art historian based in Sussex. A graduate of the University of East Anglia, she has written, lectured and broadcast on Lambert Barnard's work since the 1980s. A member of the Chichester Cathedral Fabric Advisory Committee, she collaborated with the Hamilton Kerr Institute, University of Cambridge on the recent conservation of Barnard's important paintings in the transepts of Chichester Cathedral and is currently completing work on a comprehensive monograph of the painter.

Matthew Dimmock is Professor of Early Modern Studies at the University of Sussex. His work focuses on the field of cultural encounter and amongst other publications he is author of *New Turkes: Dramatizing Islam and the Ottomans in Early Modern England* (2005) and *Mythologies of Muhammad in Early Modern English Culture* (2013), and is the editor of *William Percy's* Mahomet and His Heaven: *A Critical Edition* (2006).

Andrew Foster, FRHistS, FSA, FHA, is an ecclesiastical historian who has written largely about bishops, dioceses, clergy, parishes and cathedrals in the early modern period. He is active in the Historical Association both nationally and locally, is a well-known lecturer in the south of England, and a Literary Director of the Sussex Record Society. He is currently working on several interrelated projects: the dioceses of England and Wales, c. 1540–1700, the papers of Archbishop Richard Neile, and church surveys of the diocese of Chichester for the early seventeenth century. Andrew is an Honorary Senior Research Fellow at the University of Kent.

Andrew Hadfield is Professor of English at the University of Sussex, Visiting Professor at the University of Granada and Vice-Chair of the Society for Renaissance Studies. He is the author of a number of books on the literature and culture of Early Modern England including *Edmund Spenser: A Life* (2012), *Shakespeare and Republicanism* (2005) and *Literature, Travel and Colonial Writing, 1540–1620* (1998). He is also the editor of the *Oxford Handbook to Early Modern Prose, 1500–1640* (2013).

Nigel Llewellyn is Head of Research at the Tate and a member of the AHRC Advisory Board. He is the author of *The Art of Death: Visual Culture in the English Death Ritual, c.1500–1800* (1991) and *Funeral Monuments in Post-Reformation England* (2000) and, with Lucy Gent, the editor of *Renaissance Bodies: The Human Figure in English Culture c.1540–1660* (1990).

Elizabeth McCutcheon is Professor of English, Emerita, at the University of Hawaii, Manoa. A former Guggenheim Fellow, she is the translator and editor of *Sir Nicholas Bacon's Great House* Sententiae (1977), the author of *My Dear Peter: The Ars Poetica and Hermeneutics for More's 'Utopia,'* (1983), the co-editor of two issues of *Moreana* (1994, 2002), and the author of many studies of Thomas More, Erasmus, Margaret More Roper, Renaissance humanism, and rhetoric – including a chapter on More's rhetoric in *The Cambridge Companion to Thomas More* (2011).

Michael Questier is Professor of Early Modern History at Queen Mary, University of London and has interests in, among other things, the local history of the English Reformation. He is the author of *Conversion, Politics and Religion in England, 1580–1625* (1996), *Catholicism and Community in Early Modern England: Politics, Aristocratic Patronage and Religion, c.1550–1640* (2006) and, with Peter Lake, *The Trials of Margaret Clitherow: Persecution, Martyrdom and the Politics of Sanctity in Elizabethan England* (2011).

Paul Quinn is a Post-Doctoral Fellow in the School of English at the University of Sussex. His current research on the culture of Early Modern Sussex will culminate in a major exhibition in 2015. He has taught at the University of Chichester, Birkbeck College and at Oxford and his research interests include staged anti-Catholicism, intra-Protestant debate, and representations of martyrdom in popular texts.

Duncan Salkeld is Reader in Shakespeare Studies at the University of Chichester. He is author of *Madness and Drama in the Age of Shakespeare* (1993), *Shakespeare Among the Courtesans: Prostitution, Literature and Drama 1500–1650* (2012), and numerous chapters and articles on Shakespeare and Renaissance drama. He is assistant editor for the New Variorum edition of *Twelfth Night* and writing a book on *Shakespeare and London* for Oxford University Press.

Daniel Starza Smith is British Academy post-doctoral fellow at Lincoln College, Oxford, having previously lectured at University College London and the University of Reading. He is the author of *John Donne and the Conway Papers* (2014) and co-editor, with Joshua Eckhardt, of *Manuscript Miscellanies in Early Modern England* (2014).

Introduction

Contesting Early Modern Sussex

Matthew Dimmock, Andrew Hadfield and Paul Quinn

Figure I.1   John Speed, *Sussex Described and divided into Rapes with the situation of Chichester cheife citie thereof* (1610), by kind permission of the Syndics of Cambridge University Library.

Sussex is now effectively a home county with impressive links to the rest of the country. It has a significant London commuter population who are in easy reach of the capital by car or rail. There is an international airport, the second largest in the United Kingdom. It contains a substantial city, Brighton, and Hove, the largest seaside resort in England, with a population of some 250,000 people, and the nearest access to the sea for many Londoners – in hot weather, the city almost doubles in size for the day. The same city is also celebrated for its cosmopolitan nature and culture, well-known as the gay capital of Britain and, perhaps a little less plausibly, as its San Francisco. Although Sussex has only one other major city, Chichester, there are a number of large towns: Bognor, Crawley, Eastbourne, Hastings, Bexhill, Lewes and Worthing. The county has a population of 1.6 million and a population density of 425 per km, slightly above the national average of 407 per km. If counted as one unit Sussex contains a larger number of people than its neighbours, Kent, Hampshire and Surrey, and is the fifth most populous county in England. Sussex's relative affluence and its growth in the last century have been based less on heavy industry, which plays a small role in the county, and more on its service and retail industries and proximity to the capital.

In contrast, early modern Sussex was an unwieldy, complicated and often obscure region (see Figure I.1). An uneasy concatenation of residual Roman Catholic and Protestant communities ranging from the orthodox to the extremely radical made governmental and ecclesiastical administration a challenge, with such difficulties further compounded by a long and often remote coastline and a notoriously parlous road network. Very few travelled through Sussex to another region. Sussex was close to the seat of royal power in the realm, but that proximity did not bring wealth or stability. On the contrary, Sussex never gained the riches and commerce of its neighbours, and its nearness to London made the county a potential beachhead for invading forces and a key location in recusant itineraries. Besides Chichester, Lewes and Rye, there were few towns of any major significance (although the progressive silting up of Rye harbour reduced its prominence from its medieval heyday). Sussex was an anomaly: a southern county with a religious dynamic more in keeping with those of the north, connected to the Continent as much as to the rest of the country, an entity that resisted easy co-option into Elizabeth I's 'little Israel of Englande'.[1]

If only for this reason, Sussex is worth studying now. The county's complicated and tense history in the sixteenth century provides a direct challenge to long-held assumptions that the south-east was largely comfortable with the Reformation and, broadly speaking, Protestant and loyal to the crown, and that rebellion was the product of Catholic resistance in the north and south-west.

---

[1]   John Norden, *A Chorographicall discription of the severall Shires and Islands of Middlesex, Essex, Surrey, Sussex, Hamshire, Weighte, Garnesey, & Jersey, performed by the traveyle and viewe of John Norden* (1595) sig. E.1r [BL Add. MS31853]. This copy is incomplete, and the map of Sussex as well as part of the accompanying description of the county is lost. There is a later copy extant in the Northamptonshire Public Record Office, probably made for Sir Christopher Hatton, and catalogued as Finch-Hatton MS. 113. Norden's map of Sussex was printed on loose sheets without commentary in 1595 (only one copy remains extant, now in the library of the Royal Geographical Society).

Recent research has placed far greater emphasis on local and regional factors in understanding the complex progress of the Reformation, so that Sussex now seems a particularly interesting case of a county in which religious change is not only related to a host of other issues – social, political and personal – but is only resolved after generations of anxiety, friction and conflict.[2] As elsewhere in the country, the Elizabethan Religious Settlement spawned a variety of winners and losers, as recent work on Sussex has begun to demonstrate.[3] For every eulogy of Sussex's devotion to the crown, there was a complaint of its persistent unruliness and resistance to proper government.[4]

Even in its shape, Sussex proved awkward. Christopher Saxton's 1575 map of the county – the first substantial and detailed one of its kind – avoided the problem by combining Kent, Surrey and Middlesex with Sussex.[5] The county was then somewhat deformed in order to fit onto one of William Bowes' playing cards (1590) featuring England's counties and based on Saxton's *Anglia* (1579).[6] When Sussex came to be mapped as part of what became John Norden's *A Chorographicall discription of the severall Shires and Islands of Middlesex, Essex, Surrey, Sussex, Hamshire, Weighte, Garnesey, & Jersey, performed by the traveyle and viewe of John Norden* (1595), a volume presented to Elizabeth I, Norden had to adapt his cartographic skills in innovative ways to fit the county to the page.[7] The pronounced tapering of the coastline from Rye, Oxney and Camber in the north-east down to the Selsey Peninsula in the south-west meant that a large proportion of the page was blank sea – a space Norden filled with allegorical

---

[2]   John M. Adrian, *Local Negotiations of English Nationhood, 1570–1680* (Basingstoke: Palgrave, 2011).

[3]   Michael Questier, *Catholicism and Community in Early Modern England: politics, aristocratic patronage and religion, c.1550–1640* (Cambridge: Cambridge University Press, 2006); Graham Mayhew, *The Monks of St Pancras Lewes Priory, England's Premier Cluniac Monastery and its Dependencies 1076–1537* (Lewes: Lewes History Press, 2013); Anthony Copley, *A Fig for Fortune* (1596), ed. Susannah Breitz Montana (Manchester: Manchester University Press, forthcoming).

[4]   R. Manning, *Religion and Society in Early Modern Sussex* (Leicester: Leicester University Press, 1969), *passim*.

[5]   For more on Saxton's mapping of Sussex, his sources and his influence, see David Kingsley, *Printed Maps of Sussex, 1575–1900* (Lewes: Sussex Record Society vol. 72, 1982), pp. 3–11.

[6]   Kingsley, *Printed Maps*, pp. 12–13 – Sussex was the tenth card of the 'South' suit. Bowes' set of playing cards was reissued around 1605, and Sussex became the 10 of Spades.

[7]   See Frank Kitchen, 'John Norden (c.1547–1625): Estate Surveyor, Topographer, County Mapmaker and Devotional Writer', *Imago Mundi* 49 (1997): 43–59, and Kitchen's doctoral thesis, 'Cosmo-choro-polygrapher: an analytical account of the life and work of John Norden 1547?–1625' (Unpublished doctoral thesis, University of Sussex, 1992).

figures and an inset map of Chichester, the county's cathedral city, the first time
this had been done on any such map.[8]

This same inset device would be adopted and augmented in the most famous
and influential of the early maps of Sussex, John Speed's *Sussex Described and
divided into Rapes with the situation of Chichester cheife citie thereof* (1610) –
Figure I.1.[9] Speed's attempt to accommodate Sussex's ungainly elongation retains
Norden's inset map of Chichester, but moves it to the upper left of the page. The
rest of the space he fills with pageant and incident. Alongside the giant breaching
fish of cartographic convention, Speed fills 'The British Sea' with warships
and erupting cannon – presumably a reference to England's great victory over
the Spanish Armada of 1588, which skirmished along these coasts – and an
elaborate heraldic device featuring the arms of Earls of Arundel and Sussex from
the twelfth to the sixteenth centuries. To the east, we can watch as the army of
William 'the Bastard, Duke of Normandy' disembarks from his tightly packed
fleet to beach at Pevensey Haven. The epochal significance of this moment for
any history of Sussex and for the realm is emphasised in the cartouche in the
bottom right corner noting the details of the invasion and subsequent conquest,
with particular attention paid to the battle determining the future of the English
crown between William and Harold that took place on 'the 14. of October ...
beyng Satterdaye, nere Hastings' in 'ye yere of Christs incarnation 1066'. Speed
notes further that

> ...the place where they fought, ever since doth in memory thereof beare the name of
> *Battayll*, where the Heptarchie of the Saxons was Brought to ye last period. Having all
> their lawes altered, their Nobles displaced, and all men disherited: all seased into the
> Normands hande, whoe made him selfe Lorde of all.

As if to reinforce the inscription of this history into the landscape of Sussex, on
the north-east fringe of the map, the battle itself is played out, close by the town
named in its honour.

The marginal elements of Speed's map combine to celebrate a county with
an illustrious history that is a model of civic and ecclesiastical order, affirmed by
the prominence of Chichester Cathedral in the top left inset and by the royal
coat of arms benignly presiding from the top right. The map itself would seem
to complete this vision of provincial hierarchy and allegiance, with the careful
delineation of its fenced parks and forests, and its easy division into Norman

[8]   Kingsley, *Printed Maps*, p. 14.
[9]   Speed's map is discussed in detail in ibid., pp. 20–24.

rapes rather than a clutter of hundreds and parishes (as with much of the detail, this followed Norden).[10] Sussex's beacons, mills and towns, as well as its ruins, are detailed, while its famously troublesome roads are absent (again following Norden), overlooked in favour of a highly detailed rendering of its coastline and extensive river network, an indication of how important water was for the county and for its cartographers. Here is Sussex described and defined, wrestled by Speed, and before him Norden, into an acceptable shape for royal and public scrutiny.

As the chapters in this volume eloquently demonstrate, Sussex rarely conformed to the idealised harmony of Speed's map. Approached from a different angle, the map yields clues to that persistent unwieldiness. The discharging ships and invading fleet suggest the Armada and the Norman Conquest, but also hint at the county's suspect allegiances and its leakiness as a conduit for contraband, for recusants, and – potentially at least – for foreign armies. Sussex was vulnerable in this regard: in his accompanying description of Sussex, John Norden had noted the French destruction of Rye in 1377 and of Brighthelmstone in 1514 and 1545 (as well as Jack Cade's capture at Heathfield by Alexander Iden, later the sheriff of Kent, an incident most famously recounted in Shakespeare's *Henry VI, Part II*).[11] The lack of any reference on the map to the High Weald, an area of sandstone and clay dominated by ancient forests that ran from Kent across the north of the county into Hampshire, is also revealing. Over centuries, the Weald had gained a reputation for being beyond state and church control, providing a haven for Lollard and early Protestant congregations, and it was the cradle of Sussex's important iron industry, work that employed a high proportion of skilled migrant labour and which led to the rapid destruction of the county's forests to feed the blast furnaces.[12] Just as the jurisdictional complexities of the county are neatly contained in Norman rapes, the erasure of the Weald helps tidy up a county that in its variety and contradictory adherences ran contrary to Norden and Speed's cartographic aims.

A close consideration of the heraldic device that runs along the bottom of the map further confirms Sussex's problematic status. A depiction of 'the arms of such Nobles as have been dignified with the title of Earles since the conquest', it

[10]   Ibid., pp. 14–15.

[11]   John H. Farrant, 'John Norden's "Description of Sussex" 1595', *Sussex Archaeological Collections* 116 (1978): 269–75, p. 274.

[12]   J.S. Hodgkinson, *The Wealden Iron Industry* (Stroud: The History Press, 2009), and Brian Awty and Christopher Whittick (with Pam Combes), 'The Lordship of Canterbury, iron-founding at Buxted, and the continental antecedents of cannon-founding in the Weald', *Sussex Archaeological Collections* 140 (2002): 71–81.

juggles lineages, moving from William d'Aubigny (d. 1176) and the first creation of the Earldom of Arundel to John Fitzalan (1224–67), but then misses out Richard Fitzalan (1267–1302) the first of the second creation of the Earldom. The third creation is accurately represented by Philip Howard (1557–95), whose Roman Catholicism led to long imprisonment and the forfeiture of his title in 1589, and the list is concluded by Robert Radcliffe (1482/3–1542), the first Earl of Sussex of the second creation of that title. The first Earls of Sussex, John de Warenne and his son of the same name (together 1231–1347) are overlooked. Although it gives the appearance of a tableau that celebrates aristocratic order and allegiance, the detail reveals muddled histories, absences and elisions, with a famously traitorous earl at its centre.

Speed's map was the dominant representation of Sussex in print until the newly detailed survey provided by Richard Bugden in 1723. Speed had presented a post-Reformation vision of a loyal and God-fearing county of churchgoers that glossed over the complex religious settlement of the late sixteenth and early seventeenth centuries, as the detail of the aristocratic cartouche suggests. The incomplete nature of the Reformation in Sussex was compounded by the dominance of local politics by a small group of Roman Catholic families whose prominence in county politics continued until the 1580s; the effective end of the 'reign' of the 'five families' – headed by the Earl of Arundel and Lords Lumley, Montague, De La Warr and Buckhurst – was heralded by the exclusion of Anthony Browne, Lord Montague, from the Lieutenancy of Sussex in 1585.[13] With Browne sidelined, Thomas Sackville, Lord Buckhurst, shared the joint lieutenancy of Surrey and Sussex with Howard of Effingham from 1586.[14] This signals the terminal point for the Catholic nobility in Sussex in terms of their political domination, with their replacement by the Protestant/conformist Buckhurst. Up until this point, the Catholic families' security was relatively certain, even to the extent that they defied – and ultimately defeated – the vigorous attempts to reform them and the western half of the county by Edmund Curteys, the controversial Bishop of Chichester. The 1577 summons issued by Curteys to Sir Thomas Palmer, Thomas Lewkenor and Richard Ernley requesting that they appear before the consistory court resulted in a complaint to the Privy Council and the probable censure of the Bishop of Chichester who thereafter adopted a 'more humble

---

[13]   Manning, *Religion and Society in Early Modern Sussex*, p. 221; Questier, *Catholicism and Community in Early Modern England*, p. 63.

[14]   Manning, *Religion and Society*, p. 223.

tone', apologising to Palmer that his "'dealynges ha[d] breadd great offence"'.[15] This episode demonstrates two important features of early modern Sussex: on the one hand, the long-established Catholic families were prepared to defend themselves against the activities of a bishop who was determined to evangelise the county; on the other hand, Curteys did not receive support from the Privy Council, showing just how fractious quarrels often were and how complicated allegiances and networks could be.

Roger Manning suggests that Palmer's complaint would almost certainly have been passed to Sir Francis Walsingham and Walter Mildmay 'a pair of Puritans who were not likely to be well-disposed towards a bumbling bishop'.[16] If Manning is correct, then this affair reveals the extent to which English Protestantism was riven with intra-confessional rivalry. Curteys was already aware of this breach, evident in his problems with the cathedral chapter when he was Dean of Chichester in 1567. He found a particular rival in William Overton who may have had designs on the See of Chichester before Curteys was made bishop.[17] Sussex provides evidence of the national situation in which competing factions in English Protestantism sought dominance within the religious and political establishment. This rivalry is also evident in the clash between competing Protestant authorities in Rye.

Rye was probably the most Protestant of all Sussex towns. It gained a reputation as a 'godly commonwealth' well before the end of the reign of Henry VIII and there was strong opposition to the imposition of the mass during Mary I's reign. As a Channel port with a reputation as a bastion of the reformed faith, Rye had always attracted Protestant refugees from the Continent. In the wake of the French Wars of Religion, the resistance of the Low Countries to Spanish rule, and most importantly the St Bartholomew's Day Massacre (24 August 1572), Rye had a significant influx of immigrants who reinforced the Protestant nature of the town. However, shared religious faith did not necessarily make life harmonious. There was considerable conflict between native and foreign churches – as there was elsewhere in England – in both doctrinal and economic matters. At times, such disputes must have seemed more disruptive than the often settled relations between Protestants and Catholics in Sussex.[18]

---

[15] Ibid., p. 89.

[16] Ibid., p. 89.

[17] Ibid., p. 67. Thomas Drant's animus towards Overton may have been partly a result of Overton's relationship with Curteys. See Matthew Dimmock and Andrew Hadfield's chapter on Drant and Copley in this volume.

[18] Graham Mayhew, *Tudor Rye* (Falmer: Sussex Centre for Continuing Education, 1987).

Curteys's defeat in his attempt to investigate Non-conformity may also demonstrate the government's willingness to tolerate recusancy among the Sussex families as long as they remained loyal and politically reliable. What is striking about many of the major Sussex Catholic families was their stated loyalty to the crown, either from conviction or self-interest. Catholics in the early modern period had to decide whether to compromise their beliefs and practise them in secret for their own good and that of their families, or whether to place their trust in the success of opposition, Nonconformity and even open rebellion, as the case of Antony Copley outlined below indicates.

The foremost among the loyal county Catholics was Anthony Browne, Viscount Montague. Montague's removal from the Lieutenancy was not punishment for his own actions, but was rather a sign of a loss of patience with those members of the Sussex gentry who became involved in the Northern Uprising (1569), the Ridolfi Plot (1571) and the Throckmorton Plot (1583). Montague's loss of office was collateral damage, his loyalty was always clear and accepted as such by the government.[19] The Curteys affair and the fallout from over a decade of questionable actions and associations on the part of the Sussex families suggests that the government's principal concern was political stability rather than the expunging of Romanism.

This continuing toleration of Roman Catholic practice can be observed in the reaction to the behaviour of Magdalen, Dowager Lady Montague. On the death of her husband in 1592, Lady Montague withdrew to Battle Abbey, the Brownes' seat in the east of the county (and a key point on Speed's map).[20] Once there, she seems to have provided a focal point for the local Catholic community with the establishment of what was known as 'Little Rome'. The account of the chapel given by the future Bishop Richard Smith – Lady Montague's then chaplain – suggests a continuation of pre-Reformation modes of worship, with 'a sermon preached every single week and on solemn feasts, Mass ... celebrated "with singing and musical instruments" ... with as many as one hundred and twenty people ... attend[ing] Mass'.[21] Although there were reports about the state of religion in Battle, and complaints about the apparent overt practice of Roman Catholicism, there does not appear to have been any moves made to

[19]   Arnold Pritchard, *Catholic Loyalism in Elizabethan England* (Chapel Hill: University of North Carolina Press, 1979), pp. 44–9; Manning, *Religion and Society*, pp. 160–62.

[20]   The fact that the Brownes owned Battle Abbey, former monastic land obtained following the Dissolution, demonstrates how doctrinally 'loyal' Catholics benefited financially, and politically, from the Henrician Reformation.

[21]   Smith, quoted in Manning, *Religion and Society*, p. 159; Questier, *Catholicism and Community*, pp. 209–23.

suppress 'Little Rome'.[22] This tacit acceptance is observable in the obfuscation in the Ecclesiastical Returns of 1603, in which two householders in Catsfield are declared to 'neyther usually resorte to church nor receyve the holy communion and yet not suspected for recusants but they depend on the Lady Viscountesse Montague's protection'.[23] The only logical way to read this entry is that the two householders were known to be recusants but were under the protection of the Brownes. As late as 1603, the protection afforded to the Brownes in matters of religion was still active.

Again, the position of Sussex's religious minority and their interaction with the Protestant State demonstrates how the government negotiated the existence of a sizable Roman Catholic population in the nation as a whole. It appears odd in a southern context in part because of geography, but also because Sussex was the site of the third largest number of burnings during the reign of Mary I. Nevertheless, the case of 'Little Rome' suggests long-standing political loyalty was repaid by a form of toleration. The Catholic Sussex families who suffered imprisonment or financial ruin were, for the most part, those involved in the conspiracies against Elizabeth.[24] The eighth Earl of Northumberland was essentially sent into internal exile in Sussex following the Uprising of 1569. His fall was completed on the discovery of the Throckmorton Plot in 1583. The Throckmorton Plot also saw the personal ruin of William Shelley.[25] Shelley was fortunate to escape with his life. In 1583, Charles Paget was smuggled into England, making landfall at Arundel Haven in September 1583. Paget travelled four miles north to Patching where he stayed for ten days. While there he met Shelley, or his representative, in order to discuss a plan formulated in France which would have seen 5,000 Spanish, German and Italian troops led by the Duke of Guise land on the Sussex coast (again a context hinted at in Speed's map of Sussex) and march to Petworth – where Northumberland lived – and Arundel Castle. A second, larger force would land in Lancashire and to be joined by an uprising of English Catholics.[26] Shelley's and Northumberland's role in the planned invasion of England reveals there was some truth to the suspicions directed against Sussex Catholics. Bishop Curteys may have exaggerated their

---

[22] Manning, *Religion and Society*, pp. 162–5; Questier, *Catholicism and Community*, pp. 207–31.

[23] *Ecclesiastical Returns, 1603*: Catsfield.

[24] Shelley and Gage were both imprisoned after the arrest of Campion: Questier, *Catholicism and Community*, p. 35.

[25] Ibid.

[26] Stephen Alford, *The Watchers: A Secret History of the Reign of Elizabeth I* (London: Allen Lane, 2012), p. 155.

potential for disloyalty,[27] but the actions of Shelley and Northumberland stand in stark contrast to those of Anthony Browne. Lady Browne's actions are perhaps somewhere in between the two positions: politically loyal while doctrinally dissident. The latter was tolerated but it became more dangerous after the legislation passed in 1581. Harbouring priests and 'reconciling' to Rome suddenly became far more dangerous.

Again, the geographical location of Sussex make it the ideal landing site for missionary priests. In Sussex, there was a Catholic community who could harbour such figures on their journey to London. The Sussex families, with their London homes, could continue to provide shelter for the fugitive priests. However, after the increased legislation of the 1580s aimed against the missionary priests, a commitment to the continuing observance of Catholicism rendered those among the Sussex Catholic community who harboured the priests guilty of treason.[28] What is notable is that no member of the Sussex gentry or nobility was charged based on that legislation, or that a large uprising ever took place in Sussex despite a sizeable Catholic population, entrenched and prepared to defy, in a very limited fashion, an attempt to supplant them politically, and to pursue Reform with any kind of zeal. In that, the western half of Sussex appears out of step with much of the country, in the same way that the attempt to impose a Godly magistracy in Rye also appears out of sympathy with the general trends of English Protestantism. West and East Sussex frequently appear to be inversions of each other during the early modern period; the county as a whole is both indicative of the fundamental changes which occurred in England during the period, but it is also an idiosyncratic region which seems to operate in an entirely different fashion to the rest of the State.

Religion and religious division were probably the most significant features of early modern Sussex and, therefore, many of the chapters included in this volume explore the complicated and fascinating nature of confessional allegiance and division in the eastern and western halves of the county. Paul Quinn explores the important case of Richard Woodman, one of the most celebrated martyrs in John Foxe's *Acts and Monuments of the Christian Church* throughout its four editions (1563, 1570, 1576, 1583). Woodman was one of the 'Sussex martyrs' burned in Lewes on 22 June 1557, one of the most significant acts of the Marian

---

[27]   Manning, *Religion and Society*, p. 81.

[28]   Richard Topcliffe identified two main routes through Sussex which necessitated the priests staying in the homes of the Brownes, the Gages, the Copleys and the Shelleys, see ibid., p. 157. Again, the notion of a Catholic conspiracy found in popular texts is not entirely without some merit. The complicating factor is the overt conjunction of the maintaining of pre-Reformation religious practice with treason.

authorities, which has come to define 'Bloody' Mary's reign.[29] In examining the well-known story, Quinn is able to contrast a more complicated and contested reality to the straightforward narrative of nineteenth-century martyrology which celebrated Woodman as an English incarnation of the spirit of Protestant heroism resisting the dark forces of foreign Catholicism. Woodman's reputation is largely in line with the factual record and he was a brave and committed man prepared to die for his faith. However, Quinn demonstrates that not only were the Marian authorities in Sussex rather less bloodthirsty than is generally assumed, and often allowed their opponents to slip the noose when they could, but the other Sussex martyrs were a diverse group of believers, including some whose religion seems to have descended from fifteenth-century Lollard opposition to the late medieval Church.

The chapters by Andrew Foster and Michael Questier can be read together as complementary analyses of the networks of Protestants and Catholics existing side-by-side in the county, and clearly known to each other. Foster shows how Chichester Cathedral functioned like other educational institutions in the period, notably an Oxford or Cambridge college, providing food, shelter and intellectual companionship to a number of scholars of all ages, some staying for a whole career, others just passing through. The cathedral linked country and court and was a major centre of activity in Sussex. Questier's wide-ranging analysis shows how the Church of England also contained a vast network of Catholic clerics, eager to protect and promote their flock and able to do this through the use of the Established Church as a conduit to create what we might see as a 'state within a state', or, 'a church within a church.'

But, of course, religion was not always just religion. Daniel Starza-Smith and Karen Coke, also concentrating on Chichester and its cathedral, provide further evidence of the significance of the institution in the period. Starza-Smith explores the vast library of Henry King (1592–1669), the long-lived, controversial and intellectually brilliant Bishop of Chichester (1642–69). King had what was by any standards a colourful and eventful career. He is best remembered for his moving poem on the death of his wife, 'The Exequy', outlining her virtues and the extent of his loss. King was a close friend of John Donne (one of Donne's books survives with his signature in the library at Chichester) and wrote an elegy after his death (as he also did for Ben Jonson). He had a reputation for being relatively aggressive as a youth but became a pillar of the establishment as he got older, and he was deprived of his bishopric during the Civil War, being reinstated at

---

[29] Most recently, see Eamon Duffy, *Fires of Faith: Catholic England Under Mary Tudor* (New Haven, CT: Yale University Press, 2009).

the Restoration (1660). He was a major collector of books but his library was seized and dispersed in 1643 and what has been recovered in Chichester consists mainly of his theological books; many of the remainder are now lost. Even so, as Starza-Smith points out, it is a major early modern collection even for a bishop (bishops invariably had significant libraries) and tells us a great deal about reading habits in and beyond the county.[30]

King was not the only writer associated with early modern Sussex: the chapter by Dimmock and Hadfield analyses two more important but neglected figures: Thomas Drant, translator of Horace, and Anthony Copley, author of the first (Catholic) literary response to Edmund Spenser's *The Faerie Queene*. Other major figures of Sussex origin include Andrew Boorde (1490–1549), the physician and author, a notably eccentric figure who also had several jest books attributed to him, and John Fletcher (1579–1625), a playwright who was as celebrated as Shakespeare in the seventeenth century and who collaborated with his older contemporary to write *Henry VIII*, *Two Noble Kinsmen* and the lost play, *Cardenio*.

The chapters by Coke and Nigel Llewellyn explore the art produced in the county. Coke's chapter analyses the career and work of Lambert Barnard, who painted the murals in Chichester Cathedral for his patron Bishop Richard Sherbourne during the reign of Henry VIII. Lambert was probably English, but he was a technically accomplished artist who brought a wealth of knowledge of recent developments in European art to his work. Through a series of complicated and elaborately constructed narratives, Lambert paints an allegory of the Church supporting the monarch, but also demonstrating its independence and reminding the king, who came on a progress to Sussex, that he needed the Church too. Lewellyn explores the distinctive funeral art on seventeenth-century funeral monuments in the county, showing how inscriptions – which often expressed coded opposition to the central authorities – gave way to more figurative and visual commemorations of the dead in the second half of the century. Llewellyn shows that Sussex's relative isolation led to a distinctive artistic culture alongside its particular religious identity.

It is important to remember that if Sussex was isolated, it was hardly cut off from wider political currents in England. Not only did Henry VIII eagerly pursue a progress into Sussex, but his daughter, an even more enthusiastic traveller throughout her realm, went on two to the county, one to East Sussex

---

[30]   Another major Sussex library is that of Samuel Jeake of Rye, who also amassed an unusually substantial library in the mid-seventeenth century: Michael Hunter, *A Radical's Books: The Library Catalogue of Samuel Jeake of Rye, 1623–90* (Woodbridge: Boydell & Brewer, 1999).

in 1573 (really an addition to her progress to Kent), and a more significant venture into West Sussex in 1591. Caroline Adams analyses these in her chapter which opens the volume, showing how Elizabeth was relatively uncertain in her first venture, but that she had worked out exactly how she wanted the operation to be run later in her reign. Elizabeth visited the major Catholic families who dominated the west of the county, notably the Brownes at Cowdray and the Lewkenors, further showing that many Catholic families were loyal to the regime, undoubtedly having too much to lose through antagonising the crown. More about the culture of the county, in particular its Catholic culture, is revealed in Elizabeth McCutcheon's chapter on the education of Mary Arundel, the younger daughter of Henry Fitzalan, the twelfth Earl of Arundel. Here we witness the life of a well-educated, extremely intelligent young woman who was encouraged to develop her talents and who was forced to read far less religious and far more secular, classical material than many might have presumed. The study of early modern Sussex reveals as many surprising as expected results.

Chapter 1

Elizabeth I's Progresses into Sussex

Caroline Adams

The year 2012 saw the building of a new Record Office for East Sussex at Falmer, whereas the one for West Sussex has experienced the effects of local government financial constraints.[1] It makes us reflect again how, from a government point of view, Sussex has always been divided into two. Although Sussex was considered a single county and there was one lord lieutenant, one sheriff and one clerk of the peace for the whole of Sussex, the Quarter Sessions were divided into western and eastern divisions, time out of mind. Elizabeth I treated the two halves of the county separately on her visits: west Sussex was involved in the grand progress of 1591, whereas eighteen years earlier, in 1573, some of the east Sussex gentry were visited out of the Kent progress. However, the gentry involved may not have been as focused on county boundaries and communities as we are led to believe from the surviving records,[2] and the people and events on the progresses point to a society which was cross-border in nature. Thus royal progresses shed light on the development of local politics and cultural identity, and also deepen our understanding of the important role of hospitality and the impact of such visits on rural gentry society. For example, Anthony Browne was the owner of Cowdray and host of a week of celebrations on the progress in 1591, so was he typical of the hosts and their connections? How much preparation did the hosts have to make, and what was the practical side of making such a visit work? What of the social hierarchy – who was missed off the invitation list, and why? How much did the progress interrupt a normal summer of such a landowner, and did it really bankrupt a would-be host? This chapter considers these questions in the light of the two Sussex progresses by Elizabeth.

---

[1]   This chapter has arisen out of my PhD thesis 'Queen and County: The Significance of Elizabeth I's Progress in Surrey, Sussex and Hampshire in 1591', University of Southampton, 2012. Sussex is now divided into two counties, but in the sixteenth century, there were two formal administrative 'divisions' in place – I have kept the epithets 'west' and 'east' as indicators of these.

[2]   Local government records tend to be kept administratively under counties, whereas there was much more cross-border cooperation that they suggest.

Figure 1.1   Map of Elizabeth I's 1591 Royal Progress in West Sussex and
              Hampshire. © Author.

Nearly every summer, the queen and her court left the comparative comfort
of her London palaces, and embarked on a tour of her subjects' houses, usually for
five or six weeks.[3] She took the opportunity of the summer season, and the need to
leave London for health reasons, to travel around the southern part of the kingdom,
visiting loyal nobility and gentry, and sometimes being entertained magnificently.
She usually stayed with her hosts, using the system of purveyance to subsidise their
expenses, and the visits were accompanied by feasting and entertainment. The

---

[3]   Her itineraries have been printed in E.K. Chambers, *The Elizabethan Stage* (Oxford:
Clarendon Press, 1923) and M.H. Cole, *The Portable Queen: Elizabeth I and the politics of ceremony*
(Amherst: University of Massachusetts Press, 1999). Many original sources were collected by the
antiquarian, John Nichols, and published in three volumes: *The Progresses and Public Processions
of Elizabeth I* (London, 1788–1823).

area she knew best was what we now term the 'home counties', including the area slightly north of them, but not the far south-east, and she did not venture north of the Wash, or west of Bristol. It is surprising that Elizabeth visited the relatively accessible west Sussex only once in a long reign of 45 years; she also visited east Sussex only once, in 1573. This account considers the more important progress of the two – that of 1591 first (see Figure 1.1) – and then considers the similarities and differences in 1573, and the modus operandi for both.

The Route of the Progress of 1591 in West Sussex and Hampshire

We take a look first at a brief outline of the progress of 1591 and whom the queen visited. The 1591 progress into west Sussex and Hampshire was one of the longest and most important of her reign. The royal party left Nonsuch Palace on 2 August, and made their way along the top side of the North Downs through Surrey to Leatherhead and East Horsley, and then on to Loseley, and Farnham Castle. At Loseley and Farnham, the host was William More, a gentleman of some standing with the Privy Council, who had been involved in the planning of the progress. On 14 August, they stayed the night with Edmund Mervyn at Bramshott Place, near Liphook, and then on Sunday, 15 August, the royal party crossed the border into West Sussex.[4] The queen reached Cowdray, seat of Sir Anthony Browne, Viscount Montague, about 8 o'clock that evening. A pamphlet published later the same year gives an account of this fascinating visit.[5]

From the moment she approached the house she was greeted by poetry and music, and symbolism emphasizing the queen's grace and eternal power, and the whole visit was themed towards these Renaissance ideas. Various mythological figures, such as the Pilgrim, the Wild Man and the Angler appeared to make speeches throughout the visit. More practically, there were three hundred for breakfast the morning after her arrival. The queen's visit was filled with hunting, for which 'delicate bowers' or standings (their definition in the records depended on the author of the pamphlet, or the clerk writing the accounts) had been specially set up in the park, and deer were driven towards her. There was also a banquet at the priory at Easebourne, and on the eve of her departure, meals

---

4   Chambers, *The Elizabethan Stage*, vol. 4, pp. 105–6.

5   Thomason tract: *The honourable entertainment given to the Queenes Maiestie in progresse, at Cowdrey in Sussex, by the Right Honorable the Lord Montecute, 1591* (London, printed by Thomas Scarlet, to be sold by William Wright, 1591), (British Library, C.142.dd.23), reprinted in Nichols, *The Progresses*.

were served outside at tables 24 and 48 yards long, after which there was a grand dance.[6] The cultural impact of such a visit with plays and speeches full of classical references and symbolic meanings must have been overwhelming for the people present. Like the present day, London culture and provincial society were very different, and such entertainment and the effects of the progress generally may well have made these families hanker after a social life in the capital. By the 1590s, many of the gentry in these counties were already beginning to find more permanent residencies in London, where there was greater contact with the court, and the emergence of new investment opportunities.

From Cowdray, the queen was escorted to an unspecified dining place, probably Downley in West Dean, with the Lewkenors as hosts. The harbingers, who went ahead of the royal party, made 'readye Mr Richarde Lewkenours house for her ma'tie to dyne at betwixte Cowdrey and Chichester.'[7] The queen then proceeded to Chichester, and was settled there by 22 August. The eighteenth-century antiquarian John Nichols says 'and of her Majesty's entertainment in that City there was a full account in one of the Corporation Books; but unfortunately the Book is lost.'[8] The historian T.G. Willis, writing in 1928, embellished the visit, describing the streets of the city as 'gay with flags', and a flourish of trumpets announcing the arrival of the queen.[9] He adds that the queen was welcomed by the Earl of Scarborough,[10] and taken to the audience chamber. Both agree that John Lumley prepared a house for her in East Street near the Cross in the heart of the city, with a spacious banqueting room in which she gave audience to the mayor and citizens. This is believed to be the 'Royal Arms', or 'Old Punch House'(see Figure 1.2).[11]

There is a possibility that the internal decoration was put up specially for the visit.[12] The queen does not appear to have stayed with the Bishop of Chichester, Thomas Bickley, but only at the town house. Despite assertions by Willis, it is more likely that the queen actually gave her audiences in the cathedral, which would have provided a far larger space than Lumley's town house, and which the queen's soldiers could keep secure. The harbingers'

---

[6]   Ibid.

[7]   The best source for ascertaining the route and preparations for a progress is the royal household accounts, in particular those of the Treasurers of the Chamber: TNA, PRO: E 351/541.

[8]   Nichols, *The Progresses*, III, p. 97.

[9]   T.G. Willis, *Records of Chichester: some glimpses of its past* (Chichester: T.G. Willis, 1928), p. 147.

[10]   However, the earldom was only created in 1650.

[11]   See Figure 1.2. It still exists, as do some of the sixteenth-century ceilings.

[12]   M.J. Cutten, *Some Inns and Alehouses of Chichester* (Chichester Papers, no. 46, 1964).

Figure 1.2   The Punch House, Chichester, 2013. There is some possibility that the house Elizabeth occupied included the building on the right of the photograph. © Author.

accounts give the preparation time as six days for preparing 'the Churche at Chichester' as well as an unspecified entry which just says 'at Chichester' (eight days).[13] It is likely that she would have occupied the bishop's chair at the top of the nave with the dean and bishop either side of her, or she could have occupied the Consistory Court in the south transept, which would have accommodated less people.[14] Judging from accounts of other civic visits, she would have been welcomed by the mayor and citizens, and speeches would have been made by both parties. She would have heard petitions and accepted

---

[13]   TNA, PRO E351/452, f. 152v.

[14]   I am indebted to Dr Andrew Foster for these ideas in a discussion in February 2011.

gifts. It was an important time for the city, whose last royal visit was that of Edward VI in 1552.[15]

The queen stayed in Chichester for three nights, and then moved to Stansted, five miles west of Chichester and just inside the county border.[16] Stansted was held at the time by Lord Lumley, so he would probably have accompanied the queen along the route, which must have been familiar to him. It has been thought that Lumley had ceased to be at court or known to Elizabeth by this time, yet he was host to her for four days.[17] At the time of the progress, he was delicately negotiating with the government over a debt owed by his late father-in-law, the Earl of Arundel, and the year after the progress he agreed to sell Nonsuch to the crown and lease it back.[18] As a scholar and owner of much property around Chichester, he would have been able to keep the queen in good company.

From there, she went to Portsmouth, where she inspected the troops.[19] For the second part of the progress, which took place in Hampshire, the queen was on more familiar territory. She knew the route to Portsmouth and Southampton from several previous visits,[20] and perhaps this was 'comforting' in its own way, for she had now been away from London for over three weeks. At this stage, she must have felt the progress was going well. She was on new territory from Bramshott onwards, but the choice of visiting there had worked, and presumably local gentry were pleased that one of their number had been able to play host. The entertainment at Cowdray had been magnificent enough for it to be written up and sold as a pamphlet in London.[21] The entertainments at Chichester had been well received, to judge by nineteenth-century comments on documents now lost,[22] and the visit would do the city good in economic and patronage terms. In west Sussex, she had stayed with four hosts in just under a fortnight. Two were members of the aristocracy – Viscount Montague and Lord Lumley, and two were members of the lesser gentry – Edmund Mervyn and Richard Lewkenor (at least dining with the latter). The second part of

[15] J. North (ed.), *England's Boy King: the diary of Edward VI 1547–1553* (London: Ravenhall Books, 2005).

[16] Cole, *Portable Queen*, p. 196.

[17] K. Barron, 'Lumley, John, first Baron Lumley (*c.*1533–1609)', *ODNB*, 2004; online edn, January 2007 <http://www.oxforddnb.com/view.

[18] Ibid.

[19] Cole, *Portable Queen*, Appendix 1.

[20] Ibid.

[21] BL, C.142.dd.23: see above.

[22] Nichols, *The Progresses*, I, p. 97; Willis, *Records of Chichester*, p. 147.

the progress, in Hampshire, was, however, the more important stage, being double the length of the progress in west Sussex, and Elizabeth stayed with three earls, the Bishop of Winchester and Lord Sandys. She also stayed with seven men of the same, or less, stature as Mervyn and Lewkenor. Thus the two counties had a similar profile of hosts for the progress, but the queen did not return to Sussex. The sole visit to west Sussex may not have been as odd as it seems: for a queen who kept within the home counties normally, the territory further south than the Sussex and Hampshire Downs was out of her 'comfort zone'. However, it emphasises the contrast between the image of the queen who liked new places and fresh faces and the reality of a monarch who did not actually travel far. She did not go abroad as her father and grandfather had done, or to the north or west of England, or into Wales or Ireland. The 1591 progress was a long itinerary with important meetings and celebrations, but it did not break much new ground for Elizabeth.

The Progress of 1573 into the Eastern Division of Sussex

How does the smaller visit of 1573 into the east side of the county compare with the more important one of 1591? The first thing to be noted is that the 1573 progress was actually around Kent (see Figure 1.3). The route, shows that the progress crossed and re-crossed the border with east Sussex as it made its way around the west side of the county. This begs the question of how important the border between the two counties was considered at the time, and again, whether the gentry identified themselves as belonging to a particular county, or whether, as we will see in the context of the 1591 progress, that the immediate neighbourhood and business and family ties were more important. David Grummitt has pointed out that, at the beginning of the early modern period, Kent was composed of a series of sub-communities, rather than one large county community.[23] Its coherence depended on whether the nobility were dominant or the gentry influentially independent, and each sector shared social, cultural and religious attitudes with their peers in neighbouring regions.[24] The cohesiveness of the gentry was at its best after service to the crown during the upheavals of the fifteenth century, and, as in west Sussex, governmental office-holding was dominated by a few families. These men held property on both sides of the

[23]   D. Grummitt, 'The Kentish aristocracy in the Later Middle Ages: a County Community?', paper delivered to Conference on Later Medieval Kent, 10 December 2011.
[24]   Grummitt, 'The Kentish aristocracy'.

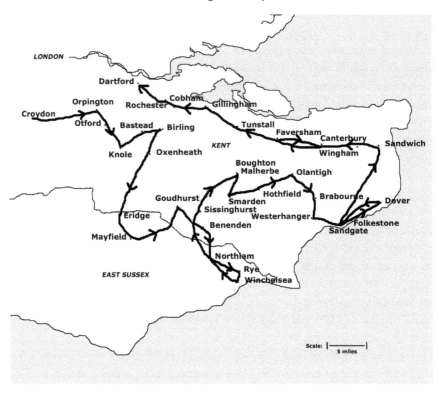

Figure 1.3   Map of Elizabeth I's 1573 Royal Progress in Kent and East Sussex
               © Author.

Sussex-Kent border, and the route of the progress suggests that strong friendship and business links were made with neighbours in the area, regardless of whether they lived in east Sussex or Kent. For the gentry of the eastern division of Sussex, these links were probably closer than those held with the gentry of the western division.

Rather than arriving in the county for a grand stay, as at Cowdray, the queen's first foray into east Sussex was from another house in Kent, after she had been on the road for about a fortnight. The royal progress had left Greenwich on 14 July, and spent the following week at Croydon.[25] On 21 July, she went on to Orpington, where she stayed three nights, and then continued to Knole, her own house, taken from Thomas Cranmer by Henry VIII. At the time of her visit, it was held by the Sackville family, who also had property in east Sussex, and they may have encouraged her to visit properties further south. Now she

---

[25]   Cole, *Portable Queen*, p. 186.

was well into Kent, and on 29 July, she seems to have dined at Bastead, a hamlet in the parish of Wrotham, before arriving at Birling on the North Downs, where her host was Lord Abergavenny. She stayed at 'Comfort', a smaller house on the estate, rather than the main house; this may have been for privacy reasons.[26] It seems that at this time, Elizabeth visited lesser gentry from her main places of stay;[27] so that she visited Sir Thomas Cotton at Oxenheath from Birling on 1 August. On the same day she crossed the border into Sussex, and moved on to Eridge in Frant, also held by Lord Abergavenny.

She then visited Sir Thomas Gresham at Mayfield, also in Sussex from Eridge, either on 2 or 7 August, or both.[28] Mayfield had been a country residence belonging to the Archbishops of Canterbury, but like Knole, had been given to Henry VIII in 1525, and had then been bought by Gresham in the 1560s. Nichols quotes an account of the room supposed to have been used by the queen at the time: ' ... one room of which was called the Queen's Chamber, and the goods and chattels belonging to it were estimated at seven thousand five hundred and fifty-three pounds ten shillings and eight pence.'[29] This account is supposed to have come from Gresham's own journal, and there may be some doubt as to whether the huge sum in fact referred to the whole property.

The queen stayed at Eridge until 6 or 7 August, when her route took her back into Kent to make visits to Kilndown, Bedgebury (held by Alexander Culpepper) and Benenden (held by Thomas Guildford). From here, Lord Burghley wrote to the Earl of Shrewsbury that the journey had been difficult:

> That the Queen had a hard beginning of her Progress in the Wild of Kent; and, namely, in some part of Sussex; where surely were more dangerous rocks and valleys as he said, and much worse ground, than was in the Peak. That they were bending to Rye; and so afterwards to Dover, where, as he added, they should have amends.[30]

On 11 August, she was back in Sussex to visit George Bishop at Northiam; the harbinger accounts suggest that this was just to dine rather than to stay there: 'To Richarde Brackenbury one of hir Ma^tes yeomen of the Chamber ... for making readie for hir Matie a dyning house at Nordeame by the space of three daies mense August' supradicti Anno xvto domine Elizabethe Regina the some

---

[26] Ibid; <http://www.visionofbritain.org.uk/>.
[27] W. Durrant Cooper, 'Queen Elizabeth's visit to Sussex', *Sussex Archaeological Collections*, 5 (1852): 190–97.
[28] Cole, *Portable Queen*, p. 186.
[29] Nichols, *The Progresses*, I, p. 333.
[30] Ibid.

of lix s.' Again two entries further on: 'To the sayde Richarde Brackenburie ... for makinge readie for her Matie at [sic] dyning house at Nordeane at hir highnes Retourne from Rie by the space of three daies mense Augistii ... .'[31]

For the purposes of dining, the work carried out by the harbingers seems to have taken less time (three days rather than the more usual six), and we may speculate that a building was put up specially, or a gatehouse altered to suit the visiting party.[32]

The purpose of the outward-bound part of this progress from London was an official visit to Rye. The queen stayed in the town 11–14 August. At this time, Rye was an important port, and one of the main channel crossings for business with France, but like other south coast ports, it was beginning to silt up to the detriment of its trading. Here the channel leading to the port was blocked, made worse by encroachment through enclosure of the low-lying salts, which was stopping the tides naturally removing the build-up of silt. Rivalry between the burgesses over power and property hindered progress on the harbour work, and in any case much of the town's wealth (up to 50 per cent) was spent on its defences because of the constant threat of invasion during these years. Although there were other natural resources besides the sea, the town was also battling with Lord Buckhurst over the use of timber and iron furnaces. As in Portsmouth and Southampton, the celebrations to mark the queen's visit may have hidden the true picture of economic stagnancy.[33] Thus Rye, like Chichester, was past its glory when the queen visited.

Rye had been devastated by a fire in the fourteenth century, and the subsequent slow building development allowed houses to be large and well spaced. Many of the leading townsmen lived in the administrative and commercial area near the church, and the queen is supposed to have stayed at Grene Hall, now known as the Customs House.[34] As in Chichester, the house she stayed in was in the centre of the commercial part of the town, and belonged to the mayor, Henry Gaymer. As the host on a progress, he was about the same level in society as Lewkenor and Mervyn; however, locally he was a leading and forceful member of the local gentry. The Gaymer family had been settled in the town for at least a century, and Henry was a jurat, an MP in three Parliaments, mayor three times

---

[31]   TNA, PRO: E 351/541, f. 148.

[32]   Northiam has a tradition that Elizabeth dined under an oak on the village green, a fragment of which is still supposed to be there – but this would have been a major security risk. She is supposed to have left a momento of a pair of slippers.

[33]   L.F. Salzman (ed.), *Victoria County History of the County of Sussex*, IX (London: University of London and Oxford University Press, 1937), pp. 44–56.

[34]   G. Mayhew, *Tudor Rye* (Falmer: University of Sussex Press, 1987), pp. 35–6.

and on several commissions. He was involved in the town's efforts to improve its port, and tried on several occasions to petition the queen or Parliament for financial help. He received the queen at Grene Hall, an older house which had been embellished with modern decorative 'mathematical' tiles on its frontage.[35] Gaymer presented her with a purse of 100 gold angels – the money given by the town to the queen as a present was part of money lent to the town by the mayor, and repaid the following Michaelmas.[36]

From Rye, the queen visited Winchelsea, another Cinque Port, in much the same trouble as the larger Rye. Camden describes it as being on such steep cliffs that the damage inflicted by the French and Spanish had been completed by the retreat of the sea, and the development of and rivalry with Rye.[37] Both towns would have been visited by the queen to inspect the defences.[38] After her return to Northiam, she then turned east, and the rest of the progress toured the county of Kent comprehensively. Thus the queen's presence in east Sussex was not as dramatic or as demonstrably powerful as in the western division of the county eighteen years later. Her visits in 1573 were for dining or brief stays, and there were no entertainments or spectacles as at Cowdray. This chapter will look at the hosts, but first we might just consider how the progresses worked, and the position of the hosts.

Practicalities of the Progresses

Elizabeth took her Privy Council with her, and business continued as normal, with arrangements made for bringing the necessary documents with them, and supplying postal services from wherever she was staying. By the time of her reign, the long baggage-train of medieval monarchs had gone, and in its place was a smart system of harbingers. The harbingers worked in teams, each with a leader who was a member of the gentry and well-versed in these practical arrangements. A case study of the 1591 progress shows that, once the itinerary was decided, each team was allotted an area, a certain number of houses to prepare and a definite time frame in which to work.[39] The days referred to in the accounts

---

[35]   Salzman (ed.), *Victoria County History,* IX, p. 44.

[36]   Cooper, 'Queen Elizabeth's visits', p. 192.

[37]   G.J. Copley, *Camden's Britannia: Surrey and Sussex* (London: Hutchinson & Co, 1977), p. 63.

[38]   G. Mayhew, 'Rye and the defence of the narrow seas', *Sussex Archaeological Collections,* 122 (1984): 107–26.

[39]   Adams, 'Queen and Country'.

represent the time taken by the harbingers and their teams of up to nine yeomen (and presumably many more workmen under them) to make the place ready for the queen to visit. For example, for the visit to Cowdray, their accounts read:

> **To** Symon Bowyer aforesaide for the lyke allowaunce of himselfe and the same number of yeomen and gromes for makinge readye my Lorde mountagues house at Cowdrey for her ma'tie by the space of 6 dayes mense Augustii 1591 as apperethe by bill signed by the Lorde Chambleyne [mark] 118s. To the sayde Symon Bowyer for the lyke allowaunce of himselfe and the same number of yeomen and gromes for makinge readye the priorye house at my Lorde Mountagues for her ma'tie by the space of twoe dayes mense Augustii 1591 as as apperethe by bill signed by the lorde Chambleyne [mark] 39s 4d. **To** him more for thallowaunce of himselfe and the same number of yeomen and gromes for making readye a lodge in the Northe parke for her ma'tie to reste as she came to Cowdrey by the space of twoe dayes mense Augustii 1591 as apperethe by bill signed by the lorde Chambleyne [mark] 39s 4d. **To** the same Symon Bowyer for thallowaunce of himselfe and thafore sayde number of yeomen and gromes for makinge readye three standinge for her Ma'tie at the lorde montagues by the space of 6 dayes mense Augustii 1591 as apperethe by bill signed by the lorde Chambleyne [mark] 118s.[40]

Here we can see that 16 days (a relatively large amount of time) were spent preparing Cowdray for the queen's arrival, and the spectacles that were to follow. From other accounts, we know that locks were changed, new hangings put in, furniture and hangings substituted, and if there was to be drama, stages and sets were erected.[41]

What part did the hosts play in all this? Some, such as Viscount Montague of Cowdray, might well have wondered. There is no doubt that much expense would have been put in by the host to accommodate the queen in the best surroundings and to give her the choicest entertainment available. Viscount Montague had much to offer. The house was by now seventy years old, and the grandest and most noble house in the western half of Sussex. It was substantial, built around a central courtyard, and on one side a huge gatehouse stood three storeys high, with guardrooms in each of its towers on either side. On the inner side of the courtyard, the kitchen tower, the pantry, brewery and larders had been remodelled to provide more space for food preparation. On either side of the courtyard were two ranges of living quarters, as big as mansions themselves. We know from later inventories that room after room was decorated and distinguished by different colour schemes

---

[40]   TNA, PRO, E351/542. Interestingly, the very last royal harbinger, Sir Henry Rycroft, was a Sussex landowner.

[41]   TNA, PRO: E351/3224–6.

with the best fustian, calico and silk furnishings. The ground floor was occupied by servants and ushers, guests were accommodated on the first floor, and Viscount Montague's own family occupied the second floor. Above them, the galleries, which would normally have been used for storage of furniture and supplies, would probably have been cleared to make them into long dormitories, and curtains and hangings strung across the space to subdivide the space into 'rooms'.[42] To this space could be added, if necessary, splendid tents owned by houses such as these, which would have normally been used for events such as jousting. There is some evidence that wooden platforms on which these could be erected were permanent features in some country houses.

There is evidence in the royal accounts that the harbingers may have overthrown a host's preparations. The practice of purveyance and the further provision of tents and supplies by the royal household was also developed into a smooth operation. They brought with them workmen who changed the order of the rooms, and dictated the accommodation.[43] The management of royal tents was important and professional, and a royal official was responsible for their correct supply for each occasion and their long-term maintenance. The tents were used not only for military events or celebrations, but on progresses, and were probably combined with those owned by the house at which the queen was staying. The harbingers may well have produced havoc with their efforts to accommodate the provisions for the royal party, taking into account everything from latrines to the queen's own furniture, and one can imagine that the host's plans and the harbingers' works may have clashed. In short, it is perfectly possible that weeks of careful preparations by hosts were ignored by these experienced royal household officials. Their work left the house owners to add to their efforts and supply as much entertainment as was feasible. However it does mean that some traditional assumptions, such as a host on a royal progress being bankrupted, or the long train of goods and people following the monarch, are not supported from the evidence of the accounts.

The Hosts and People Involved on the Progresses

A detailed look at the hosts of both the progresses reveals much about their attitudes to themselves, their neighbours and the royal court. Inevitably, in the stories of these two progresses, the hosts of 1591 stand out. The first main event

---

[42]   F.W. Steer, 'A Cowdray inventory of 1682', *Sussex Archaeological Collections*, 105 (1967): 84–102.
[43]   TNA, PRO: E351/3224–6.

of the 1591 progress was the week at Cowdray, one of the biggest celebrations in any of Elizabeth's progresses, and it gives a picture of the intellectual culture and network of patronage that existed in Sussex gentry society at the time. Anthony Browne would have gathered friends and family around him. Judging from household books and other evidence, Browne's household probably numbered more than a hundred people, possibly two hundred including servants.[44] Some of these would have been sent away during the visit, but many more people would have come, and his extended family might well have expected to not only be there, but to be staying at the house. Numbers could have swelled to as much as three to four hundred that week. From the Acts of the Privy Council, we can see that attendances of the council itself comprised fewer people towards the end of July and beginning of August, but there was nearly a full attendance during the time the court was at Cowdray.[45] From various sources, it is possible to put together a guest list of at least the main participants of the festivities at Cowdray.

First there would have been the Browne family and their kin, who included Anthony Browne himself, his second wife Magdalen, his widowed sister Mabel, Countess of Kildare, and possibly her son, Henry, the 12th Earl. Anthony Browne's own children included his sons Anthony Maria, George and Henry, his daughter Mary (widow of their close friend Henry Wriothesley) and her son Henry who was later to entertain the queen at Titchfield. Secondly, the court included Elizabeth herself, of course, and ten privy councillors, including Lord Burghley, Robert Cecil, Christopher Hatton and Lord Buckhurst, who was himself from Sussex.[46] Henry Carey was the son of Mary Boleyn, and therefore cousin to the queen. In 1545, he had sat in Parliament for Horsham as a nominee of his wife's kinsman, the 3rd Duke of Norfolk, so he had connections with west Sussex.[47] Thomas Heneage, nominally in charge of progresses at this time, had been MP for Arundel in 1559, probably through the influence of his friend and patron at the time, Henry Fitzalan, 12th Earl of Arundel.[48] He soon became a member of the Privy Council, and had been vice-chamberlain for thirteen years by 1591.

---

[44]   Evidence for the size of the household can be gleaned from inventories (WSRO, Add Ms 14858; Cowdray Ms 93, and the Cowdray Book of Orders, WSRO, Cowdray Ms 18).

[45]   J.R. Dasent (ed.), *Acts of the Privy Council of England, 1591*, new series, vol. XXI (London: HMSO, 1900). Unfortunately, the minutes for the relevant part of the 1573 progress does not exist.

[46]   Dasent (ed.), *Acts of the Privy Council* vol. XXI.

[47]   W.T. MacCaffrey, 'Carey, Henry, first Baron Hunsdon (1526–1596)', *ODNB*, 2004; online edn, May 2011.

[48]   M. Hicks, 'Heneage, Sir Thomas (*b.* in or before 1532, *d.* 1595)', *ODNB*, 2004; online edn, January 2008.

Genuine friendship with Elizabeth led to many gifts of land and offices. He may have decided on his second wife at Cowdray, for in 1594, he married Anthony Browne's eldest daughter Mary, the widow of Henry Wriothesley.[49] Many of these nobles were married to Ladies of the Bedchamber, powerful women close to Elizabeth, including Frances Brooke, wife of Lord Cobham.[50] Thus members of the Privy Council had connections with the area through family or property, and it would have made a difference to Sussex society to see the courtiers connected with their lord and the context of his life outside the locality.

Such a big event would have had an impact on the locality. The gentry of the area who would almost certainly have received an invitation to Cowdray included Henry Goring, Henry Glemham, John Carrell and Nicholas Parker who were knighted during the stay.[51] Thomas Sherley the younger, of nearby Wiston, was there with his mother – Sherley was embroiled in an argument with Robert Cecil while they were staying at Cowdray – and ended up with a brief spell in prison.[52] Local families such as the Lumleys and Lewkenors, who also acted as hosts, are mentioned in passing in correspondence and wills, and were probably there. We can speculate further – William More of Loseley, who was partly responsible for organising at least the early stages of the progress, may well have continued to accompany the royal party, as he and Anthony Browne enjoyed a strong friendship which lasted all their adult lives. John Hill, the Mayor of Chichester, was host on the next part of the trip, and so may well have come up to Cowdray to meet his guests. All these people, from the nobles downwards, would have been accompanied by servants, both personal and household.

Thus it is possible to work out from family history and local and regional sources just who attended the week of celebrations at Cowdray, and see that although the party from court was numerous, Anthony Browne had gathered friends and family around him, and these may have outnumbered his guests. It must have been important for local gentry to have an invitation to at least one event in the six-day spectacle. It would have been a sign of one's importance, and a chance to network with the local gentry as well as the court, and to offer or

---

[49]   The *ODNB* entry for Heneage says that they had probably been close friends for years, but at this time he was still married to his first wife, Anne Poyntz. Mary had had a difficult marriage to Henry Wriothesley, which had ended in separation from both her husband and son.

[50]   S. Adams, 'Brooke , Frances, Lady Cobham (*b.* after 1530, *d.* 1592)', *ODNB*, 2006; online edn, January 2008. The Cobhams had played host in Kent on the 1573 progress.

[51]   Nichols, *The Progresses*, III, p. 96.

[52]   A.J. Kempe (ed.), *The Loseley Manuscripts: manuscripts and other rare documents illustrative of English history, biography and manners from Henry VIII to James I* (London: John Murray, 1836).

receive patronage, and oil the wheels of sixteenth-century society. Did the two parties have equal footing? Although there has been discussion of the possibility that Browne and his family were wary of the queen's presence,[53] research has shown that the queen was always the most important person in the house, and that theoretically she became the host whilst she was in it.[54]

Equally important are those not invited. To miss out on this visit must have been similar to not being invited to a family wedding. It would still have been possible for local magnates and gentry to have felt snubbed through no invitation, or perhaps to send a message to the queen by non-attendance at the festivities. Most interesting of the local nobility from the point of view of the progresses were the Earls of Northumberland. Petworth House, about ten miles away from Cowdray, was owned by the Percy family, whose real authority and power was based in the north of England, but who had recently been made to live in the south by the Privy Council. At the time of Henry VIII's visits, Petworth was a modest manor house and although it was the centre of an estate which brought the family a substantial income, it had not been used regularly whilst the 6th Earl, Henry Algernon, concentrated on his property in the north of England.[55] This family was one of the most important in the kingdom, but also the most controversial. In 1537, the 6th Earl died, having broken up the family's large estates in Yorkshire, Northumberland and Cockermouth; in the same year, his brother Sir Thomas was executed for his part in the Pilgrimage of Grace, and the third brother Ingram died in the Tower. The 7th Earl of Northumberland was executed in 1572 for his part in the Northern Rising of 1569.

His brother Henry, the 8th Earl, succeeded him, managing to keep the title and estates, but was required to live in the south of England. Consequently, around 1574–76, he started to take an interest in Petworth House and undertook remedial work on the fabric. When there was a possibility in 1583 that he might be asked to act as host, the latter wrote:

> ... her Majestie will never thank him that hath perswaded this progreyse ... considering the wayes which she must come to them, up the hill and down the hill, so as she shall not be able to use ether coche or litter with ease, and those wayes also so full of

[53]   C.C. Breight, 'Caressing the great: Viscount Montague's entertainment of Elizabeth at Cowdray 1591', *Sussex Archaeological Collections*, 127 (1989): 147–66; M. Questier, *Catholicism and Community in Early Modern England: politics, aristocratic patronage and religion, c.1550–1640* (Cambridge: Cambridge University Press, 2006).

[54]   Adams, 'Queen and Country'.

[55]   E. Barrington de Fonblanque, *Annals of the House of Percy* (London: Richard Clay & Sons, 1887).

louse stones, as it is carefull and painfull riding for any body, nether can ther be in this cuntrey any wayes devised to avoyd those ould wayes.[56]

The truth was that the 8th Earl did not want her to visit, perhaps because he may have been involved in a conspiracy with Charles Paget, a Roman Catholic conspirator who was in Sussex in the same period. He was certainly being accused of it by contemporaries.[57] William Durrant Cooper, writing in the nineteenth century, says that 'although the earl expressed pleasure at the contemplated honour, every quiet mode was adopted to put aside the visit.'[58] Neighbours around Petworth must have been watching events in the family with interest. A break-up of the southern estates would affect landowners in Sussex, possibly producing opportunities for aggrandisement of their own estates.

In contrast, Henry, the 9th Earl, who succeeded in 1585, was desperately trying to change his own image, acquired in his youth, of being more fond of wine and women than of managing his estates.[59] At the time of the 1591 progress, he was just beginning to rebuild Petworth,[60] and according to Fonblanque, biographer of the Percy family, he would, unlike his predecessor, have welcomed a visit from his monarch.[61] However, in 1591, the queen chose to ignore the earl, coming down from Bramshott to Cowdray and then moving on to Chichester. The previous July, William More had been asked by Lord Hunsdon, the Lord Chamberlain,[62] to find a convenient stopping place between Farnham and Cowdray:

[The queen] is verie desyrous to go by Petworth and Cowdry, yf yt be possible; but none of us all can sett her down anie wher to be at betwene yo' house and Cowdry. And therefore I am to require you that you will set this berer some way for her to passe, and that you will let some one of y'r owne men, who is best acquaintyd wth those wayes, to be his guyde, that he may see whether they be fit for her Ma'tie or noe. And

---

[56] TNA, PRO: SP 12/181, f. 34.
[57] Fonblanque, *Annals*, p. 164. For the Sussex angle of the Throckmorton plot, see S. Johnson, 'In the wake of Throckmorton: Christopher Haynes, customer, searcher and taverner of Arundel (c. 1527–1586)', *Sussex Archaeological Collections*, 149 (2011).
[58] Cooper, 'Queen Elizabeth's visits', p. 193.
[59] G.R. Batho and S. Clucas, *A facsimile and transcript from the manuscripts of Henry Percy, ninth Earl of Northumberland at Petworth House* (London: Roxburghe Club, 2002).
[60] G.R. Batho, 'The Percies at Petworth 1574–1632', *Sussex Archaeological Collections*, 95 (1957): 1–27.
[61] Fonblanque, *Annals*, p. 193.
[62] MacCaffrey, 'Carey, Henry'.

whether yt be best goeing from yo'r howse to Petworth and so to Cowdry, or els from
yo'r howse to Cowdry. And yf you can set her downe anie place betweene yo'r howse
and Cowdry that may serve for one night, you shall do her a greate pleasure.[63]

At this point, it is clear that they were discussing Petworth as an option, and
whether to visit the Earl of Northumberland. The letter hints that the royal
party had doubts about a stay at Petworth, as had been traditional for Henry
and Edward's progresses.[64] More had replied that there

> ... is not anie convenient howse for that purpose standinge neare the way from my
> howse towardes Petworth or Cowdrey. Onlie ther is a little howse of Mr Lawrence
> Elliott's distant three miles from myne,[65] the direct waie to either of the said plac's
> and wthin tenne miles of Petworth and eleaven of Cowdray, to wch howse I directed
> Mr Constable by a servaunte of myne, who hathe viewed the same and canne make
> reporte to yo' Lo' therof. From thence is another, the like howse, in Shillinglie, of
> one Bonner's, distant five myles the direct way to Petworth, and about a myle out of
> the waie to Cowdrey, where King Edwarde dyned in his waie from Guildford Parke
> to Cowdrey.[66]

More suggested a straight route south, but one that would involve two stops,
although, as he pointed out, there was a precedent for dining at Shillinglee. It
would not have been difficult to change the route along the Arun, but More's
suggestions were not used. In the event the queen did not go to Petworth,
but went out of her way, not necessarily on better terrain, to Bramshott. Both
the route she took, and a speculative one of 1586,[67] which took in Petworth,
included a climb over the Downs. At some time, the decision was made not to
visit the earl, which must have been regarded as a snub to him, although the
queen did restore the governship of Tynemouth Castle to him that year.[68] For
the 9th Earl, it must have become evident that a visit was not in the 'giestes'

---

[63]   Kempe, *The Loseley Manuscripts*, p. 271, quoting 6729/7/84.

[64]   Henry VIII had visited often, and Edward VI had followed in his footsteps, see Adams,
'Queen and Country', pp. 45–65.

[65]   Kempe suggests this is Busbridge, near Godalming.

[66]   Kempe, *The Loseley Manuscripts*, p. 272, quoting 6729/7/83. There is no other evidence
that Edward visited Shillinglee.

[67]   See Adams, 'Queen and Country', p. 138.

[68]   Mark Nicholls, 'Percy, Henry, ninth earl of Northumberland (1564–1632)', *ODNB*,
2004; online edn, January 2008.

because he chose to visit Bath[69] as the progress set off, and he does not appear to have been on any of the guest lists for the progress. Although he was friendly with Montague, he was not necessarily part of the gentry network in that area of Sussex.[70]

Nor does the queen appear to have stayed in 1591 with the Bishop of Chichester, Thomas Bickley. Lord Lumley was her host in the city, not the Bishop of Chichester. The relative importance of this bishop is therefore contrasted with the position of Thomas Cooper, the Bishop of Winchester, who played host three times during this progress (twice at Farnham and once at Bishop's Waltham) and was well used to entertaining royalty at his palaces.[71] The Bishop of Chichester should have carried similar local weight and influence. However, as possibly the oldest man consecrated under Elizabeth, Bickley has been seen as 'a tired old man slumbering away in his diocese ... the most procrastinatory bishop in England'.[72] Kenneth Carleton is kinder:

> The balance of probabilities, however, is that he continued into old age as a conscientious administrator who monitored nonconformist activity, at least within the immediate vicinity of Chichester itself, and attempted to provide for regular sermons and other measures of control in a diocese where Catholicism remained more strongly entrenched among the ruling élite than anywhere else in the home counties.[73]

Bickley was 73 at the time of the progress. He may have been too old to fulfil his duties as host, and been excused. The bishop's palace was probably the largest residence in the city,[74] but the queen was not always disposed to stay in the biggest places available.

The main host for the lesser progress of 1573 was Henry Nevill, Lord Abergavenny (or Bergavenny). The Nevills were an important family both locally and at the royal courts, and held estates in Sussex, Kent, Surrey, Essex, Suffolk, Norfolk, and in the west country and west midlands. At this time, Nevill was married to Frances Manners, and they must have considered Birling

---

[69] WSRO, PHA 425 for 1591.

[70] Fonblanque, *Annals*, p. 201 suggests that the earl was indifferent to his magisterial duties in the south, and was reproached by Lord Buckhurst for declining to join the justices of Sussex in stopping the export of corn and munitions from the county.

[71] Chambers, *The Elizabethan Stage*, IV, appendix A.

[72] R. Manning, *Religion and Society in Elizabethan Sussex* (Leicester: Leicester University Press, 1969), p. 204.

[73] K. Carleton, 'Bickley, Thomas (c.1518–1596)', *ODNB*, 2004.

[74] R. Morgan, *Chichester: a documentary history* (Chichester: Phillimore, 1992), p. 160.

their main home, as she was buried here three years later;[75] in 1587, Henry also died at Comfort and was buried at Birling. Of the places visited on this progress, he held Comfort, Birling and Eridge, and he may have been the patron of the gentry who became hosts to the royal party of a night or a meal.

Edmund Mervyn and Richard Lewkenor, who were hosts at Bramshott and West Dean respectively in 1591, were interesting men in their own right, powerful landowners, but without the access to the Privy Council held by William More of Loseley. Edmund Mervyn held property in Durford in the north of west Sussex, Petersfield and Bramshott, the latter two being on the Hampshire/Sussex border.[76] He married Elizabeth, daughter of Sir Edmund Pakenham, and some of his twelve children were baptised (and some of those buried) at Rogate in Sussex.[77] Bramshott had been bought by his father Henry in 1580, and he and his sons were involved in the very active land market at this time. Edmund and Henry appear in numerous deeds,[78] collecting small parcels of land, and building a power-base at Bramshott. It is believed that the gatehouse, which still stands, was built in honour of Elizabeth's visit.[79] It is too small to entertain more than one or two people there, but may well have been considered a fashionable novelty.

Richard Lewkenor of Trotton and Downley in West Dean, west Sussex was a proficient and prominent lawyer in the region. He was admitted to Middle Temple in 1560, JP for Sussex from 1583, serving on many commissions, searjeant at law from 1594, and Recorder of Chichester 1588–1600. In 1588, he was presiding justice at the Chichester Sessions, where he sentenced four seminary priests to death. He was MP for Chichester from 1572 to 1598, and surveyor of lands for the Bishop of Chichester from 1571; he was knighted in 1600. He witnessed or took part in many exchanges of property in west Sussex in 1580s and 1590s, and in 1589 bought the manor of West Dean from Lord Lumley, where he entertained the queen in 1591. Despite this, he may have had Catholic leanings, but his first loyalty was to the crown.[80]

---

[75] Elaine V. Beilin, 'Neville , Frances, Lady Bergavenny (*d.* 1576)', *ODNB* (Oxford: Oxford University Press, 2004), G.E. Cokayne, *The Complete Peerage of England, Scotland, Ireland, Great Britain and the UK, extant, extinct or dormant*, vols I–XII (new edn revised, enlarged, edited by the Hon. Vicary Gibbs) (London: St. Catherine's Press, 1912–53).

[76] Roy McCaughey, 'Mervyn, Sir Henry (*bap.* 1583, *d.* 1646)', *ODNB* (Oxford: Oxford University Press, 2004).

[77] WSRO, Par 159/1/1/1: Rogate composite parish register 1558–1744.

[78] WSRO, add mss. collection, etc.

[79] Owner of present house, interviewed by Diane Ladlow, 2012.

[80] P.W. Hasler, *The House of Commons 1558–1603* (London: HMSO, 1981), II, pp. 474–5.

In contrast, some of the hosts of the earlier 1573 visit to Sussex, other than Henry Nevill, do not appear to have been as active locally. The harbinger accounts do not mention the hosts other than Lord Bergavenny, Sir Robert Cotton [*sic* – it was actually Sir Thomas Cotton], Mr Guildford and Mr Savage.[81] Alexander Culpepper, Thomas Guildford, George Bishop and Mr Savage may have been chosen through the patronage of Nevill, rather than in their own right. Sir Thomas Cotton was an exception, an active justice of the peace in Kent, and a landowner around Rye, enclosing land, and in contact with the Privy Council on behalf of Lord Bergavenny.[82] Guildford was probably a justice of the peace.[83] The harbinger accounts do not mention Mayfield and Sir Thomas Gresham at all.[84] The latter would have been well known to the queen as a leading mercer in the City of London, a financier and founder of the Royal Exchange.[85] Both Culpepper and Guildford were knighted at Rye, along with Thomas Sherley the elder of Wiston and Francis Walsingham.[86] Otherwise, the men were not well known to the Privy Council. It may be that the culture of the progresses was not as defined as twenty years later. The years 1574 and 1575 saw two big progresses into the midlands, both culminating in important visits to Kenilworth, courtesy of Robert Dudley. Much has been written about these, and they were certainly important defining events in the history of Elizabeth's progresses. After them, the queen was more confident of her routes and the receptions she would receive. The Kent progress took place before this development, and she may have relied heavily on Nevill's patronage to find hosts.

Detailed case studies within the two progresses offer evidence on how the relationships of the participants worked. They show that the most important people were not necessarily those we might first think, and it gives a clearer idea of relationships within the gentry, and of their relationship with the monarch. As far as the hierarchy of local gentry was concerned, there are two ways of looking at the progresses. It could be said that the natural order of local society was given a shake-up by the progress because Elizabeth stayed with certain gentry who were just small landowners, and did not stay with some important nobles. However, it is more likely, on the other hand, that the progress may have reflected what was already happening within the community. The dominance of Henry Nevill

---

[81] TNA, PRO, E 351/541.

[82] Dasent (ed.), *Acts*, vol. VIII, pp. 34, 144, 349.

[83] Ibid., pp. 123, 308, 316, 326.

[84] TNA, PRO, E 351/541.

[85] Ian Blanchard, 'Gresham, Sir Thomas (*c*.1518–1579)', *ODNB* (Oxford: Oxford University Press, 2004); online edn, January 2008.

[86] Cooper, 'Queen Elizabeth's visits', p. 191.

is marked by the 1573 progress, and his control over events; whereas in 1591, the Earl of Northumberland evidently was not taking part in the governance of the region, and his visitors seem to have been recusants and men who were not approved by the Privy Council. At the other end of the scale, Edmund Mervyn was a rising member of the gentry in 1591, whose success was confirmed by the queen's visit, but in 1573, the gentry seemed to have been involved at the behest of Lord Abergavenny. The visits on the progresses may have confirmed what was already taking place.

There were, however, practical consequences of a royal progress. It would have inconvenienced local society routine at harvest-time, when men were busy checking their estates, even going on small progresses of their own. There was a 'calendar' for local nobility and gentry, dictated by the rituals of the church and agricultural year, which would have been disrupted by preparations for the arrival of a monarch. At the same time, those preparations may have made travel and accommodation easier for other travellers once the progress had moved on. The work carried out by local gentry to maintain the provision of goods and services and keep communication lines open would have contributed to the stability and success of the progresses. Travel in the region was dictated by the chalk of the Downs, the marshy area between the Downs, and the rivers – but the summers at the end of the sixteenth century tended to be warm enough for these not to hinder travellers. Progresses opened up the countryside by extending the number of available places to stay for future progresses, whether carried out by the monarch or other officials.

Secondly, the tenor of the 1591 progress shows that local religious leanings were respected or at least tolerated in this period after the defeat of the Spanish Armada. The people visited and the entertainments given suggest that the monarch and government were comfortable in west Sussex and not overly worried about their Catholic nature. As the 1590s progressed, the government would tighten up again, but this case study demonstrates a certain amount of satisfaction with the local governance and its efforts against recusancy in the county, despite the misgivings of Thomas Cooper, the Bishop of Winchester. The Privy Council seem to have been prepared to work with Catholics where loyalty to Elizabeth could be – and needed to be – displayed.

The progress became a multi-functional device under Elizabeth. She was able to undertake such progresses for her own uses, such as meeting new people and seeing new landscapes. Whereas Henry, Edward and James always stayed with friends who were generally nobility, Elizabeth chose to stay with lesser gentry, whom she might not have met before, and used this to confirm her position in regional society and with the Privy Council. Her practice and ability to do this shows that she had few worries about her own security. She may have been checking the loyalty of such people, but the progresses in this region show that she was able to do so in a relaxed style, and there were no political repercussions for the region itself after 1591. Equally, she chose to raise the importance of small landowners by dining with them, and by receiving gifts and giving audiences in Chichester, and in this way she showed her interest in local society. The Privy Council members may not themselves have wished to stay or dine at smaller places such as West Dean or Northiam, but 'she preserved her authority by reinventing herself by the media of the times ... .'[87] Elizabeth took a stronger interest in regional society than any other monarch, and it has echoes of the present Queen Elizabeth and her 'walkabouts'. In doing so, she confirmed and helped develop new social networks in local communities.

The details of the progresses also show the inequality of the places at which she chose to stay: a small manor house such as at Comfort, Northiam, or Bramshott is in direct contrast to her stay at Cowdray. Sometimes there must have been very little entertainment for the queen (which we do not hear about), and at other times the cultural impact must have been overwhelming for people in the region, because some of the refined noble entertainment was up to courtly and London standards. To those gentry invited to host or dine at less important places, the sight of the grand occasions must have increased the lure of taking up a residence in London, where the new sophistication brought fresh treats and 'novel devices'.

Although Elizabeth stayed with 'lesser' gentry in 1591, they were still men of property. The dissolution of the monasteries had brought about a significant increase in the local land market, and also changes in perception of hospitality. After the wholesale alienation of estates from the crown in the 1530s and 1540s, there had been huge activity in buying and selling property throughout the mid-sixteenth century. By the 1570s, many small pieces of property were being bought, sold and exchanged, and a local study such as this highlights a fast-growing expanding land market. The men involved in the progresses were the same men who were increasing the standing of their families by buying up a messuage or a few fields adjacent to land they already held. With their new-found wealth, they were also building and rebuilding their country houses. The fortunes of country houses in the area changed over the sixteenth century, as local country house architecture was influenced by a desire to offer hospitality to important people, and their ability to host a progress was that much greater.

---

[87]   Cole, *Portable Queen*, p. 170.

The increased availability of estate land also provided a new culture in which the old orders of hospitality were questioned. The idea that good hospitality was expected from nobility and gentry did not change, but it was also a means of giving and receiving patronage, and this was highlighted in the progresses. Hospitality became more self-serving during the sixteenth century, and more an expression of power and wealth, and kinship ties were most important as men sought to increase the power of their families. The men who could welcome a monarch into their homes found dealings with the local poor awkward: they were expected to pick up the responsibilities of the local dissolved monasteries, but they did not see it as their duty to keep philanthropy as personal as it had been in the past. The changing rules on the duties of hospitality were one of the consequences of the progresses.

So hosts became aware that new trends in architecture and hospitality mattered, and they interpreted this in their own way. Viscount Montague and the Earl of Hertford were able to build houses to reflect the number of guests they were hoping to entertain. Other houses in the area, such as New Place, Pulborough, or Bramshott, were given new gatehouses. The development of 'visitor flow', so obvious, for example, in the alterations to Lacock Abbey in Wiltshire,[88] required changes to the design and structure of a country house, which were taken up in the bigger houses in this region, such as at Cowdray. In the sixteenth century, there were more than sixty houses in Sussex which might have been attractive to the planners of a progress.

What does such close inspection of two royal progresses in the south tell us? First, it offers a spotlight on local society and reveals who was favoured by the queen. It may also reveal whom she respected or wished to win over to her cause. The progress hosts were both the great landowners whose power and wealth needed to be recognised, and also gentry who were influential in their own locality, but not necessarily known to the Privy Council or at court. The queen appears to have been happy to spend one or two nights with these men of less importance, and the Privy Council seems to have been as happy to hold their Council meetings in many of these places. This suggests a certain amount of trust and satisfaction in the way the hosts were conducting local business and government, even with those who were obviously Catholic. This study also throws light on patterns of patronage and power at court and in government. The local gentry would have used the progress to further their own careers – through mixing with courtiers and Privy Councillors and by seeking opportunities for patronage. Authority within the progress would have led to

---

[88]   Adams, 'Queen and Country', chapter 6.

respect and patronage outside it. It might have introduced some of the gentry to court, or increased their status within it. It was an opportunity for local and national government to meet, and local concerns to be discussed with men of importance.

Secondly, through various family and local government papers, the practical aspects of the progress can be established, working at a grass-roots level – a level which people on the progress may not have fully appreciated. In 1573, Elizabeth was still experimenting with the ways in which she would conduct her progresses, but chose to visit two towns on the south coast successfully. The route in 1591 shows a confidence that summer travel could be undertaken in relative safety. It was one of the grander and longer progresses of Elizabeth's reign, and there is no evidence of the changes of routes and events that happened with the greater ones in the 1570s.[89] Looking at the region's affairs in the light of the progresses therefore gives new insight into interaction between the centre of government and a local community. Such studies confirm the emergence of a new class of gentry, who were rising in importance for the Privy Council. Their relationships were tight-knit, and they knew each other through working on commissions of the peace and the musters. At the same time, the notion of a 'county community' (the notion that the gentry in a given county created a strong faction deliberately within those limits) is refuted. It is an important point that there were circles of gentry working across county borders within the region defined by these royal progresses, and this situation was as true for 1591 as it was for 1573. A study of the progresses themselves confirms the cross-border operation of responsibilities, governance and friendship.

---

[89] For example, the 'giestes' [itinerary details and programme] of the 1575 progress, including the visit to Kenilworth, were radically altered when the queen decided to return early; information from 'Kenilworth Revisited: Perspectives On The Castle And The 1575 Festivities' in September 2005, held at the University of Warwick and Kenilworth.

Chapter 2

Two Sussex Authors: Thomas Drant and Anthony Copley

Matthew Dimmock and Andrew Hadfield

The Reformation took its toll on Sussex. While the county is now largely remembered for its Protestant martyrs (the reason for the vigorous celebrations on 5 November), in the late sixteenth century, it was a complicated and divided region, riven by confessional battles and the divergent forces of conflicting loyalties. The country was largely loyal to the old religion, dominated by ancient Catholic families: the Howards at Arundel Castle, the Percys at Petworth House, the Gages at Firle Park, the Brownes (the Lords Montague) at Cowdray Park, and the Palmers at Parham House, as well as other more minor dynasties such as the Lewkenors and the Shirleys. The towns, notably Rye and Lewes, as in the rest of south-east England, were much more likely to be controlled by Protestants, if not Protestant in orientation. Outsiders found the county's loyalties hard to fathom and to negotiate; insiders often found themselves caught between the heroic desire to resist the central authorities and the pragmatic need to survive in the hope that more favourable times might lie ahead.

This chapter explores the experiences of two important but largely neglected writers and intellectuals: Thomas Drant (c. 1540–78) and Anthony Copley (1567–1607). Drant was very much an outsider. He was born in Lincolnshire, educated at Cambridge and then began a career in the Church, securing a number of ecclesiastic positions in Sussex, including the archdeaconry of Lewes, through his connections to Richard Curteys, the controversial Bishop of Chichester. Drant was embroiled in a number of ecclesiastical disputes which were clearly well-known to many, in part because of Drant's position in the Church but more significantly because he secured a formidable reputation as a poet, translator and writer, completing a book of epigrams and a now-lost treatise on poetry, translating Horace's satires and his treatise on poetry, as well as the *Lamentations of Jeremiah* and a large number of feisty sermons. Drant's career cannot simply be explained in terms of the character of early modern Sussex, but the nature of religious dispute in the county played its part in developing the confrontational nature of his ecclesiastical life and his writing. Copley, in contrast, was an insider. He was the son of the prominent recusant Sir Thomas Copley (1534–84), from Roffey (Roughay) near Horsham, and was very close to the Browne family at Cowdray. Copley spent a large part of his adult life abroad in Rome and in the service of the King of Spain, but returned to England in 1590, whereupon he alternated between the risk of serious danger and morally compromised service to the crown. Copley, like Drant, developed a reputation as a hot-tempered, angry man. However, his poetry, which included a substantial book of varied epigrams and *A Fig For Fortune* (1596), the first sustained literary response to Edmund Spenser's *The Faerie Queene*, was often read as a plea for the toleration of Catholics, a project that might well be linked to Drant's early attempts to balance classical and Christian learning. Copley's career can largely be explained in terms of its engagement with the religious culture of early modern Sussex. While Drant was part of an attempt to impose a centralised will to conformity on the county, Copley was part of a concerted desire to resist in the name of an ancient faith.

I

Thomas Drant was brought to Sussex as a prominent member of a group of nearly forty Cambridge graduates enlisted by Richard Curteys, Bishop of Chichester, to vigorously impose uniformity on the county's notoriously errant clergy.[1] Drant had gained initial preferment from Curteys (and his friend and colleague Edmund Grindal) when at St John's, Cambridge, where Curteys was a senior fellow and deeply embroiled in the vestarian controversy, a failed attempt to impose conformity on the college in matters of clerical dress. Drant's later religious work – particularly his published sermons – indicate how deeply Curteys's position in these continuing controversies influenced his thinking.[2]

Bishop Curteys's zeal for the reformation of Sussex focused on charismatic and learned preaching (for which Curteys and Drant were celebrated, with

---

[1]   The details of Thomas Drant's biography are considered at greater length in R.W. McConchie, 'Drant, Thomas (c.1540–1578)', *Oxford Dictionary of National Biography*, Oxford University Press, 2004; online edn, January 2008.

[2]   A good example of this is the sermon Drant preached before the court at Windsor in 1570, decrying excesses in attire – it was printed in the same year as the second of *Two sermons preached the one at S. Maries Spittle on Tuesday in Easter weeke 1570 and the other at the court at Windsor* (London: John Daye, 1570).

both publishing a number of sermons) throughout Sussex, the deprivation of unschooled or recalcitrant local clergy, and the enforcement of conformity on the more conspicuous elements of the local populace.[3] Such tactics generated a great deal of ill feeling and controversy, particularly amongst the local gentry who conformed to the Elizabethan Church often unwillingly and on their own terms. Curteys was a firm Calvinist, with a conviction that 'the popular reformation had not yet begun or at least was not finished in some parts of England' – and especially in Sussex.[4] His zealous pursuit of that aim earned the enmity of Sir Thomas Palmer of Parham Hall in particular, and Palmer's accusations of misconduct brought Curteys the rebuke of the Privy Council on at least two occasions.[5]

When he officially arrived in Sussex, first as rector of Slinfold, then prebendary of Firle, and finally as archdeacon of Lewes, all in 1570 (the same year Curteys became Bishop of Chichester), Drant was therefore an incomer, an imposition from without. It seems that despite his duties at the cathedral he was resident in Chichester only infrequently, and his defence seems to have been that 'he is a preacher, and may do much good abroad in the country thereby', suggesting again the importance he and Curteys attached to this activity.[6] Even so, the number of benefices offered to him in 1570 indicate there was a serious attempt to lure him to the county. Drant's chief competitor for the archdeaconry of Lewes had been William Overton, client of the Earl of Leicester, son-in-law of the previous bishop, William Barlow, and later Bishop of Coventry and Lichfield. Overton was already treasurer of Chichester Cathedral and pressing for the bishopric at Barlow's death; frustrated in this attempt, he turned his attentions to Lewes, which was also given to Drant by his patron Curteys, no friend to Overton. Thereafter, Drant and Overton became bitter enemies, and their conflict represents deeper factions within the Sussex community.

Drant's position and some sense of his temperament can be found in an anonymous record of a sermon he gave at 'Lyncolne' (perhaps more likely to have been Lincoln's Inn than Lincoln Cathedral?), now among the Lansdowne manuscripts in the British Library and later partly transcribed by John Strype in

---

[3] Bishop Curteys's campaign in Sussex is analysed in detail in Roger Manning, *Religion and Society in Early Modern Sussex: A Study of the Enforcement of the Religious Settlement, 1558–1603* (Leicester: Leicester University Press, 1969), pp. 63–125. See also Roger Manning, 'Curteys, Richard (1532?–1582)', *Oxford Dictionary of National Biography*, Oxford University Press, 2004; online edn, January 2008.

[4] Manning, *Religion and Society*, p. 71.

[5] Ibid., pp. 93–4.

[6] Reproduced in Manning, *Religion and Society*, p. 73.

his *Annals of the English Reformation.*[7] Strype – sympathetic to the apparently more emollient Overton – describes how Drant 'most rudely aspersed him openly ... in most indecent language, no way beseeming the mouth of a preacher in so public a place, betraying his own malice, and envy, and pride, and conceit of himself'. The account begins with considerable verve:

> He sayd yt doctor Overton, was a very hypocrite, a noble, a gloriuse and everlastinge
> hipocrite & nothing els butt a meare sachel of hipocrysie. That he was brimfull,
> toppfull, overruninge full, toto full of hipocrisie and thought he damned in the nett
> of hipocrisy yett he would disrobe hym, & whipp hym withall.[8]

The substance of Overton's extreme hypocrisy lay, it seems, in pretence; an attempt to disguise a lack of zeal – issues at the heart of Curteys's reforms. Rather than crypto-Catholic, however, Overton's deceptions were more subtle. Drant accuses him of being 'lyke a vyce in a playe' – he represents 'a graver mans p[ar]t' but has 'no gravity'; he swells with the title of a doctor and yet has 'no doctryne'. Drant goes further: Overton is covetous as a treasurer, a spoiler of the county's woods, a keeper of 'excessive fare', heaping 'dishes upon dishes' at his table, just as he did with benefices. Worse, Overton does not even understand his own sermons, nor could any divinity be found in them (the focus on preaching once again a reminder of its importance to Drant's and Curteys's vision of faith and strategies for uniformity). This theme is continued in Drant's assertion that this 'doltyshe doctor' came by his degree 'by some sinister means' and that Drant, along with two others, had 'taken more paynes in london, and broughte more things to passe amongst the sqeamish heads of ye londyners, then ever did this doctor, or iii of the best doctors that ever dubbed him a doctor had done'.[9] At its root, Drant's argument hinges on the differences established between his own devotion to his calling and its transformative effect, and Overton's careerist, mercenary attitudes. For Drant (and for Curteys), the true church of God had no place for such men.

Later in the account – which was surely compiled by an ally of Overton, perhaps for the attention of the Privy Council in the context of their suspension of Bishop Curteys from the exercise of his episcopal duties in 1578 – the

---

[7]   John Strype, *Annals of the Reformation and Establishment of Religion* (Oxford: Clarendon, 1824: reprinted by Cambridge University Press in 2010) Vol. 2, part 2, p. 379. Strype ignores the title on the manuscript – suggesting instead that this sermon took place in Chichester.

[8]   BL Lansdowne 110, f. 56v.

[9]   Ibid.

bitterness of this dispute gives way to Drant's sense of himself and of his theology.[10] When commenting on this section, Strype suggested that it indicates how 'in an overweening conceit of himself, he was disturbed in his mind.'[11] The anonymous author records that Drant 'began to boast of his forwardness in the Hebrewe tongue, & his great skyll in the arte of Rhetorik'.[12] Furthermore, in a short postscript that purports to record another sermon at St Giles in Cripplegate, London, Drant then argued that those who had 'translated the Bible understood not the Hebrewe tongue as he did, and therefore had translated it falsely'.[13]

Drant's facility in languages was well-known: he was an accomplished translator and scholar, and it had been his reputation for 'learning' that had hastened his appointment to the prebendary at Chichester in early 1570.[14] For all its boastful self-aggrandisement, Drant's assertion of intellectual and spiritual superiority was part of an ideological template for reform in which he saw himself as an exemplar of what a clergyman should be: educated in the biblical languages and thus up to date with new exegetical possibilities, and trained in the arts of rhetoric in order to stir the hearts of local congregations. In the battle waged by Curteys, Grindal and others for control of the Anglican Church – in some quarters characterised as a struggle between the forces of Christ and Antichrist – Sussex became a key battleground, with Thomas Drant on the front line.

Drant's position suggests he, and by extension Curteys, were necessarily unimpeachable. But the vigorous efforts of their opponents ensured that this was not the case, with accusations of venality, bribery, simony, gambling, drunkenness, adultery and nepotism made at Curteys and his supporters (it was the last of these, centred upon Curteys's brother Edmund as vicar of Cuckfield, that finally led to his suspension).[15] Neither did Drant escape censure, and Gabriel Harvey's well-known references to him as 'your gorbellyed Maister' and as 'a fat-bellied Archdeacon' might suggest not simply that Drant was a substantial man, but also that he exercised the same gluttonous hypocrisy Drant had attempted to use to tarnish William Overton.[16]

However, while Harvey laughed at Drant's ponderous figure, he and his protégé, Edmund Spenser, took Drant very seriously as a translator and,

---

[10]   Curteys's fall mirrored that of Archbishop Grindal in the previous year. The circumstances are thoroughly analysed in Manning, *Religion and Society*, pp. 113–25.

[11]   Strype, *Annals of the Reformation* 2.2, p. 381.

[12]   BL Lansdowne 110, f. 56v. Strype does not transcribe this or the following section.

[13]   Ibid., f. 57v.

[14]   Manning, *Religion and Society*, p. 72.

[15]   Ibid., pp. 113–25 and his 'Curteys, Richard', *ODNB*.

[16]   Manning, 'Curteys'.

especially, as a theorist of poetry. In his published correspondence with Harvey, Spenser grants Drant two favourable mentions. First, he chides Harvey – partly in jest – for making a 'breach in Maister *Drants* Rules', and secondly, when he provides evidence that Drant's theories of metre formed the basis for the most innovative discussion of poetry in the late 1570s:

> I would hartily wish, you would either send me the Rules and Precepts of Arte, which
> you obserue in Quantities, or else followe mine, that *M. Philip Sidney* gaue me, being
> the very same which *M. Drant* deuised, but enlarged with *M Sidneys* own judgement,
> and augmented with my Obseruations, that we might both accorde and agree in one.[17]

Spenser's comments cannot be taken quite at face value, as he is clearly trying to establish a wider literary community – the Areopagus – than may really have existed, in order to add weight to his own contribution and importance at the start of his literary career. But what these comments do indicate is that Drant, who appears to have written a now-lost treatise on quantative metre, was regarded as one of the key literary theorists of the late 1570s. The fact that the experiments with quantative metre proved to be a dead end has obscured Drant's significance and eminence in the years before and after his death.[18]

Drant was supposedly discouraged from continuing his poetic and classical career by Grindal, as he suggests in his dedication to the Archbishop prefacing *Thomae Drantae Angli Aduordingamii Praesul Eiusdem Sylua* (1576).[19] Grindal evidently felt that Drant's talents would be better suited in the service of the Church. This was no small sacrifice on Drant's part, as the Harvey-Spenser comments indicate. Drant had already forged a considerable reputation as the first English translator of Horace, a bold, innovative and astute decision. Ben Jonson, a conspicuously Horatian poet, did not translate the *Ars Poetica* until the very end of his career.[20] Drant published two major editions of Horace's *Satires, Verse Epistles*, and *Art of Poetry* in his mid-thirties.

Drant's poetry has often been rather harshly judged, although C.S. Lewis valued Drant's 'homely and pungent manner', which was at least compatible

---

[17]   Edmund Spenser, *The Prose Works*, ed. Edwin Greenlaw et al. (Baltimore, MD: The Johns Hopkins Press, 1949), pp. 12, 16.

[18]   Derek Attridge, *Well-Weighed Syllables: Elizabethan Verse in Classical Metres* (Cambridge: Cambridge University Press, 1974), pp. 130, 139.

[19]   McConchie, 'Drant'.

[20]   Ben Jonson, *Horace His Art of Poetry, Made English by Ben Jonson*, ed. Colin Burrow, in *The Cambridge Edition of the Works of Ben Jonson*, eds David Bevington, Martin Butler and Ian Donaldson, 7 vols (Cambridge: Cambridge University Press, 2012), VII, pp. 1–67.

with Horace's style, albeit nowhere near as urbane.[21] In the one recent article dedicated to Drant's translations, Neel Mukherjee sees Drant's Horace as a monolithic and leaden text which demolishes the nuances of the Latin original, 'foreclos[ing] any possibility of movement and accommodation by its intolerant overtones'.[22] The work warrants far more serious analysis because of its significance in English literary history, its intrinsic quality, and for its crucial relationship to his ecclesiastical career.

A superficial reading of Drant might seem to support Mukherjee's judgement. Drant's writing does not always strike the right note and he can appear to be lacking in sophistication and subtlety with his vigorous, demotic and Anglicised style of writing. Drant renders Horace's ironic warning against the over-exuberant pursuit of virtue in his epistle to his friend, Numitius, in flat, clumsy lines that seem oblivious to the subtle nature of the original Latin:

> The wyse man maye be counted mad, the righteouse man vniuste,
> If he after virtue virtue it selfe more then enough do luste.[23]

Elsewhere the lines have a jolly jingle that can seem trivial. In the fifth satire of the first book, Drant replaces Horace's thoughts on movement and journeys with his reflections on the state of worship in the contemporary English Church, with mixed results:

> My thinks this church, this englishe churche,
> Is clogged at this daye,
> With ceremonies more than nedes,
> To tell you at a worde,
> I would haue all thynges iuste as they
> Were left vs by the Lorde.[24]

---

[21] C.S. Lewis, *English Literature in the Sixteenth Century, Excluding Drama* (Oxford: Oxford University Press, 1954), p. 256.

[22] Neel Mukherjee, 'Thomas Drant's Rewriting of Horace', *Studies in English Literature, 1500–1900* 40 (2000), 1–20, p. 18. See also Fred Schrink, 'Thomas Drant', in Garrett A. Sullivan and Alan Stewart, eds, *The Encyclopedia of Renaissance Literature* <www.literatureencyclopedia. com/subscriber/uid=4905/tocnode.html?id=g9781405194495_chunk_g97814051944957_ ss1-17&authstatuscode=202> (accessed 21 December 2012).

[23] Thomas Drant, *Horace His Arte of Poetrie, Pistles, and Satyres Englished* (London, 1567), sig. D1r.

[24] Thomas Drant, *A Medicinable Morall, that is, the two bookes of Horace his satyres, Englyshed accordyng to the prescription of saint Hierome. The wailyngs of the prophet Hieremiah, done into Englyshe verse. Also epigrammes* (London, 1566) , sig. C8r.

Such lines have a simple power, and are clear and easy to understand, but they bear no resemblance to the poetry of Horace. However, the next few lines seem rather more promising:

> This knewe I was the deynte dyshe,
> that so theyr passions fed:
> I am not nowe to learne I trowe,
> to bring a babe to bed.

The sentence neatly links two images. The first disparages the epicurean nature of those who wish to add ceremonies to the basic ones – those whom followers of Grindal like Drant abhorred – but the second then surely hints at the problems that clerical marriage might impose on learned divines who knew little of family life.[25] There may, of course, be a further joke at his own expense, given Drant's corpulence. Perhaps Drant was rather more Horatian than his critics have allowed.

At its best, Drant's version of Horace has an idiomatic flavour that would have reminded literate readers of John Skelton, one of the many English poets co-opted by Protestants as an internal critic of the late medieval Church.[26] The concluding lines of Horace's last satire (Book 2, satire 8), attacking greed, are a good example:

> Therfore some people parasites,
> that they may seeme to passe,
> Wyll spende out maluesey, muscadell,
> and fumyshe hypocrasse.
> And make their cookes looshiously,
> theyr delicates to dresse
> Their very meates in insensiue
> brought in, in suche excesse:
> That I doo lothe them more in mynde,
> as thynges more full of harme,
> Then, if that witche, that Canadie,
> had cursed them with her charme (sig. R6r).

Drant adapts and updates Horace, who had described blackbirds 'served with breasts slightly charred' and 'pigeons minus their rumps', which the guests

---

[25]   For the background, see Mukherjee, 'Drant's Rewriting of Horace', pp. 3–7.

[26]   John N. King, *English Reformation Literature: The Tudor Origins of the Protestant Tradition* (Princeton, NJ: Princeton University Press, 1982), pp. 11–12, 254–6.

wolfed down without tasting in order to escape the tedious lectures of their host. Horace's guests would have enjoyed the feast in other circumstances, but Drant's description of the feast with its array of expensive spiced drinks is something to be avoided at all costs (is there a recollection of January drinking a collection of spiced wines to fortify his sexual prowess in *The Merchant's Tale*, as Chaucer was another author appropriated by a Protestant literary tradition?).[27]

Drant's translations of Horace were published alongside his version of *Lamentations* in *A Medicinable Morall*, the aim being to make readers understand that the classics and the Bible could be understood to contain similar wisdom, holding up a mirror to the excesses of contemporary life and so, through the use of example and satire, exhorting mankind to virtue and proper behaviour. Each verse translation looks exactly the same on the page, a deliberate ploy that involved dividing the fourteeners of the translation of Horace published the previous year into two so that both texts alternate between lines of eight and six syllables. The rather tinny opening of the third chapter of *Lamentations* sounds very like any number of passages in the satires:

> I am that wight, that abiecte wighte,
> whiche mine owne neade haue seene,
> Whilste that, the massie rod of God,
> vppon my backe hath bene.[28]

What Drant was trying to achieve was incredibly difficult and involved a whole range of poetic experimentation, as he sought to produce a version of English writing that could accommodate the Bible and the most important Latin poetry, making both accessible to a wide audience. That his output might seem uneven should not surprise us. What he did achieve shows just how skilled and resourceful a linguist, rhetorician and poet he really was. That he wrote in a Skeltonic style at times, and yet was also able to berate his fellow Biblical translators for lacking Hebrew, speaks volumes for his ambition and for the complexity of the tasks he set himself.

Drant's translations suggest further that the aggressive style he adopted in his sermons, which shocked John Strype, was, rightly or wrongly, a conscious decision that abuse of his opponents was required for him to make his point,

---

[27] *The Satires of Horace and Persius*, trans. Niall Rudd (Harmondsworth: Penguin, 1973), p. 113; Geoffrey Chaucer, *The Merchant's Tale* (Fragment IV, line 1807) in *The Riverside Chaucer*, ed. Larry D. Benson et al. (Oxford: Oxford University Press, 1987), p. 160.

[28] Drant, *A Medicinable Morall*, sig. R5v.

not simply a failing of character and temperament. Drant obviously meant to use his skills to make his message fit into the correct medium. Furthermore, it is a sign of the times and the urgent need many saw to accelerate the progress of the Reformation in key areas of the British Isles that Drant was asked to abandon his scholarly and literary career to wage confessional war in Sussex against lukewarm Protestant backsliders and Catholics of every hue. Priority had to be given to dangerous areas that needed to be forced to conform. Drant was not made in Sussex, but was seen as exactly the sort of man who could change the county and help impose uniformity in the south of England. The English Reformation was, as Brian Cummings has argued, a literary phenomenon, its makers quick to see the need for the literate and the literary to make it work.[29]

II

If Thomas Drant was involved in the imposition of religious uniformity in Sussex, Anthony Copley spent his life resisting and negotiating that uniformity. Born into a family that was embedded within a network of Catholic gentry that focused on Sussex but extended into Surrey and Hampshire – the Shelleys of Michelgrove, the Gages of Firle, the Kempes of Slindon, the Thatchers of Priesthawes and the Apsleys of Pulborough, and beyond them, the Viscounts Montague of Cowdray and the Earls of Southampton – Copley's contrary and controversial trajectory was a product of the struggle for early modern Sussex that so animated Thomas Drant.[30]

For recusant priests seeking access to English Catholic communities, Sussex had a series of advantages. It had a long and largely ungovernable southern coastline, and a road system that (outside of key routes northwards into London) barely functioned, which together facilitated ease of clandestine movement. It had a ready-made network of sympathetic gentry, with familial connections and land that stretched across the county, from Cowdray and Midhurst in the west to the dowager Lady Montague's Catholic stronghold at Battle in the east.[31] It also had a store of young men – the product of these closely allied families – prepared to cross and re-cross the Channel to keep English Catholicism alive, whether by

---

[29] Brian Cummings, *The Literary Culture of the Reformation; Grammar and Grace* (Oxford: Oxford University Press, 2002), p. 5.

[30] Manning, *Religion and Society*, p. 155.

[31] Ibid., pp. 159–63.

fighting for Catholic armies or by taking holy orders. The State Papers report numerous Sussex men – Edward James, Rafe Crocket, John Owen and many more – who were 'made priest beyond the sea' and had been apprehended on their return into England.[32]

Anthony Copley was another such product of the Elizabethan settlement in Sussex. In his teenage years, he trod the familiar paths of English Catholic exile, living with his parents in Rouen, spending time in Rome and gaining a pension from Pope Gregory XIII secured by his kinsman the Jesuit Robert Southwell, and then serving (and gaining another pension) with the Duke of Parma's Spanish army in the Low Countries. Yet he was well connected in England as a kinsman of the Queen, Lord Burghley and Francis Walsingham. Following the death of his father, and the award of a £30 annuity in the will, Copley returned to England in 1590, aged 23.[33] Unlike some of his kinsmen and many of his contemporaries, he was not compelled by his religion to do so as a recusant priest, but returned instead – so he claimed – as 'a true subiect toward Prince & Countrey'.[34] He was arrested, suggesting the Privy Council were well aware of his movements, and was interrogated by the clerk of that council, William Waad. The four reports in Copley's hand that survive from between late October 1590 and early January 1591 seem to be responses to the Privy Council's demands for ever more detail about the movements, resources and opinions of English Catholics (and some significant others – most notably Parma) whom Copley had either met or heard about.[35] This level of detail, coupled with Copley's desperate protestations of loyalty – he asks that his death 'in her Ma[jes]ties service in the behalf of my Country make amends hereafter for such my offence'; his heart is guilty only of 'love and duty to my Country' – indicates that, despite immediate imprisonment in the Fleet for his recusancy, he was prepared to turn informer when necessary and that he saw his future as an English Catholic in England.[36]

Despite his willingness to accede to demands for specific information on individuals, Copley is still circumspect – he is careful only to incriminate those

---

[32]   Strype, *Annals of the Reformation* 4, p. 256.

[33]   Detailed in Michael A.R. Graves, 'Copley, Anthony (b. 1567, d. in or after 1609)', *Oxford Dictionary of National Biography*, Oxford University Press, 2004; online edn, January 2008.

[34]   BL Lansdowne 64 f. 25r. This letter is also transcribed in part in Strype, *Annals of the Reformation* 4, pp. 379–85.

[35]   They begin at BL Lansdowne 64 f. 25v, f. 31v; Lansdowne 66 f. 74v, f. 116v. There is an earlier report that is incomplete but in similar handwriting that concerns English Catholics abroad – this too may be from Copley – Lansdowne 63 f. 154r. The first two of these reports are transcribed in part in Strype, *Annals of the Reformation* 4, pp. 379–85 and 386–93.

[36]   *Acts of the Privy Council of England*, 1591–92, p. 163; BL Lansdowne 64 f. 29v.

he feels have acted treacherously, and displays a commitment to toleration commensurate with that espoused by Anthony Browne, Viscount Montagu (and kinsman to Copley) as well as by Henry Percy, ninth Earl of Northumberland (who was based nearby in Petworth) and others.[37] When considering English Catholics abroad, Copley takes care to note:

> In fine, my good lords, so it is, that divers English gentlemen there are beyond the seas, whose faith to England and her majesty's happy estate is most sincere and loyal; and who only for their conscience (for ought I could ever know to the contrary) have betaken themselves to foreign infelicity and misadventures; willing, if occasion were, to lose life and all for England and her majesty, might they by your honours favours be but permitted to live at home.[38]

This was as much a plea for himself and for his exiled father's memory as for his comrades and his country, but it does suggest the vision he had of a state governed not according to the policing of conscience, but on the basis of individual loyalty – one in which politics and religion remained distinct. Such a vision was anathema to the one propounded in Sussex by Bishop Curteys and Thomas Drant, but it seems that Copley had no intention of subscribing to their brand of uniformity: after his release he moved to his ancestral lands in Roffey, near Horsham, in the north-west of the county, where he began to use translation and writing to press his own tolerationist agenda.[39]

Given the pressures increasingly exerted on the Catholic communities in Sussex, it should be no surprise that Copley's existence was erratic. The state's chief interrogator and hunter of recusants was Richard Topcliffe, who was tasked with tracing the routes used for smuggling priests through Sussex to

---

[37]   As Manning notes, 'Lord Montague's unique position as the most important Catholic in Sussex and perhaps the most influential Catholic in England derived from his unquestioned loyalty to the queen and his unscrupulous moderation in religious matters' – a position Copley's mirrors: *Religion and Society in Early Modern Sussex*, p. 160. Whilst both Henry Percy, the eighth Earl of Northumberland and Philip Howard, Earl of Arundel and Surrey fell foul of mixing politics and Catholicism, the ninth Earl approached the future James I to advocate tolerance for English Catholics.

[38]   BL Lansdowne 64 f. 29v.

[39]   Copley's father Thomas was also a translator, similarly seeking to press a vision of religious unity, and translated *Certain Treaties ... Touching the Doctrine of Good Works* and *A Treatise of justification. Founde among the writinges of Cardinal Pole of blessed memory* both published in Louvain in 1569. His letters among the State Papers indicate that he was on occasion an informer on English Catholics abroad to the Privy Council, but spent much of his life abroad struggling to maintain the queen's favour.

London, and to whom Copley and his family were probably well known. Before Anthony's return to England, the family and their extended network of recusant contacts had come under intense official scrutiny: in September 1586 (two years after her own return to England), Lady Copley had been apprehended and transported to London on the orders of Francis Walsingham after a priest named Nicholas Smith (alias Phelps) had been discovered at her house in Roffey.[40] The examinations of Lady Copley and her daughter Margaret indicate that Smith was their kinsman, that she had supported him at both her houses at Gatton and at Roffey, and that only the night before he had been at Edward Gage's house at Firle.[41] All parties were interrogated (and Lady Copley would be apprehended – along with 'other dangerous persons remaining with her' – again, nearly ten years later, apparently for the same crime).[42] As late as 1613, long after Anthony had left the country in disgraced exile, the family were still under suspicion: Anthony's elder brother William (earlier one of the Queen's wards) would be described in official documentation as 'a recusant convict'.[43]

The tensions and pressures that the imposition of religious uniformity on Sussex placed on the Copley family go some way to explain Anthony's otherwise curious behaviour and inform his writing. In June 1592, Topcliffe wrote to the queen reporting on an examination of the Jesuit Robert Southwell, with whom Copley was 'most familiar'. In the course of that report, he refers to Copley as the 'most desperant yowth yt lyuethe', and goes on: 'Coplay did shoote at a gentilman the last summr, & killed an Oxe wth a muskett, & in horsham Church threwe his dagger at ye p[ar]ishe Clarke & stuck it in a Seat in ye Church. There lyueth not ye lyke I think in Engl[and] for sudden attempts.'[44]

Unpredictable bursts of violence, particularly in a parish church setting, suggest Copley's boiling frustration and the limits of his toleration: the opportunities for advancement and patronage for an English Catholic poet and translator were rapidly shrinking, his family were under close scrutiny, and there

---

[40]   Letter from Francis Walsingham to the Justices of the Peace, 11 September 1586. *A Catalogue of the Harleian Manuscripts in the British Museum*, eds Robert Nores, Stebbing Shaw, Joseph Planta, Francis Dacre and T.H. Horne (London: Record Commission, 1808), p. 417.

[41]   Examinations dated 9 September 1586. *Calendar of State Papers Domestic, 1581–1590*, p. 352.

[42]   Letter from Lord Buckhurst to Sir Walter Covert, 28 January 1595: *A Catalogue of the Harleian Manuscripts*, p. 418. This may, of course, be a later Lady Copley, perhaps Anthony's sister-in-law.

[43]   A Licence for William Copley, 19 May 1613. *Acts of the Privy Council of England*, 1613–14, p. 44.

[44]   BL Lansdowne 72 f. 113v–113r. See also Strype, *Annals of the Reformation* 4, p. 186.

was no shift in the religious and political landscape in prospect. His writing was shaped by the same forces.

Copley was undoubtedly a writer of great, eccentric talent, eager to experiment and forge new forms of writing, achievements that provide yet another link to the life and work of Thomas Drant. In other ways, Drant would have been rather less keen to be associated with the younger writer. One remarkable facet of Copley's writing is his resolute refusal to disguise his beliefs, his connections and his knowledge, perhaps an indication of how securely he felt protected by his patrons, or his arrogance and devil-may-care attitude. Certainly no one reading Copley's work could have had any doubts that he was a Catholic with links to Europe. By the time he published his collection of proverbs, jokes and parables, *Wits, Fittes and Fancies* in 1595, Copley had spent two years in Rome and served the Spanish crown in Flanders. The dedicatory epistle to George Clifford, third Earl of Cumberland (1558–1605), makes it clear that the work is largely a translation from a Spanish source:

> I hope the generalitie of the matter, ioint that the Author is a stranger, will, if not priuiledge such amisse, yet at least wise holde it excused in your favour. It seemeth the *Spaniard* for his part (for so he was) did not basselie conceipt this matter, that did dare direct it to so high a State as *Don Iohn* of *Austria*, his Lieges brother. But how ere it were blameworthy or innocence in him I recke not, neither yet force I howe *Don Iohn* conceipted it, so your Lordship daigne it in gree.[45]

By any standards, this is an unusually bold, casual and familiar form of address to a major court figure. Copley assumes an almost intimate association with the earl, publicly denigrating a foreign prince as unworthy of his care, and adopting a conversational style ('I recke not'). Certainly this letter reads more as one between equals rather than one from a supplicant to a potential patron. Clifford could well have been discomforted by this dedication: he was born into a Catholic family and then brought up a Protestant under the wardship of the Protestant Russells. He fought against the Spanish as a privateer in the 1580s with some success – on the opposing side to Copley – but he was never granted the post that he felt his rank deserved.[46] Interestingly enough, there is no record of any further contact between Copley and Clifford – in marked contrast to the enduring relationship between Copley and Anthony Browne, Viscount

---

[45] Anthony Copley, *Wits, Fittes, and Fancies* (London, 1595), sig. A2r–v.

[46] Peter Holmes, 'Clifford, George, third earl of Cumberland (1558–1605)', *Oxford Dictionary of National Biography*, Oxford University Press, 2004; online edn, January 2008.

Montague, to whom his next work, *A Fig For Fortune*, was dedicated – which would suggest that this offering did not lead to any substantial gains. Copley hopes that Clifford will enjoy the work, again, in terms that sound like the familiar musings of a friend rather than a humble offering to a patron: 'I did intende it to your late sea-voyage, to the ende it might haue pleased you to passe away therwith some vnpleasant houres. But as it was not ripe ynough for that season, so now I pray God it come in due season to your good liking.'[47] Copley is perhaps assuming rather too much about the earl's tastes and habits, at least in public.[48]

The text itself consists of translations from a Spanish work, *La Floretta Spagnola*, interlaced with additions of Copley's own, and concludes with a long dialogue poem, 'Love's Owl'.[49] The work is divided into thematic sections, many of which further advertise their origins, notably one entitled 'Biscayans and Fools'. The tales and jokes here point out Spanish inequalities and prejudices with a laconic humour: 'A *Biscayn* being demanded what Countri-man he thought God was, he answered: Questionles a Castilan, for that neuer in all my life could I yet loue him hartily.'[50] Is Copley showing what a good, loyal subject he is in declaring his knowledge of England's chief enemy and revealing how divided and fractious Spain really is? Possibly. Other tales are perhaps darker and more self-reflective. In the section 'Of Fellons and Thieves' we find the sentence: 'A Scholler being to be hang'd for robbing his father in law, at the very instant that he was to be throwne off the ladder, said: *Dulce mori pro Patria*.'[51] The reference, of course, is to Horace's 'Ode' (III, 2), but it surely cannot have escaped Copley's attention that he had already been forced to plead for his life against charges of treason and had followed the path he had taken because of his family's allegiances. The section, 'Of Equivocates in Speech', seems extraordinarily prescient given the role that Henry Garnett played in the aftermath of the Gunpowder Plot.[52] Again, this might seem to be loyal exposure of a foreign threat or a sly warning that Copley himself, who was never entirely loyal to the crown, was not quite what he seemed to be. Even more confrontational is a joke in the next section,

---

[47]   Copley, *Wits, Fittes, and Fancies*, sig. A2v.

[48]   A few others were translating similar material from Spanish in this period, but rarely so flagrantly. Those examples that remain extant are anonymous and in manuscript – see, for example, the English translation of the Catalan romance *El Deseoso* (1589) now in the Beinecke Library (Osborn MS.a.41).

[49]   Graves, 'Copley'.

[50]   Copley, *Wits, Fittes, and Fancies*, sig. S2r.

[51]   Ibid., sig. X1v.

[52]   See David Jardine, ed., *A Treatise of Equivocation* (London: Longman, 1851).

'Extravagant Speech': 'A Recusant making water against a church-wal, the Church-warden seeing it, excepted thereunto, as prophanely done. Whereunto he answered: It is my Church, not yours.'[53] Surely this does rather more than expose a mindset and advertises Copley's true loyalties.

However it was read, *Wits, Fittes and Fancies* proved popular and was reprinted the next year and again in 1614, by which time Copley was either in exile or dead. *A Fig For Fortune* (1596) was his only other literary work, suggesting that Copley may have decided to abandon literature in the mid- to late 1590s, perhaps because it was too risky a pursuit (his last published works before he was involved in the Bye Plot and went into exile were anti-Jesuit tracts pledging Catholic loyalty, published in 1601–02). The poem, consisting of 355 six-line stanzas, has long been recognised as a Catholic adaptation of Edmund Spenser's *Faerie Queene*. Book 1, 'The Legend of the Knight of Holiness', is specifically a plea for the toleration of loyal Catholics. Throughout, Copley shows that he is, if nothing else, a careful and confrontational reader of Spenser, bold enough to provide the first poetic response to a writer celebrated as England's premier poet.[54] *A Fig For Fortune*, the title further suggesting Copley's chutzpah alongside the theological sub-text of trusting God above earthly things, contains numerous echoes of Spenserian vocabulary and reveals how closely he has read the older man's work. But Copley has cast Spenser in his own idiom and the poem is only intermittently Spenserian. (It is not written in Spenserian stanza, does not often sound like Spenser, or use Spenserian vocabulary; it contains only one plot, and has a relatively simple allegorical message.)

Copley reverses Spenser's representation of Duessa as a figure for Catholic deception with his own figure of Doblessa, the evil female spirit of the Church of England. In doing so, he repeats the familiar Catholic taunt to Protestants: 'Where was your church before Luther?' His description of the evil goddess begins with a rhetorical question that celebrates the Catholic martyrs, that is, the Jesuits whom he later publicly attacks:

> How manie Sionits of choise esteeme
> Brave men of woonders have beene sent from thence
> To teach Doblessa (Errors dreary Queene)

---

53   Copley, *Wits, Fittes, and Fancies*, sig. Y3r.

54   Paul J. Klemp, 'Imitations and adaptations, Renaissance (1579–1660)', in A.C. Hamilton, ed., *The Spenser Encyclopedia* (London and Toronto: Routledge/Toronto University Press, 1990), pp. 395–6.

Their Temples sanctimonie and innocence?
How many worthies have dispenst their blood
To doe th' unkind Doblessa so much good.

But she, oh she accursed Sorceresse
Would never yet beleeve, nor gree their grace
But still persisteth in her wretchednesse
Warfaring with bloody broile this happy place;
Yea, had she might according to her malice
Sion had been a ruine long ere this.

She was a Witch, and Queen of all the Desert
From Babell-mount unto the pit of Hell,
She forc'd nor God, nor any good desert,
She could doe any thing save doing well:
Her law was Libertie, her lust was Pride
And all good awe and order she defi'd.

Erst ere this Temple was established
She had no being at all above the earth
But ever lay in deepest hell abyssed;
Why did not God confound her in her birth?
Oh, t'was because his Temple might attaine
Through her assaults to be more soveraigne.[55]

Copley associates Doblessa with Babylon, a clear allusion to Spenser's representation of Duessa as the Whore of Babylon; for good measure, he also associates her with lust and pride, further allusions to Duessa's behaviour in Book I, and to Lucifera's house of Pride (Canto 5).[56] Her temple – that is, the Church of England – exists in Hell before brought to earth with the permission of God who sees its persecuting force merely serving to validate the true Catholic Church through the creation of martyrs (an argument used by both sides of the confessional divide in early modern England).[57]

---

[55] Anthony Copley, *A Fig For Fortune* (London. 1596), sig. K2v.
[56] For further analysis of Duessa, see D. Douglas Waters, *Duessa as Theological Satire* (Columbia: University of Missouri Press, 1970).
[57] Susannah Breitz Monta, *Martyrdom and Literature in Early Modern England* (Cambridge: Cambridge University Press, 2005).

Copley ends his poem with what Frederick Padleford has described as 'a duplicity nothing short of sublime in its daring', when he has the narrator mistake the Virgin Mary for Elizabeth:

And still I call'd upon Elizas name
Thinking those Roses hers, that figure hers,
Untill such time as Catechrysius came
And pointing me unto his faithfull teares
(Teares of the zeale he bare t'Elizas name)
He told me No; she was an Esterne Dame.

With that I case mine eye into the East
Where yet I might discerne the region bright,
Much like as when the Sunne downe in the West
Newly discended, leaves us of his light
Some Rubie-Rellickes after: Oh, deer God
Why made she not with us more long abod.
Rapt with these woonders, wrapt in virgin-Roses
And faire be-Sioned against misfortune,
I suddainly was gone from these reposes
Sollicited with an especiall importune
Of home-ward zeale and of Elizas name,
Wherto I bend, and say; God blesse the same.[58]

The lines are disingenuous, to say the least. Elizabeth was the Supreme Governor of the Church of England and the first half of her reign had been a struggle to define and create a state Church that would be acceptable to as many of her subjects as was possible.[59] Copley cannot have been ignorant of this fact and neither, surely, were most of his readers in England, making it less than clear what he was hoping to achieve through his clever but far from persuasive allegory. Perhaps the point was to produce a poem for English Catholics, a rewriting of the work that many saw as a celebration of the Protestant queen, regardless of the consequences.[60] It is little wonder that Copley was described in such disparaging

---

[58] Copley, *A Fig For Fortune*, sig. M2v.
[59] William P. Haugaard, *Elizabeth and the English Reformation: The struggle for a stable settlement of religion* (Cambridge: Cambridge University Press, 1968)
[60] That Spenser's religious and political affiliations are notably complex is now an accepted facet of modern criticism: see Andrew Hadfield, *Edmund Spenser: A Life* (Oxford: Oxford University Press, 2012). Evidence does, however, suggest that Catholics saw Spenser as a

terms by Richard Topcliffe, or that he had such a complicated and difficult life in Elizabethan and early Jacobean England.

III

What can we learn from this study of two religious intellectuals in Sussex? In many ways, Drant and Copley seem to be quite similar figures. Each was confrontational and prepared to challenge enemies in a provocative manner – although Drant had a more obviously aggressive style, while Copley was as insolent and reckless as he was satirical and dismissive. Each took their religion seriously and were convinced that they were right, their opponents deluded, and both were more than happy to engage in polemic. They were both learned, Drant in a rather more scholarly way than Copley. Both were particularly interested in literature, kept abreast of current developments in literary culture, and were eager to experiment. As a result, both were closely engaged in thinking about the relationship between literature and faith, Drant trying to reconcile sacred and classical language through his juxtaposition of the language and style of Horace and *Lamentations*, a manoeuvre that was not to everyone's taste, while Copley, a careful and close reader of Spenser, sought to appropriate Protestant literature for Catholic ends. Both explicitly brought the Church of England into their literary work; both saw themselves as reforming forces and craved a return to an original purity – visions forged through their immediate experiences of that Church in Sussex. The combination of ferocity and toleration in the work of both men was, of course, not unusual in this period, but each exhibited what we might see as a contradiction today in a relatively exaggerated manner.

What separated the two men was not simply their religion, but the forms that their particular religious faiths took in Sussex. Copley was acutely aware that he was from an ancient Catholic family and clearly believed that times would change and the legitimate form of worship would eventually return to replace the new-fangled apostasy that had temporarily replaced it. Hence, the hauteur that Copley's writing often exhibits and, perhaps also, the apparently casual manner in which he was prepared to be reconciled to the Elizabethan authorities, as well as the way in which he was nearly destroyed in the false dawn that James I's accession represented for English Catholics. Drant, on the other hand, was a committed anti-Catholic who was determined to extirpate all trace

Protestant: Richard Peterson, 'Laurel Crown and Ape's Tail: New Light on Spenser's Career from Sir Thomas Tresham', *Spenser Studies* 12 (1989): 1–36.

of superstitious popish forms from the county. Indeed, that was the very reason why he came to Sussex. The stories that the lives of Copley and Drant tell us were not unique, as early modern England provides ample evidence of tales of such striking divisions. They are, however, an accurate testimony of the fractured religious life that characterised Sussex in this period of reform and resistance.

Chapter 3

Lambert Barnard, Bishop Shirborn's 'Paynter'

Karen Coke

As an early sixteenth-century Tudor painter, Lambert Barnard is of immense significance to the cultural history of Sussex and England. His work, created in the environment of a regional episcopal court for Robert Sherborn, Bishop of Chichester, was varied in subject and significant for the glimpses it allows of the nature and uses of painting away from the particular, often transitory, demands of the London court. Created between 1513 and 1537, narratives in Barnard's *oeuvre* are particularly informative, reflecting the cultural ambience of the county and the changing concerns of ecclesiastical and state politics immediately prior to the Reformation; they provide sure example when, elsewhere in the country, there is little contemporary comparative material.

Unusually, Lambert Barnard appears to have worked only in and around Chichester. His career was determined by the same type of patronage, extended by king, cardinal and courtier in which novelty, costly material – even the status afforded to his patron through the act of employing a foreign or especially gifted craftsman – combined in a conspicuous display of wealth, loyalty and learning, designed to reinforce the special status of these individuals. Barnard, like the court painters of mainland Europe, was expected to fulfil a similar and wide range of commissions; however, in spite of his episcopal patronage, no evidence of purely devotional or religious material by him has survived.

Time has not been kind to his paintings; damp, neglect and iconoclasm has meant that all his work has undergone restoration and, in some cases, drastic overpainting that has obscured much fine detail. Recent conservation of his largest scheme has revealed him to have had greater skill and a more delicate hand than previously believed.

Apart from a brief period in the 1880s when antiquarian interest was focused on the re-discovery of a series of his painted panels executed c. 1526, little attention was given to the rest of Lambert Barnard's *oeuvre* until 1957 when Edward Croft-Murray, recognising the singularity and significance of the painter's work, published the first, albeit brief, monograph on the painter.[1] More recently attempts have been made to examine the political and social conditions under which his paintings were produced, how these same conditions shaped his art, the circumstances of his employment and how, as a painter working in England, he relates to wider European practice. It is impossible to overestimate the importance to Barnard's work of the catalyst that was his episcopal patron.

Robert Sherborn, Bishop of Chichester, belonged to that group of churchmen whose career had followed paths of academic, secretarial and ambassadorial responsibility. The recipient of many emoluments, he was admitted as Dean of St Paul's in 1499 and consecrated Bishop of St David's in 1505 before his translation to Chichester in 1508. Previously, c. 1492–1505, he was a secretary to Henry VII, and remained, even in retirement from public service, a useful, though circumspect, servant of his king.

In common with other bishops of his generation, Sherborn was a prolific, if conservative, builder and renovator.[2] However, it was not until he settled into old age, and his Sussex diocese, that he is known to have employed a painter. Few of his personal accounts survive and it is his book of donations[3] that provides the only account of benefactions and gifts made during his years in Chichester. As non-portable objects, Barnard's schemes are not singled out within this inventory, so there is no indication of the cost of his commissions or materials. Similarly, the bishop's remaining letters and papers[4] contain no instruction to his painter; neither are there any extant contracts for Barnard's paintings. However, from Barnard's remaining *oeuvre*, it is clear his paintings are as much a demonstration of the generosity, status and learning of his patron as they are a fulfilment of specific allegorical, narrative, or decorative programmes.

How and at what date Barnard first entered the bishop's employment is unknown. The first documentation of Lambert Barnard 'pictoris' is in 1529,

---

[1]   Edward Croft-Murray, 'Lambert Barnard: An Early Renaissance Painter', *Archaeological Journal*, 113 (1957): 108–25.

[2]   The completion of the cloisters at Christ Church, Oxford; the erection of a timber-framed loggia and work to the Master's Lodge at St Cross Hospital, Winchester; the rebuilding of the church of St Thomas's Hospice in Rome and major alterations and improvements to the Bishop's Palaces at Lamphey and St David's pre-date improvements to his Sussex manors at Amberley, Aldingbourne and Cakeham, his palace at Chichester and within Chichester Cathedral.

[3]   In Chichester there are four copies in the West Sussex Record Office, hereafter 'WSRO' (WSRO Cap/I/14/1, WSRO Cap/I/14/2 and 3 and Cap/I/14/5), another two copies are at New College, Oxford (MSS. 313 and 313A), and the final manuscript is at Winchester College (Chest II, 168).

[4]   BL Add. MS. 34317.

when he was named as a tenant of the bishop's manor of Lathorne,[5] but we must be grateful for an undated leaf bound into another register, that unequivocally states him to be 'Lamberto Barnard B^p Shirbornes paynter'.[6] Further occasional documentation regarding the painter exists in the cathedral's Chapter records, but dates from after the bishop's death and is concerned chiefly with the payment of his annuity or rent.

Comparative works in this country are scarce, but Barnard's work can be counted alongside such examples as the Hastings and Oxenbridge Chantries in St George's Chapel, Windsor. The Hastings Chantry with panel paintings of *Scenes from the Life and Death of St Stephen* dates from about 1499 and is most likely the work of an English painter,[7] whereas the later paintings of the Oxenbridge Chantry, *Scenes from the Life and Death of St John the Baptist* (*c.* 1522?), are believed to be the work of a painter from the Low Countries. Nearby, Eton College Chapel offers an example of educated ecclesiastical patronage, and has retained substantial parts of its painted *Miracles of the Virgin* and *The Story of the Empress*, executed 1477–88 at the charge of Provost William Wayneflete. The composition of the Eton workshop is still undecided but probably comprised a mixed nationality team under the direction of William and Giles Baker.[8] The Eton murals can be grouped tentatively with a less accomplished set of *Miracles of the Virgin* commissioned (1510–20)[9] by Prior Silkstede for his chantry in Winchester Cathedral. Again the composition of the Winchester workshop is unsure, elements within the painting connect them to the Eton cycle but they are less well-executed. Typologically, the Windsor, Eton and Winchester cycles accord with paintings, manuscripts and tapestry of the Low Countries and France. In sum, this handful of projects lay down a pattern of ecclesiastical and secular patronage hinting at a greater body of large-scale works, not unlike those still to be found in the churches, town halls and private houses of continental Europe.

---

[5]   Bishop Sherborn's Donations, WSRO Cap I/14/3, f. 29r.

[6]   Communar's Accounts, WSRO Cap I/23/2, f. 18r. The phrase appears, almost as an afterthought, squeezed into the lower margin of the manuscript without continuation on f. 18v. The page is believed to have formed part of the White Act Book, WSRO Cap I/3/0 dated 1472–1544.

[7]   For information regarding these two chantry chapels, see W.H. St John Hope and P.H. Newman, 'The Ancient Paintings in the Hastings and Oxenbridge Chantry Chapels, in St George's Chapel, Windsor Castle', *Archaeologia*, 63 (January 1912): 85–98.

[8]   Emily Howe, 'The Fifteenth Century Marian Scheme in the College Chapel' in Emily Howe, Henrietta McBurney, David Park, Stephen Rickerby and Lisa Schekede, *Wall Paintings of Eton* (London: Scala, 2012), p. 47.

[9]   David Park and Peter Welford: 'The Medieval Polychromy of Winchester , in John Crook (ed.), *Winchester Cathedral. Nine Hundred Years 1093–1993* (Chichester: Phillimore, 1993), p. 134.

As with the Eton and Winchester painters, Barnard's nationality is uncertain and of some interest to art historians keen to assess the number and dispersal of English painters' workshops in this period. The myth of his Italian origin, a misconception based on the occasional Latinisation of his name in Chapter records, persisted alongside nineteenth-century antiquarian recognition of Netherlandish and northern French influences in his work. It was not until 1957 that Edward Croft-Murray suggested Barnard might, in fact, be English. His suggestion was based on a combination of documentary evidence and stylistic analysis, though given the lack of current evidence, he cautiously reserved the possibility of Barnard's being of Netherlandish descent.

In support of Croft-Murray's thesis, following combined technical and historical research, a clearer picture of English late-medieval painting is now emerging and revealing the extent to which English workshops dominated the production of late fifteenth- to early sixteenth-century painted rood-screens in East Anglia.[10] These workshops owed their stylistic trajectory to a small number of immigrant painters who had taken advantage of long-established trade connections to settle in that region. Cornwall and Devon also reveal a similar pattern believed to be a result of continental shipping trade. Sussex's coastal proximity to the Low Countries might offer suggestions that clusters of Barnard families established within south-east England from as early as the thirteenth century could owe their origin to similar patterns of migration. More recently, in the fifteenth century, a large number of French ironworkers settled in the Sussex Weald but the Barnard surname is not found among them. This, though, is to ignore the fact that the name had a wide geographical distribution, even in areas where there was little or no immigration from Europe, and that several Barnard family units are recorded living within the Chichester area from the fifteenth into the eighteenth century. Lambert Barnard's own line continued in Chichester with a further three generations of painter-stainers.[11] Intriguingly, not so far afield, records show two painters by the name of William Barnard 'of London' resident in the capital in the fifteenth century.[12]

---

[10]   I am grateful to Lucy Wrapson of the Hamilton Kerr Institute for sharing her findings related to her continuing and extensive study of East Anglian rood screens.

[11]   His long-lived son Anthony (1513?–1619), grandson Lambert (1583–1655) and great-grandson Lambert (1627–79).

[12]   A William Barnard, citizen and stainer is named in a Letter of Administration in London in 1414, [Reg 2. 276 v.]: Marc Fitch (ed.), *Index to Testamentary Records in the Commissary Court of London (London Division), Now Preserved in the Guildhall Library*, 1, 1374–1488 (London, HMSO, 1969), p. 12. The second William Barnard of London, painter, occurs in the reign of Richard III, National Archives documents CP40/888, AALT (1484) to be seen on <http://aalt.

One previously overlooked document can now be added to the evidence: in 1544/5 a brief entry in the accounts of the Supervisor of the Guild of St George in Chichester, shows 'Lambart Paynter' paying his 4d. entry fine.[13] The rate was in accordance with that of other town craftsmen such as the fuller and glazier's widow listed next to him. It was usual practice for guilds to charge double fines for aliens, often making a note of their nationality at the same time, but no such entry is made here. Similarly, Sherborn's provision, in December 1533, of an annuity for his painter refers to him solely as 'Lambertum Barnard pictorem de civitate Cicestrie';[14] had Barnard been an immigrant practitioner, it seems odd that nowhere in his surviving documentation, particularly in Sherborn's indenture and the guild entry, is such a reference ever made.

French, Flemish, Burgundian, Germanic and Italian – all have been applied in attempts to describe the appearance of Barnard's paintings, an overwhelming accumulation of styles and influence from differing areas and eras that should alert the historian to exercise caution. Though his hand may appear primarily Flemish in style, he stubbornly avoids obvious comparison with any known examples; there is a demonstrable lack of a convincing connection to a contemporary continental workshop either stylistically or biographically. Searches for his name and its variants amongst continental painters' guild records have proved unfruitful, neither has any surviving record of his denization or naturalisation in England been traced. Given this accumulation of negatives, it is tempting to see Barnard having been apprenticed to an English workshop.

Assessments made during the recent conservation of Barnard's scheme, the *Charter Paintings*,[15] hanging in Chichester Cathedral, reveal his method was up-to-date with northern European practice, even sometimes in advance – being remarkably experimental at times – yet simultaneously adhered to some well-established and by then rather old-fashioned English techniques such as

---

law.uh.edu/AALT3/R3/CP40no888/bCP40no888dorses/IMG_0940.htm> the digital archive assembled by Robert C. Palmer and Elspeth K. Palmer, *The Anglo-American Legal Tradition*, available at <aalt.law.uh.edu/aalt.html>, accessed 16 July 2012. My thanks to Lucy Wrapson for bringing this last reference to my notice.

[13] WSRO CHICIT AE/2 membrane f. 3r. Accounts of the Supervisor of St George's and of the Customar, the Reeve, and the Steward. As a member of the bishop's household, his 1523 Lay Subsidy Taxation record would have been included within that now-lost group of records for the clergy and their households. My thanks are due to Dr Steven Gunn and Caroline Adams of the WSRO for communicating this reference.

[14] WSRO Cap I/3/0, f. 132 r. and v. I am grateful to Alison McCann of the WSRO for supplying a transcription and new translation of this document.

[15] Work carried out in 2011, by a team of conservators from the Hamilton Kerr Institute, Fitzwilliam Museum, University of Cambridge.

the use of lavish gilding and heavy black outline, the latter still in common usage with largely native East Anglian workshops;[16] although, it should be recognised, the use of copious gilding might also reflect a patronal preference. Significantly, in spite of his absorption of new techniques, his representation of pictorial depth, though reasonably effective, remained relatively unsophisticated and often clumsily contrived. Except for where his imagery is directly copied from contemporary examples, he lacked the sense of dynamism, expression and gesture common to the painters of the Low Countries and Italy.

Through Bishop Sherborn's local and London connections, Barnard had ready access to imported works of art, particularly tapestries, as well as opportunities to make contact with foreign workshops working within England. Tellingly, all his visual sources seem to have been either directly accessible to him in England or transmittable, as will be seen, verbally. There is no evidence in his work that he ever travelled or studied outside of England. The weight of current evidence, therefore, leans towards Barnard's being English.

Sherborn's employment of Barnard was of a permanent nature. Not only was he seemingly held on a retainer funded from the bishop's Privy Purse, but in December 1533, he was granted a life annuity of £3 6s. 8d. payable from the income of Lathorne Manor to be administered by the Dean and Chapter following the bishop's death. In case of Barnard's continued employment within the cathedral and close, a set figure of £14 8s. per annum was to be allotted 'pro stipendio et victu suo ac servitoris quem ad sibi serviendum in arte huius modi propriis conducet expensis quatuordecim libras et octo solidos per annum' and 'ultra onera omnium colorum ac ultra aurum et argentum arti sui necessum.'[17]

This long relationship gave rise to an extraordinarily informative body of work but one that is frustratingly lacking in secure dating. The most that can be said is that Barnard may have been at work in the cathedral as early as 1513, continued under Sherborn's patronage and probably completed his remaining commission for the bishop in 1537, a year after his patron's death. Thereafter, he appears to have produced no major works, and remained in Chichester until his own death in 1567, leaving behind a son, Anthony, and apprentice, John Foster, to continue his small workshop.

---

[16] Christine S. Kimbriel, Alison Stock, Lucy Wrapson with contributions from Krista Blessley, Abigail Granville, Karen Coke and Esther Rapoport, *The Charter Paintings, Monarchs and Catalogus of Bishops in Chichester Cathedral*, Hamilton Kerr Institute, *Conservation Report* (2011), Part I, p. 96.

[17] WSRO Cap I/3/0, f. 132 r. and v: 'his stipend and subsistence, for his servant whom he hires to help him in his work at his own cost' and 'besides the charges of all the colours and besides the gold and silver needed for his work'.

His work for Sherborn was varied. At Chichester Cathedral, Barnard covered the vaults of the nave, side aisles and Lady Chapel with a trailing floriated design displaying the badges of the royal house, Sherborn's arms and mottoes together with those of notables associated with the cathedral since its original foundation at Selsey in 681. On the west wall of the south transept is Barnard's largest and most ambitious project, *The Charter Histories*,[18] comprising two narrative sections showing *St Wilfrid petitioning King Cædwalla for lands on which to build his monastery and Cathedral of Selsey* (the 'Wilfrid narrative') and *Bishop Sherborn petitioning King Henry VIII to confirm Cædwalla's gift, now the See of Chichester* (the 'Sherborn narrative'), plus two attached sections, *The Early Monarchs*, containing portrait heads in roundels of the kings of England from William I to Edward VI as well as a lost component now replaced with *The Later Monarchs*, portraits in ovals of Mary I to Charles I probably continued by Barnard's family. In continuation of these sections a separately framed *Catalogus Episcopi*, a series of invented portrait heads of bishops of Selsey and Chichester enclosed in roundels,[19] once hanging opposite, was removed to the north transept following the fall of the cathedral spire in 1861. The *Charter Paintings* and *Catalogus* contain several black-letter painted inscriptions with biographical material of St Wilfrid, St Richard and Bishop Sherborn together with shorter descriptions of the bishops and biblical quotation.

Also in the cathedral, Barnard painted the woodwork of the choir stalls of which three of his black-letter, gilded stall-plates have survived and remain on show in the treasury. He is known to have repaired a painted cloth of the *Crucifixion* in 1545,[20] but it is not known if he painted the image originally.

Within the cathedral close, Barnard decorated an internal wall, once part of the prebendal residences, with a painted textile pattern and improving biblical text in dry-fresco, and a splendid Italianate oak ceiling, in the bishop's Chichester palace, datable through genealogical evidence to 1524–28. Outside the city walls, for the bishop's manor at Amberley, he produced c. 1526, a series

---

[18]   See also Jonathan Woolfson and Deborah Lush, 'Lambert Barnard in Chichester Cathedral: Ecclesiastical Politics and the Tudor Royal Image', *Antiquaries Journal*, 87 (2007): 259–81, and Karen Coke, 'Bishop Robert Sherborn and Lambert Barnard: An English response to Italian practice?', in Paul Foster and Rachel Moriarty (eds), *Chichester: The Palace and its Bishops*, Otter Memorial Paper No. 27 (University of Chichester, 2011), pp. 146–58.

[19]   Because of their complex arrangement, historically different titles and general difficulty referencing the component parts, the Hamilton Kerr Institute and I have attempted to introduce a standard nomenclature for the panels that are now grouped together under the name *The Chichester Cathedral Charter Paintings*.

[20]   WSRO Cap I/23/2, f.64r.

of *Worthy Women* or *Heroines of Antiquity*, now displayed in Pallant House Gallery, Chichester;[21] while at Boxgrove Priory he was commissioned to paint yet another heraldic scheme on its vaults for the la Warr family. These works are all that remains of what might have been a larger *oeuvre*.

Barnard has also been suggested as the author of several miniatures in BL Roy MS 18 D II,[22] a copy of John Lydgate's *Troy Book* and *Story of Thebes*, whose owner, Algernon Henry Percy, the fifth Earl of Northumberland, commissioned between 1516 and 1523. Percy's southern seat, Petworth House, was less than twenty miles from Chichester and so it is possible that he knew of Barnard; yet stylistically it seems unlikely Sherborn's painter had a hand in their production.

In common with other painters of the age, Barnard was equally at home using dry-fresco or oil technique. None of his preliminary drawings or studies exist but under-drawings revealed by infra-red photography during recent conservation work on the *Charter Histories* reveal a sure and precise hand, confirming his painterly style was far more lyrical, delicate and detailed than their present heavy eighteenth-century overpainting would suggest.

Nowhere is Barnard's painting more lyrical than on the Lady Chapel vaults (see Figure 3.1). Using a palette of soft grey-greens for his delicate trails of vegetation, the effect is of looking upwards through the leafy canopy of a paradise garden to the periphery of the divine world beyond. Interwoven amongst the flowers are the badges of the royal household, including the Beaufort marguerite and Scottish thistle. The presence of these two suggests the ceiling could have been completed as early as 1509, before the death of Lady Margaret Beaufort, the king's grandmother or, as the marguerite and thistle may be a combined reference to Princess Margaret Tudor, no later than 1513 following the death of her husband, King James IV of Scotland and her re-marriage to Archibald Douglas, Earl of Angus following a short period during which she was Regent of Scotland (1513–14). A flurry of activity in the Lady Chapel associated with the making of a new altar suggests a dating of 1513 when payments were made for the construction of scaffolding, and 'ye partycyon between ye paynter and ye new aulter';[23] though inconclusive, this might be an indication of Barnard at work.

---

[21]   For more information concerning the Amberley paintings, see Karen Coke, 'The Amberley Castle Panels and a Drawing by William Henry Brooke', *Sussex Archaeological Collections*, 145 (Lewes, 2007): 137–52.

[22]   Croft-Murray, 'Lambert Barnard: An Early Renaissance Painter', p. 123, images accessible on <http://www.bl.uk/manuscripts/Viewer.aspx?ref=royal_ms_18_d_ii_fs001r>.

[23]   WSRO Cap I/23/1, f. 131r.

Figure 3.1   Lambert Barnard, Lady Chapel Vault decoration (c. 1513?),
              by kind permission of the Dean and Chapter of Chichester
              Cathedral; © Author.

The decorated vaults of the Priory of St Blaise and St Mary, Boxgrove follow
a similar decorative approach. This is Barnard's only project not undertaken for
Sherborn, instead being most likely commissioned by Thomas West, 9th Baron la
Warr, a close friend of the bishop and patron of the priory. The scheme decorated
the monk's choir, and therefore not intended for the public eye, the paintings
were designed to display West's genealogical connections through intermarriage
with local families and in effect demonstrate his family's long attachment to the
priory and the right to be buried in its chancel. Less fluidly painted than the
Lady Chapel vaults, the painted escutcheons surrounded by fields of appropriate
heraldic flowers, complement the naturalistic Renaissance *putti*, angels and
heraldic animals of la Warr's 1532 chantry, situated in the second bay of the
south arcade. West is believed to have employed Franco-Flemish carvers for his
chantry and as part of his commemorative programme in the priory it is likely
the ceiling was also commissioned around this time.

Barnard's floriated designs are of a type widespread throughout France, Belgium and the Netherlands, as well as Denmark and southern Sweden, with a few examples occurring in northern Italy and England. Such designs are often interwoven with biblical scenes, portrait roundels and heraldry. Those at Boxgrove appear to have been drawn from early illustrated herbals such as that attributed to Mattheus Platearius of Salerno; his *Circa Instans*,[24] known to have been widely circulated and used in university medical schools, is therefore a not improbable source given that Bishop Sherborn graduated as a Bachelor of Medicine.

The linear elegance that is so much a feature of the Lady Chapel vaults is also evident in the series of Worthy Women, painted for Sherborn's newly created upper chamber at Amberley Castle and known as the 'Queen's Room'. The earliest description of the scheme in 1813 describes it as 'the remains of the portraits of ten ancient monarchs and their queens, with their coats properly blazoned; and on the ceiling are the portraits of six warriors carved in wood'.[25] Its accompanying illustration shows some of the panels set high on the wall with what appear to be accompanying full length figures beneath.[26]

Remnants of the panelling suggest an overall colouration of dark red, the dado painted to represent grained wood with Sherborn's mottoes and heraldry, above this may have been a range of kings, or male worthies.[27] The upper range consisted of a row of modest-looking, smiling ladies with downcast eyes, partially armoured, bearing weapons and shields with apocryphal escutcheons, gazing down on the room below. These were set behind a painted round-arched arcade, fronted by painted *trompe l'oeil* parapets with panels bearing verse legends. Each figure was separated from its neighbour by a panel of leafy 'antick' design with striped poles attached to the stiles. The overall effect, heightened by Barnard's use of gold and silver, would have been one of glowing colour and great richness.

Eight of the panels remain;[28] they depict a group of militaristic, empire-building women composed of three Middle Eastern queens (Semiramis, Thomyris and Sinope), three Amazon queens (Hippolyta, Lampedo and Menalippe) and one prophetess (Cassandra) (see Figure 3.2).

---

[24]   Also known as the *Liber simplici medicina* or *Secreta salernitana*.

[25]   Frederic Shoberl, *The Beauties of England and Wales*, 14 (London, 1813), pp. 87–8.

[26]   See Coke, 'Amberley Castle Panels', pp. 138–9 for a history of their later resitings.

[27]   My original belief that there was an additional figure, perhaps a tenth worthy, above the west door was erroneous.

[28]   On the sale of the contents of Amberley Castle in 1983, they were purchased by Chichester District Council with the aid of the National Heritage Memorial Fund and are now displayed at Pallant House Gallery, Chichester.

Figure 3.2   Lambert Barnard, *Cassandra* panel from *The Ladies Worthy, or Heroines of Antiquity* (c. 1526), Pallant House Gallery, Chichester, UK (Chichester District Council); purchased with the support of the National Heritage Memorial Fund (1938); © Author.

The identity of the remaining eighth panel is not known, nor is that of a missing sister panel, now visible only in a drawing made by W.H. Brooke in 1820.[29] It is impossible to guess at their identity as unlike their male counterparts, the women

---

[29]   Coke, 'Amberley Castle Panels', pp. 138 and 143–4.

worthies were chosen from a long list of possibilities and invariably differ from example to example, neither do their emblazoned arms offer any clues.[30] From the fourteenth century onwards, the topos of the Ladies Worthy, as remarked, usually though not invariably a group of nine, formed a favourite subject of literature, pageant, domestic decoration, tapestry and even playing cards, and was popular in northern European countries, especially the Burgundian court. Viewed as possessing characteristics worthy of a Christian prince and, allied to images of Good Government and Virtues, they were accepted as particularly suitable exemplars for princes.

The Nine Worthies made their first appearance in 1389, in Eustace Deschamp's poem, *Il est temps de faire la paix* and widely disseminated through literature such as Giovanni Boccaccio's *De Mulieribus Claris* (1361–75). Important for the concept of the Amberley series is Tommaso III di Saluzzo's poem, *Chevalier Errant* of 1395 which verses were used to illustrate a series of eighteen Worthies – nine male, nine female – depicted life-size on the walls of the Sala Baronale in the Castello della Manta, Piedmont; they were painted in the 1420s during the ownership of his illegitimate son Valerano Bastardo da Saluzzo.[31] They are accompanied by descriptive black-letter verses from Tommaso's poem and one figure, Hector of Troy, was given the features of Valerano. At Amberley, seven of the eight remaining panels of Barnard's allegorical scheme are still identifiable, but unlike the single poetic source of La Manta, their verses are an amalgamation of literary quotations, in particular Eustace Deschamps' undated poem *Si les héros revenaient sur la terre, ils seraient étonnés* and the *IX Ladyes Worthy*, the anonymously authored poem 31 in MS. R. 3. 19, Trinity College Cambridge.[32]

The remains of a series of Cardinal Virtues showing *Temperantia* and *Fortitudo* frescoed on the walls of a house in Vlamingstraat, Bruges, provide a close example of a late medieval domestic depiction of a related subject (see Figure 3.3).[33]

[30]   Planché, J.R., 'The Nine Worthies of the World: An Illustration of the Paintings in Amberley Castle', *Journal of the British Archaeological Association* (1864): 315–24.

[31]   Until recently ascribed tentatively to Giacomo Jacquerio (Jacques Iverny), they are now ascribed merely to an Unknown Master. Interestingly, there are Sussex connections with the Saluzzo family. Alesia da Saluzzo, daughter of Thomas I, married Sir Richard Fitzalan, eighth Earl of Arundel sometime before 1285.

[32]   For further discussion of this topic, see Coke, 'Amberley Castle Panels', pp. 144–9.

[33]   Marjan Buyle, 'Indrukwekkende Laatmitteleeuwse Deugden op de Muren van een Brugs Woonhuis', *Monumenten, Landschappen &Archaeologie*, 25(3) (2005): 33–56.

Figure 3.3   *Temperantia*, wall-painting (second half, fifteenth century),
            Vlamingstraat, Bruges; photo by Oswald Pauwels; © Flanders
            Heritage Agency.

The Virtues, depicted three-quarter length and with banderoles of text,
are clearly derived from images of female saints. They are clothed in similar
fanciful brocades and heavy chains and, as did the Amberley models, occupy
a position along the upper part of the chamber. However, typologically closest

Figure 3.4   Unknown. *Sibyls*, (c. 1526) Château de Piquecos; © Ministère
              de la Culture – Médiatheque du Patrimoine, Dist. RMN-Grand
              Palais/Violle A.

and contemporary to Barnard's series were the Sibyls painted for Sherborn's
contemporary, Jean IV des Prés-Montpezat, protonotary apostolic and Bishop
of Montauban 1519–39 (see Figure 3.4).[34]

These frescoes were painted along the upper edge of the wall in his chapel at
the Château de Piquecos, Tarn-et-Garonne, as part of renovations undertaken
during his bishopric. Though not pictured within a fictive Renaissance
architectural framework like the Amberley Worthies, the Sibyls carry attributes,
wear fanciful costume and all have black-letter descriptive verses painted below.
The lower half of the wall was painted with strips of alternating coloured
brocade in a fashion similar to that of Barnard's South Street wall decoration.
The treatment of this sister episcopal commission, reveals the extent to which,
though crudely executed, such themes had penetrated these regional sites.

Unfortunately, no direct connection can be made between the two bishops
in spite of their Vatican links, neither has Barnard any traceable relationship

---

[34]   More images of these can be accessed on <http://www.culture.gouv.fr/public/
mistral/memoire_fr?ACTION=CHERCHER&FIELD_98=LOCA&VALUE_98=%20
Piquecos&DOM=Tous&REL_SPECIFIC=3>.

with the anonymous painter of the Piquecos Sibyls, so it must be assumed that a well-dispersed generic model for these works once existed, possibly in the form of a French or Franco-Flemish tapestry similar to *Penelope at her Loom*, (c. 1480–83), a fragment from the *Story of the Cimbri Women*, itself part of a series of *Virtuous Women* produced for Bishop Ferry de Clugny in the last part of the fifteenth century.[35]

If the resemblance of the Amberley figures to tapestry counterparts lies chiefly in their fanciful costume, their architectural presentation owes more to Italian series of male Worthies such as that found in the Palazzo Trinci, Foligno, c. 1415, who appear, within a round-arched colonnade. The decoration of this palace, as Anne Dunlop demonstrates,[36] effectively presents a history lesson. Other rooms were given over to several separate series depicting historical personages, many of them accompanied by verse legends derived from literary sources and incorporating portraits of contemporary figures. As was also noted by Dunlop, the Trinci programmes are above all, preoccupied with the 'differentiation of past and present', a theme which will be seen to motivate Barnard's *Charter Histories*.

At Amberley, the series might therefore be said to be a continuation of these two types, for if Worthies, as a group, are based not so much on human achievements as Christian ideology and abstract concepts of virtue, the Amberley examples also celebrate the virtues of contemporary figures, in particular (discussed below), those of Queen Catherine of Aragon. In this respect, they are part of a long tradition reaching back to the now-lost allegorical painting of *Vanagloria* attributed to Giotto in which his patron, Azzone Visconti (1302–39), figured as a Christian worthy alongside Charlemagne – a conceit that gained currency amongst many European rulers.

On a leisurely summer progress in 1526, while staying at Arundel Castle, Henry VIII dined with Bishop Sherborn, most probably at nearby Amberley. The king's days were spent hunting and making merry and the bishop's estate at Amberley, conjoining that of Fitzalan, Earl of Arundel, would have provided further opportunity for the king's entertainment. One of Henry's party, William Fitzwilliam, noted in a letter to Thomas Cromwell 'sundry and diverse devices', 'right commodious and proper',[37] words believed to refer to Barnard's curious decorative scheme. The chamber, recently created by Sherborn as part

---

[35]   To be seen in the Boston Museum of Fine Arts, Maria Antoinette Evans Fund, Inv. 2654.

[36]   Anne Dunlop, *Painted Palace*, (Pittsburgh: Pennsylvania State University Press, 2009), pp. 186–208.

[37]   Letter from William Fitzwilliam to Cardinal Wolsey of 3 August 1526 in the National Archives, TNA SP 1/39, 26–7.

of his improvements to the castle, may have been intended for several uses and was ideally suited, in its positioning as an upper apartment, for occupation by the queen. Had Catherine accompanied Henry in 1526, she would have found her own regal merits flatteringly reflected in the qualities of the women Worthies depicted. Having distinguished herself as interim ambassador for the court of Spain following Prince Arthur's death, after her marriage to Henry VIII she acted as his regent during his absence in France in 1513; at that time, she not only attended to provisioning the English army in Flanders but also ordered an army to be raised against James IV of Scotland's attempted invasion of England. Following his defeat at Flodden Field, in an action worthy of Thomyris (pictured among the Amberley Worthies), who, legend relates, cut off Cyrus's head and threw it into a goatskin containing the blood of his captured generals, Catherine sent James's bloodied surcoat to her husband with the suggestion he should use it as his banner; she would have sent the king's body too but felt that the 'Englishmen's hearts would not suffer it.'[38] A further suggestion of there being a subtext woven into these depictions is to be found in the figure of Hippolyta, who carries a long-bow and sheaf of arrows in reference to one of Catherine's badges, a pun on her name.[39]

The concept for the Amberley scheme must have originated with Sherborn, for it was he who had sufficient knowledge, not only of the literary topos but of its painted application perhaps encountered at first hand at La Manta when he travelled in Milanese territory in 1496.[40] Even had the Amberley series originally also included kings, the inclusion of references to Catherine suggest a theme aimed, if only partially, at celebrating the qualities of queenship. Here it is done by using a comfortably familiar theme particularly suited to a female audience; in the same way, the city magistrates of Tournai, seeking a suitable gift to express their loyalty to her, in 1513 presented Queen Margaret of Austria with a set of tapestries illustrating Christine de Pisan's *Cité des Dames*. Not only do the Amberley Worthies stand as symbols of moral excellence, as do the ladies of the *Cité des Dames*, but they also highlight Queen Catherine's

---

[38]   Quoted in Garrett Mattingley, *Catherine of Aragon* (London, Jonathan Cape, 1950), p. 121.

[39]   Neil Samman, 'The Henrician Court during Cardinal Wolsey's Ascendancy *c.* 1514–1529' (unpublished PhD thesis, University of Wales, 1988), p. 144; and also for other instances of a sheaf of arrows as a reference to Catherine.

[40]   A letter, dated 1 April 1496, from Henry VII to Ludovico Maria Sforza, Duke of Milan, requesting free passage across his territory for 'his Secretary, councillor and ambassador' to the Roman Court. *Calendar of State Papers and Manuscripts in the Archives and Collections of Milan*: 1385–1618 (1912), pp. 293–310 <http://www.british-history.ac.uk/report.aspx?compid=9227 8&strquery=Roberto Date> accessed 1 November 2009.

Figure 3.5   Lambert Barnard, detail of Tudor Room ceiling, Bishop's
Palace Chichester (c. 1529), by kind permission of the Bishop
of Chichester; © Author.

embodiment of these virtues. The subject matter may have been conservative,
even old-fashioned, but the use of earlier medieval literature married to an
essentially Italian presentation brought an element of novel modernity to this
scheme in Sussex.

The same courtiers who met and entertained Henry during the 1526 progress and who formed Sherborn's circle of local influence also took their place on the parlour ceiling in Sherborn's Chichester residence (see Figure 3.5).

Though this and Boxgrove Priory display the heraldry of local families, they differ in intent. Boxgrove was essentially a mark of ownership subsumed to piety, but the parlour, known now as the Tudor Room, separate from Sherborn's private chambers, provided a social space or audience chamber, in turns public and private, where the bishop would hold court, receive petitioners, lords, ladies and other ecclesiastics and was on occasion also used as a dining room. Barnard's magnificent, brightly coloured and heavily gilded, heraldic ceiling would have dominated the furnishings, but its purpose was far more than merely decorative.

This type of ceiling was not unusual in England, the polychrome and gilded ceiling of the Bayntun Chapel in St Nicholas's, Bromham dates from the end of the previous century and Abbot's Parlour at Thame Park, Oxfordshire, a carved example also Italian in style, from the 1520s. Though different in arrangement, the painted oak ceiling of Prior Simon Senhouse's Tower at Carlisle of c. 1520, also contains both his and the arms of local nobility together with mottoes. All were based loosely on Italian coffered ceilings, stone-carved examples of which had also appeared in France by this period.

At Chichester, the space was broken into four sections with 32 individual compartments. Each section contained in order the naturalistically painted arms set within Renaissance roundels or medallions together with their initials of Bishop Sherborn; Thomas Fitzalan, Lord Maltravers, later Earl of Arundel; Thomas West, Lord la Warr of Halnaker House and Henry Owen of Cowdray. These arms were alternated with 16 compartments showing the Tudor Rose badge, again set within three-dimensionally painted roundels and the initials 'H' for Henry VIII and 'K' together with the Aragonese pomegranate for his queen. Painted curling ribbons enliven the spaces between the escutcheons and all was richly coloured and originally heavily gilded. Bishop and courtiers were thus permanently intertwined in a display of regional loyalty. These individuals were Sherborn's most powerful neighbours; their influence was not only based on the extent and spread of their estates that covered a substantial part of the western end of Sussex, but also as intimates of the king, being attendants (in 1520) at the Field of the Cloth of Gold and, at various times, members of the Privy Chamber. It must be remembered that proximity to the king not only allowed them to accrue high office, titles and estates, but was a necessary factor in their retention. It was vital that they remained in royal favour, and were seen by others to occupy a place in that charmed circle.

To do this required constant demonstrations of loyalty. One such method was in the private presentation of costly New Year's Gifts to Henry and another was a reassuring, public, overt, visual display of allegiance.

Sherborn's intentions therefore were twofold: he needed to emphasise, not just his own and his circle's loyalty to the king, but this demonstration of connection also underscored his power-base, the secular authority he could bring to bear. Consequently, this statement of authority was better made if underscored with materials of conspicuous wealth, status and high fashion. This ceiling demonstrates how after 1526 Barnard turned increasingly to exotic Italianate models for his inspiration. Its dating of 1524–28, based on genealogical information, places its execution firmly within national trends.

This eclecticism is most obvious in Barnard's final commission for Sherborn; the *Chichester Cathedral Charter Paintings* were painted as a response to the devastating changes being imposed upon the structure of the Church in the first half of the 1530s (see Figures 3.6 and 3.7).

Unusual in that they afford a window into the opinions, reservations and fears of a conservative cleric at this difficult time, they additionally provide a fascinating exercise in reportage, a visualisation of the delicate state of dependence of the Church on monarchy. The entire composition, which covers over 85 square metres, was placed high on the east and west walls of the south transept. As this part of Chichester Cathedral was reserved for the activities of both Chapter and Consistory Court, so combining secular and ecclesiastical power, this massive scheme would have been an imposing and supportive presence in an area set aside for the exercise of the Church's jurisdictional authority.

Except for the far smaller (65 x 85 cm) late sixteenth-century *Tabula Eliensis* in the south transept of Ely Cathedral and the 1596 painted cloth of the same subject on the walls of Coughton Court that might be intended to show a similar interdependence by the retelling of local history,[41] nothing on the scale of the Chichester narratives survives in any other part of England. A recently discovered wall-painting in the manor house at Milverton, Somerset, once belonging to the Archdeacons of Taunton, depicting Henry VIII enthroned, is thought to be of later date, c. 1540,[42] but is not accompanied by such a complex narrative as the *Charter Histories*.

---

[41] Possibly a copy of a painting believed to have been on the refectory walls at Ely. Forty of William I's knights were quartered on the abbey; each became so friendly with the monk assigned to him that the monks regretted their leaving and commemorated the event by painting their portraits and the knights' arms on the refectory walls. My thanks are due to Elizabeth Stazicker for sharing her current research on the *Tabula*.

[42] Currently being researched by Prof. Michael Liversidge and Dr Tatiana String.

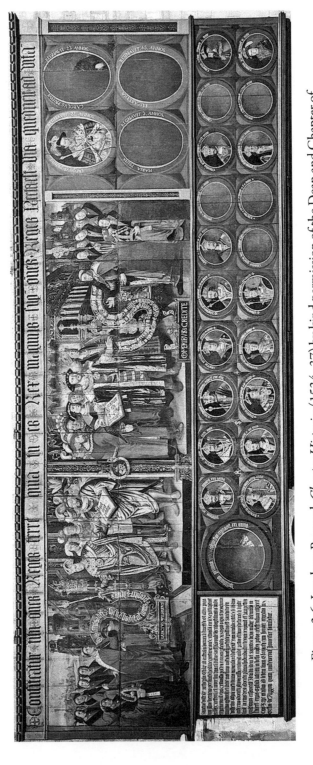

Figure 3.6 Lambert Barnard, *Charter Histories* (1534–37) by kind permission of the Dean and Chapter of Chichester Cathedral; Photo by Chris Titmus, © Hamilton Kerr Institute, University of Cambridge.

Figure 3.7 Lambert Barnard, *Catalogus Episcopi* (1534–37) by kind permission of the Dean and Chapter of Chichester Cathedral; Photo by Chris Titmus, © Hamilton Kerr Institute, University of Cambridge.

Figure 3.8   Lambert Barnard, 'Cain and Abel', detail of *Charter Histories* (1534–37), by kind permission of the Dean and Chapter of Chichester Cathedral; Photo by Chris Titmus, © Hamilton Kerr Institute, University of Cambridge.

The threads binding the components of the *Charter Histories* are too complex to discuss in full here and, given this complexity, it is clear that Sherborn's was the creative intellect behind this exercise in visual rhetoric with Barnard being the executor. Sherborn's concept required the illustration of multiple events, occurring at differing historical periods, with each narrative containing more than one time-frame. In order to effect this, Barnard arranged individual scenes, first as a linear history reading from left to right, separated by painted pilasters each bearing a grisaille roundel with an Old Testament scene. A single-handed clock is set on the bell-tower in the background of each of the two chief narratives. One dial has since been over-painted and lost its hand, but it is likely they were set originally to different times and are indicative of the passage of time between the two scenes.

The one remaining grisaille roundel carries an image of *Cain killing Abel*, traced directly from a pre-1517 woodcut of the same subject by Jan Gossart (see Figures 3.8 and 3.9).

The subject of the now-lost partner roundel originally in place on the second pilaster is unknown, but if typology as it occurs in tapestry and painting was followed, it too represented an Old Testament story. This placing of elements one in front of the other in the three-dimensional space of the painting creates another illusion of time advancing away from the onlooker. Thus Old Testament events precede the events of Wilfrid's and Sherborn's time, in the distance of the 'Wilfrid narrative' the yet-to-be-erected monastic cathedral of Selsey is balanced, in that of the 'Sherborn narrative' by the rather shakily pictured, classically styled architecture of the 'New Rome' envisaged by Henry VIII.

Figure 3.9   Jan Gossart,
*Cain killing Abel with a
Jawbone* (before 1517) (British
Museum); © Trustees of the
British Museum.

This physical placing of time
in separate spaces signals an
episodic reading of the *Charter
Histories*, again common to late
fifteenth-century tapestry. The
'Wilfrid narrative' illustrates
primarily the foundation of the
See of Selsey by Royal Charter
following   Wilfrid's,   then
Bishop of Northumberland,
petitioning of the South Saxon
king Cædwalla;[43] the scene is
then reproduced in near-mirror
image as the second episode,
the 'Sherborn narrative' (see
Figure 3.10). This shows Henry
VIII in the possibly apocryphal
act of acceding to Bishop Sherborn's request for confirmation of the status of
his cathedral re-founded in Chichester on the orders of William I in 1075.
The two scenes together reading from left to right and front to back, therefore
constitute a persuasive, large-scale visual 'charter' commemorating the royal gifts
of land to the See of Chichester. In their creation, Barnard has drawn on existing
portraiture for the features of the Kings of England, though his depiction of
Henry VIII as a full-length figure, pre-dating Holbein's iconographic version,
has him standing arms open in an image of royal munificence. The accompanying
kings whose portraits, now heavily over-painted, were based on contemporary
examples, and the bishops, whose features were largely invented, provided the
historic participants and witnesses to these events.

---

[43]   Historically, the gift of lands was made by Cædwalla's predecessor Aethelwealh. For a
discussion of the charters, see S.F. Kelly (ed.), *Charters of Selsey, Anglo Saxon Charters VI* (Oxford:
Oxford University Press for the British Academy, 1998), and for Cædwalla's contribution of part
of the Isle of Wight see Susan Kelly in, Mary Hobbs (ed.), *Chichester Cathedral: An Historical
Survey* (Chichester: Phillimore, 1994), p. 3.

Figure 3.10   Lambert Barnard, *Cædwalla*, the column, horseman and victim,
                detail of *Charter Histories* (1534–37), by kind permission of the
                Dean and Chapter of Chichester Cathedral; Photo by Chris
                Titmus, © Hamilton Kerr Institute, University of Cambridge.

Barnard then introduces a second reading. In the 'Wilfrid narrative', the story
now told is of the early Christianisation by conversion of Sussex and the black-letter
biography of St Wilfrid included beneath his image, tells of the events leading to
this point. The subtext of the founding of the Roman Church itself is signalled
by a group composed of a porphyry column, composite in order, wound with

bronze oak leaves and fretted in a Düreresque fashion: the abacus carries a bronze statue of a knight on horseback.

Very difficult to see clearly from the ground, the group is often excusably believed to be a representation of St George and the Dragon; however, close inspection reveals the 'dragon' beneath the horse's hooves to be the half-naked body of a vanquished barbarian. Variants of this popular classical equestrian imagery are associated with Constantine, Marcus Curtius and Santiago 'Matamoros', all adopted as symbols of the triumph of Christianity through the application of military might, pious belief and personal sacrifice. The iconography of columns appearing in paintings is a complex subject but in the context of Wilfrid's conversion of Sussex and Cædwalla's own conversion, Barnard's painting

Figure 3.11   Lambert Barnard, *Monkey*, detail of *Charter Histories* (1534–37), by kind permission of the Dean and Chapter of Chichester Cathedral; Photo by Chris Titmus, © Hamilton Kerr Institute, University of Cambridge.

of the mounted rider on a rearing horse poised on the porphyry column, is here to be read as a double symbol of imperial rule and of the presence of the Christian faith or Christian Church. As such, it becomes a reference to the Emperor Constantine's vision-led victory over Maxentius at the Milvian Bridge in 312, and his consequent authorisation of the Christian religion's supremacy in the Roman Empire. The group is placed prominently in the centre of the picture space and is one of the first of several references to Constantine within the two narratives.

The theme of conversion is expanded by the fettered monkey in the centre foreground of the 'Wilfrid narrative' (see Figure 3.11). The symbolism of this

Figure 3.12   Albrecht Dürer, *Virgin and Child with Monkey*, engraving,
c. 1498 (British Museum); © Trustees of the British Museum.

animal in painting changed subtly over time[44] but by now was representative of
the yearning for salvation, achievable by man but unobtainable because of the
creature's baseness or folly. In this instance the monkey, contentedly fettered to
the column and seated at Cædwalla's feet, is symbolic of their having overcome
their base and barbarian natures and accepted the bonds of Christianity. Scattered
about the monkey's feet are walnuts broken to reveal their kernels, a symbol of
Christian reward (Salvation) to be enjoyed by the faithful and quite literally by
the monkey, who having persisted in breaking open the nut is now about to enjoy
the fruits of his labours. The allegory combining all three elements of monkey,

---

[44]   W. Janson, *Apes and Ape Lore in the Middle Ages and the Renaissance* (London: Warburg
Institute, 1952), p. 150.

Figure 3.13 (Left) Lambert Barnard, *Courtier*, detail of *Charter Histories* (1534–37), by kind permission of the Dean and Chapter of Chichester Cathedral; Photo by Chris Titmus, © Hamilton Kerr Institute, University of Cambridge.

Figure 3.14 (Right) *Courtier*, detail of *The Adultery of David* (1526–28), tapestry, Brussels, Musée National de la Renaissance Ecouen; © RMN-Grand Palais/Gérard Blot.

nuts and reward is often erroneously ascribed to St Augustine but is actually to be traced to the monk and fabulist Odo of Cheriton (c. 1185–1246/47), who used the same combination to illustrate his moral fable *De Symia*. The fables remained a popular and widely distributed text. This little group, therefore, is absolutely central to the overall narrative, in that it not only celebrates the triumph of the Church and Christianity over the heathen by referencing Wilfrid's missionary work in Sussex that led to Cædwalla's acceptance of the faith and his subsequent donation of lands, but also celebrates in its subtext the foundation and longevity of the imperial Roman Church itself.

From this narrative emerges a statement of the history of Constantine as the founding and enduring source of papal jurisdiction, not just across the ancient Roman Empire but extending far beyond that, reaching through time to Sherborn's present, his known Christian world. Because the two narratives are balanced in a constant and tensioned equivalence, we should expect to find a transmutation of this theme within the 'Sherborn narrative' to determine if or how a similar programme of 'inherited' historic authority is deployed. So just as Cædwalla stands with the figure of a classically clothed man with Renaissance breastplate, possibly intended as Constantine immediately behind him, in a line illustrating the descent of authority, so too is Henry VIII positioned forward of his father Henry VII from whose line he draws his imperial pretensions and royal authority. That Cædwalla might have served as a secondary reference to Cadwaladr, the king of the Britons whose invisible inclusion in the narrative was to be interpreted as a sign of Sherborn's support for the Tudor dynasty, was pointed out by Woolfson and Lush.[45] Britain's ancient histories were scoured by Henry VIII's advisers for authentication of his royal line as descending from Cadwaladr through Arthur; however, shortly before this painting was commenced, an episode involving Ambassador Chapuy and his plainly cynical attitude to the claims of Arthur's imperial status,[46] meant that focus was quickly changed to Constantine the Great, who according to the ancient histories was the British-born offspring of a British mother, and from whom Henry could more realistically claim descent. This was thought to be the more credible argument and to constitute a far stronger link in Henry's chain of rhetoric. As argued by the Italian historian Polydore Vergil in his 1534 revision of his *Anglica Historia*, 'the majestie of the emperie could not perish, sithe that even at this presente the kinges of England, according to the usage of their aunciters, doe weare the imperiall diadem as a gift exhibited of Constantinus to his successors.'[47]

Was Sherborn aware of the interest in Constantine's imperial legacy that was occupying the king's advisors in the run-up to the 1532 Act of Restraint in Appeals? It must be said that the emperor and his historic relationship to the Roman Church only contributed in a small way to the complex debate concerning the nature of empire to the authors of the *Collectanea satis copiosa*.[48]

---

[45]   Woolfson and Lush, 'Lambert Barnard in Chichester Cathedral', p. 269.

[46]   'Spain: January 1531, 11–20', *Calendar of State Papers, Spain*, Volume 4 Part 2: 1531–1533 (1882), pp. 17–31 <http://www.british-history.ac.uk/report.aspx?compid=87734&strquery=Chapuys "King Arthur" Imperial Date> accessed 9 June 2013

[47]   Sir Henry Ellis (ed.), *Polydore Vergil's English History* (London: Camden Society, 1746), pp. 98–9.

[48]   Thomas Cranmer and Edward Foxe.

However, importantly for the 'Sherborn narrative', the matter remained topical as the same Constantinian persuasions in giving imperial authority to King Henry VIII, also provided a historic precedent for Thomas Cromwell to further the king's claims to Supremacy. In a letter of 1 April 1534, William Marshall wrote to Cromwell, 'I send you two books now finished of the Gift of Constantine. I think there was none ever better set forth for defacing of the pope of Rome.'[49] This first book was Marshall's recent translation of Marsilius of Padua's *Defensor Pacis* of 1324, a written attack on papal authority in refutation of the Donation of Constantine; the second was Lorenzo Valla's *De falso credita et ementita Constantini Donatione declamatio* written in 1440, first published in 1517 and known to have been translated for Cromwell. It should be noted that Henry VIII's stance, as depicted by Barnard, as well as a figuration of munificence, is also reminiscent of the attitude of prayer adopted by early Christians and by Constantine himself on his coinage where it was intended to show the imperial body as a conduit for divine power.[50]

The topicality and emphasis of these two arguments underlines the duality of the history being presented in the *Charter Histories*. Based on the narrative content of the paintings and documentary evidence of a considerable amount of scaffolding being erected in the south transept for the painters,[51] a proposed commencement date of Summer 1534 has been put forward. Following on from the preamble to the 1532 Act of Restraint, it shows Sherborn remained closely in touch with events and developments at court and the strategic inclusion in the *Charter Histories* of the same arguments as used by Henry to secure his Supremacy over the Church is a calculated and flatteringly placatory public statement of his support for the king, even if the narrative simultaneously allows a statement of the traditional Catholic view of events. The evidence from Barnard's *Charter Paintings* clearly demonstrates that Sherborn was determined

---

[49]   From 'Henry VIII: April 1534, 1–5', *Letters and Papers, Foreign and Domestic, Henry VIII*, 7: 1534 (1883), pp. 177–83 <http://www.british-history.ac.uk/report.aspx?compid=79305&strquery=constantine> accessed 8 September 2011.

[50]   'Quanto porro divinae fidei vis ac virtus in ejus animo insederit, vel ex hoc uno conjici potest, quod in aureis nummis exprimi se jussit vultu in cœlum sublato, et manibus expansis instar precantis. Et huius quidem formae nummi per universum orbem Romanum cucurrerunt. In ipsa vero regia juxta quasdam januas, in imaginibus ad ipsum vestbuli fastgium positis depictus est stans, difixis quidem in cœlum oculis, manibus autem expanisis precantis in modum' (Migne 1857–1905, X, col. 1163) from Eusebius, *The Life of Constantine*, Book IV, Chapter XV, 'He causes himself to be represented on his Coins, and in his Portraits, in the Attitude of Prayer' (1976), p. 544., quoted in Irving Lavin, 'Bernini at St Peter's', in William Tronzo, (ed.), *St Peter's in the Vatican* (Cambridge University Press, 2005), p. 163.

[51]   WSRO Cap I/23/1, f. 86r.

to maintain the status quo in the relationship between Church and State and was prepared to go to some lengths to achieve his end.

With this in mind, Sherborn's third and most obscure narrative is a poignant reminder of the betrayed woman at the centre of this debacle. The allegorical reading of Barnard's monkey as heathen acceptance of Christianity has already been noted; significantly, a similar allegorical depiction was used in a 1531[52] reworking of Lucas Horenbout's portrait (c. 1526) of Catherine of Aragon in which the queen's pet monkey seated on her arm, spurns an offered coin, reaching instead for the promise of salvation in the form of the crucifix worn around her neck. In colouration, the animal of the 'Wilfrid narrative' bears a resemblance to Catherine's pet, tentatively identified as a now-rare Marcgrave's Capuchin,[53] a species imported into Italy from Brazil by Portuguese traders since c. 1500, though its pose is more likely to have been adapted from the marmoset of Albrecht Dürer's engraving, *The Madonna with the Monkey* of c. 1498 (see Figure 3.12).

If the Amberley series celebrated Catherine as a worthy amongst worthies, could this multi-referential monkey in the *Charter Histories* also be considered a mnemonic reference to Catherine's life-long adherence to the true faith, whose refusal to deny papal authority ultimately was to deprive her of her husband and status, thus constituting a sacrifice assuring her own eventual salvation?

In support of the theory of Catherine's invisible presence is the bearded courtier standing to the far left of the 'Sherborn narrative' directly against the dividing pilaster (see Figure 3.13). This same figure appears in the same place, in a tapestry belonging to a second and more expensive set acquired by the king in 1529 depicting the *History of David*,[54] a subject recently interpreted by Thomas Campbell as playing a deliberately propagandic role aimed at raising awareness of Henry's conviction of the illegality of his marriage (see Figure 3.14).[55]

As Henry's courtier, he is clad in a red robe rather than yellow as in the tapestry, yet there is one notable difference between the two depictions: Barnard's figure is shown with an open, empty purse from which hangs either the Great or Privy Seal included ostensibly as a symbol of Henry's munificence, and symbolic of his royal generosity to Chichester. However, with this figure's presence in such a

---

[52]   Tree-ring dated to 1531.

[53]   My thanks to John Pullen, Keeper of Mammals, Marwell Wildlife and Co-Chair BIAZA Primate Focus Group for identifying the species.

[54]   Now in the Château d'Ecouen.

[55]   Thomas Campbell, 'The Art and Splendour of Henry VIII's Tapestry Collection,' in Maria Hayward and Philip Ward (eds), *The Inventory of King Henry VIII. II Textiles and Dress* (London: Harvey Miller Publishers for the Society of Antiquaries of London, 2010), p. 27.

publicly displayed tapestry, he serves also as an active reminder to all who were familiar with the affairs of the day and of the court, of the underlying causation of the imminent break from Rome.

The subject of the *Charter Histories* is therefore manifold. At a time when the crown was threatening to absorb ecclesiastical revenues and lands, Barnard is called upon to make an unmistakable statement of ecclesiastical dependence on and acquiescence to the monarchy. Secondly, through the narrative we are presented with the history of the Christianisation of Sussex – the last county of England to accept the Roman Church. This final defeat of paganism in England was achieved, the painting says, only through the cooperation of Church and monarch which successful symbiosis will ensure its continuation into the future. The historic agents of that symbiosis are depicted alongside, laid out in the form of portrait heads in roundels, a format long established in genealogical illumination and familiar from Italian fifteenth-century portrait medallions. Ruth Chavasse[56] has proposed that Sherborn was aware of a collective European movement using such imagery as a means of supporting Catholic reform, citing the humanist Thomas Mürner's 1535 manuscript, *Histoire des Papes et Empereurs*,[57] as a typical model. Historical example, she argues, provided both traditionalists and reformers with a safe 'umbrella', from which to make controversial statement, a practice of which Sherborn took full advantage.

That Sherborn was able to devise, together with his painter, a subtext in defence of the authority of the Roman Church would support Chavasse's findings. Significantly, Barnard also presented his narratives in a simplified reworking of another statement of ancient ecclesiastical authority – the *Concordantia Veteris ac Novi Testamenti*, frescoed at the order of Pope Sixtus IV on the walls of his Sistine Chapel. Completed in 1482, the scheme by Sandro Botticelli, Cosimo Rosselli, Domenico Ghirlandaio, Pietro Perugino and perhaps Luca Signorelli was, like the *Charter Paintings* afterwards, large in concept and size, placed high on the wall and arranged in the manner of a set of tapestries; it also involved Constantinian imagery, being punctuated by images of the Arch of Constantine in Rome. Individual scenes comparing the Old and New Testament stories of Moses and Christ culminating in St Peter's receiving the keys of Rome, were separated by painted pilasters of antique decoration and accompanied, not by a catalogue of kings and bishops, but by a series of full-

---

[56]   Ruth Chavasse, 'The Bishop's Portrait Medallions in their Renaissance and Reformation Context: A Note on Episcopal Authority as Interpreted by Bishop Sherborn and Lambert Barnard', in Foster and Moriarty (eds), *Chichester the Palace*, (2011), pp. 159–66.

[57]   MS 268 Humanistenbibliothek Schlettstadt. Mürner visited England in 1524 at the invitation of Henry VIII.

length images of pre-Constantinian popes commencing with St Peter. Spaced between the windows, above the *Concordantia*, the chronological arrangement of these portraits draws the eye from side to side of the nave controlling the directional reading of the stories, rather as the eye is encouraged to pass to and fro in comparison on Barnard's narratives. Significantly for Sherborn's histories, Sixtus's ideological programme was devised as a statement of his own papal authority and jurisdiction by illustrating his line of God-given authority, through St Peter and Constantine. His reign was characterised by a jurisdictional conflict with the French king Louis XI who insisted the papacy needed royal permissions for issuing decrees in France, a situation similar to that in England; simultaneously he was also preoccupied with re-capturing Constantine's Istanbul through mounting a crusade against the Ottoman. Without a doubt, Sherborn, as Orator to the Vatican and Warden of the English College of St Thomas in Rome, would have been aware of these issues, and certainly have seen and admired this remarkable cycle of paintings during his sojourn in Rome. Barnard seems not to have seen the Arch of Constantine so turned instead to that other symbol of imperial power, porphyry. Thus the *Charter Paintings* might owe their general appearance as much to Sherborn's verbal description of Pope Sixtus's programme as to a device of tapestry.

The *Charter Histories* hover on the knife-edge of being inflammatory, yet are ultimately propitiatory and flattering; for each argument that could question Sherborn's loyalties, there is a plausible counter-explanation. He plays a double game cleverly and assuredly, deftly yet resolutely stacking history and opinion. Sherborn's final and admonitory message, a suitably biblical combination extracted from Psalms – the final word of which is subtly amended from 'gods' to 'kings' – lies in the inscription above the two narratives, *Confiteantur tibi omnes reges terrae quia tu es rex magnus super omnes regesi*.[58]

For his part, Barnard is able, through his knowledge of painterly language and imagery selected from easily accessible tapestries, circulating pattern books and print sources, to piece together the complex visual narratives demanded of him; though his ingenuity, his language of symbolism and allegory must have

---

[58] 'Let all the kings of the earth confess to thee, for thou, O Lord art a great king above all kings': Psalm 138, verse 4, '*Confiteantur tibi Domine omnes reges terræ: quia audierunt omnia verba oris tui*' – 'May all the kings of the earth confess to thee, O Lord. For they have heard all the words of thy mouth' (King James Bible) and Psalm 95, verse 3, '*quoniam Deus magnus Dominus et rex magnus super omnes deos*' – 'For the Lord is a great God, and a great King above all gods' (King James Bible). The original inscription has been altered over time. My thanks to Rachel Moriarty for improving my transcription of the Latin text.

been stretched considerably by the complexity of approach required in realising Sherborn's unique vision.

Barnard's eclectic massing of such widely sourced imagery would be unthinkable without Sherborn's intellectual input, nursed as it was in the schools of Winchester and New College, Oxford, honed in the humanist atmosphere of Archbishop Morton's household, exposed to court influence and further refined through continental travel and residence in Italy. He held a profound understanding of how the example of history could be used to communicate experience, moral example and political comment not just to the present but so as to have relevance for the future. On a personal level, he wished his earthly conduct and achievements to be seen as evidence of his good governance, charity and piety – a desire encapsulated in his motto, prominently displayed on the *Charter Paintings* and on his tomb in the south aisle, 'Operibus Credite'.[59]

The public addressed through these paintings were his contemporaries, future generations and ultimately his God. Barnard's presentation and language was finely honed to the purpose of each project. Heraldry was easily read by those who themselves bore arms, thus his heraldic ceilings and vaults are relatively simple in concept and follow standardised patterns of display. At Amberley, the topos of the Worthies was entirely appropriate to the purpose of the Upper Hall as both reception room and as a private chamber with the specific and unusual inclusion of the women Worthies rendering it more so for its occupation by a princess or queen familiar with the literature it illustrated. The *Charter Histories* easily stood solely as a record of the respective foundations of the Sees of Selsey and Chichester but other purposely embedded narratives were brought to life by references drawn from the literature, histories and biblical texts that should have been recognisable to any educated person. In this latter programme, Sherborn anticipated the king's later use of propagandic imagery as a means of establishing his monarchical supremacy, but 'propaganda' is too strong a term in the context of Barnard's *oeuvre*, for it contains no deliberate untruths nor was there any intention to manipulate universal opinion, merely a heartfelt personal statement.

Barnard's images were sited in spaces that were simultaneously public and private. This ensured that the maximum number of those equipped to understand their narratives would have access to them. For those whose might not find their way through allegory and subtext, their rich colouration and heavy

---

[59]　Derived from the Vulgate, John 10:37–8, '*Si non facio opera Patris mei nolite credere mihi, Si autem facio et si mihi non vultis credere operibus credite ut cognoscatis et credatis quia in me est Pater et ego in Patre*', 'If I do not the works of my Father, believe me not. But if I do, though ye believe not me, believe the works: that ye may know, and believe, that the Father is in me, and I in him' (King James Bible).

gilding would have left an overwhelming, if not intimidating, impression of the power and status expected of a prince of the Church.

The bishop's death in 1536 effectively brought about the end of Barnard's productive career. Dean William Fleshmonger honoured the bishop's request, dutifully providing a pension that enabled the painter to continue to live in his tenement in East Street, Chichester. Barnard died in 1567 and was buried in the graveyard of nearby St Andrew Oxmarket. Together with his bishop he had created a unique and certainly significant group of images that reveal the preoccupations of a regional bishop in the years immediately prior to the Reformation. This body of work was only achievable through the building of a close creative partnership between patron and artist, where the artist brought his creative and aesthetic judgements and skills to bear on the demanding intellectual agenda of a well-educated and politically aware patron. To what extent this occurred in other regions of England is impossible to say, depending as it does on the serendipitous coming together of two such unusual individuals. However, in Sussex, the sheer variety of sources plundered by Barnard for inspiration and the wide geographical origin of this material is proof of a sustained and dynamic involvement with continental culture, and shows, at the very least, that the county was no backwater. Its diplomatic and trade links with the European mainland and proximity to London and the court, the presence in the county of a learned upper clergy and long-established politically ambitious nobility ensured a continuity that allowed Sussex to move with the times, and to remain closely connected to cultural and political, national and international developments.

Chapter 4

Intellectual Networks Associated with Chichester Cathedral, c. 1558–1700[1]

Andrew Foster

English and Welsh cathedrals of the early modern period have rarely been investigated as centres of intellectual activity. Contemporaries of the Elizabethan church settlement viewed them at best with deep suspicion, while many saw them as part of the trappings of Rome. For some, they were 'dens of loitering lubbers', and for others, profitable sinecures to bolster poor livings held elsewhere.[2] They became revitalised in the early seventeenth century when associated with the ceremonial, music and rituals of the 'Arminian' movement, but that was scarcely popular and may even have contributed to the origins of the British Civil Wars. When bishops were abolished in 1646, it was not surprising that so too were deans and chapters soon after, for by that period they had few defenders.[3]

[1] Andrew Hadfield and Paul Quinn kindly asked me to speak on this topic at a conference they hosted in Chichester in 2011. This article has benefited from the input of people who attended, notably members of our Early Modern Studies Group, and is dedicated to the memory of Dr Mary Hobbs, for many years the real librarian of the cathedral acting for the chancellor. I am grateful for illuminating discussions since with Dr Charlotte Hanson, the current librarian, and with Dr Daniel Starza Smith, a fellow contributor to this volume who has done much to revise our thinking on the 'King' library. As ever, I am indebted to the indefatigable local member of the Clergy of the Church of England Database project, John Hawkins, and Professor Kenneth Fincham. I would also like to acknowledge the Leverhulme Trust for granting me an Emeritus Fellowship to pursue work relating to the Church of England, 1540–1700, which has provided essential context to this article.

[2] Claire Cross, "'Dens of Loitering Lubbers": Protestant protest against Cathedral foundations, 1540–1640', in *Studies in Church History*, 9 (1972), D. Baker, ed.: 231–37; D. Marcombe, 'Cathedrals and Protestantism: The Search for a new identity, 1540–1660', in *Close Encounters: English cathedrals and society since 1540*, D. Marcombe and C.S. Knighton, eds (Nottingham: University of Nottingham), 1991, pp. 43–61.

[3] The demise of deans and chapters was actually only formally ratified in April 1649, by which time many of their lands and perquisites had been traded. For current thinking that offers more nuances to the arguments about cathedrals and Laudianism, see Ian Atherton, 'Cathedrals, Laudianism and the British Churches', *The Historical Journal*, 53(4) (2010): 895–918.

Yet it is possible to argue that cathedral clergy of this period have had a bad press and that they were indeed attempting to fulfil the ideals of some reformers that they might make cathedrals beacons of light and learning in the provinces.[4] Thanks in no small part to Henry VIII and Edward VI, most were associated with schools, many had prebends specifically attached to teaching/preaching roles, and all had libraries – some still of great distinction.[5] While many cathedral clergymen were indeed scarcely resident – high fliers who picked up sinecures on their road to promotion – a large number were local clergymen or came to reside in their posts.[6]

One obvious way in which cathedrals might serve their local scholarly communities might have been through their libraries. Yet the history of cathedral libraries in England and Wales between the sixteenth and seventeenth centuries, from what is already known in outline, is a story of some devastation and losses – particularly for the old monastic foundations – at the Reformation. This was followed by some stirrings to rebuild collections from the late sixteenth century, then the major setbacks caused by looting in the Civil Wars, before entering calmer waters after the Restoration, when deans and bishops set about in earnest to re-found libraries.[7] A flurry of books on cathedrals over the last few decades has confirmed this general account and supplied detailed case studies for places like Norwich, Gloucester, Ely and also Chichester.[8] While we have more details

---

[4]   Cranmer obviously had high hopes for the educational role of cathedral clergy when he fought for the establishment of the 'six preachers' at Canterbury, for which see Patrick Collinson, 'The Protestant Cathedral, 1541–1660', in *A History of Canterbury Cathedral*, P. Collinson, N. Ramsay and M. Sparks, eds (Oxford: Oxford University Press, 1995), p. 159.

[5]   It has to be noted of course that the libraries suffered during this period and many were raided for the King's collections or those of courtiers.

[6]   Andrew Foster, 'The Dean and Chapter 1570–1660', in *Chichester Cathedral An Historical Survey*, Mary Hobbs, ed. (Chichester: Chichester Press, 1994), p. 95.

[7]   For authoritative writing on this general topic, see N. Ramsay, '"The Manuscripts flew about like Butterflies": The Break-Up of English Libraries in the Sixteenth Century', in *Lost Libraries*, James Raven, ed. (Basingstoke: Palgrave, 2004), pp. 125–44; D. Pearson, 'The Libraries of English Bishops, 1600–40', *The Library*, 6th series, 14(3) (September) 1992: 221–57; C.B.L. Barr and D. Selwyn, 'Major ecclesiastical libraries: from Reformation to Civil War', *The Cambridge History of Libraries in Britain and Ireland, I, To 1640*, E. Leedham-Green and Teresa Webber, eds (Cambridge: Cambridge University Press, 2006), pp. 363–99. One should also mention the two volumes on cathedrals by Stanford E. Lehmberg, *The Reformation of Cathedrals: Cathedrals in English Society, 1485–1603* (Princeton, NJ: Princeton University Press, 1988) and *Cathedrals Under Siege: Cathedrals in English Society, 1600–1700* (University Park: Penn State Press, 1996).

[8]   *Norwich Cathedral Church, City and Diocese, 1096–1996*, Ian Atherton, Eric Fernie, Christopher Harper-Bill and Hassell Smith, eds (London: Hambledon Continuum, 1996); S. Eward, *No Fine But a Glass of Wine: Cathedral Life at Gloucester in Stuart Times* (Salisbury:

of collections, where they were located, how they were arranged, how they were paid for, and the growth of regulations that came into existence in an attempt to control borrowing, we still have scant details of what a library collection might have meant to a dean and chapter, clergy and others in the region – how it might perhaps have served as an hub for intellectual life.[9]

The key resource that might be found at any cathedral, however, was not the books they might hold, but the people. In a moderately sized cathedral chapter would be found highly qualified clergymen and lay officials. Cathedrals, particularly those of the old foundation like Chichester, with a dean, chancellor, precentor, treasurer and resident canons, together with a number of civil lawyers would form the basis of a small community that would be augmented by schoolmasters attached to the cathedral school and prebendaries required to preach or maintain residence by dint of their foundation.[10] Hence at Chichester, the Highleigh Prebend was held by the Master of the Prebendal School, the Wightring Prebendary was expected to preach, and the so-called four 'Wiccamical prebends' established by Bishop Sherbourne had places of residence in the Close.[11] Two archdeacons – for Chichester and Lewes – might also be expected to maintain close links with the cathedral and nearby episcopal palace in which there would also be some chaplains.

The Chichester Cathedral Chapter consisted of 35 post-holders, a relatively large establishment by contemporary cathedral standards.[12] That number may be

---

Michael Russell Publishing, 1985); *A History of Ely Cathedral*, P. Meadows and N. Ramsay, eds (Woodbridge: Boydell, 2003); *Chichester Cathedral*, Hobbs, ed.

[9] My research for this article originated in a desire to construct some case studies on the roles of cathedrals within dioceses in connection with preparing a book on the Dioceses of England and Wales, c. 1540–1700. It was natural to use Chichester as one of those case studies given my earlier work with Mary Hobbs.

[10] Each holder of a Chichester prebend was required to preach in the cathedral at least once a year. Nine cathedrals had establishments of over 33 clergy, including chancellors, precentors and – apart from York and Lincoln – treasurers; but it must be admitted that those of the new foundation or with amended statutes under Henry VIII had much smaller cathedral establishments.

[11] The Highleigh prebend represents an interesting special case, for until 1662, the post-holders were not required to be in holy orders, something tested when Daniel Baines was refused admission in 1664. Indeed, the post seems to have been used for quite young scholars taking a 'gap year' in their studies, several of whom went on to enjoy illustrious careers, most notably George Buck.

[12] The Chichester Cathedral 'establishment' was almost certainly amongst the top six in overall size (see below) and probably better placed than most in terms of those required to keep residence, preach and teach. Seventeen English and Welsh cathedrals had clerical establishments of fewer than fifteen clergy.

increased if one includes the bishop and the two archdeacons, neither of whom was always invited to become a member of chapter even if they might probably have passed through Chichester quite regularly. The point of 'residence' is quite important, for this large establishment should really be reduced quite dramatically when one takes account of who was involved in the day-to-day running of the cathedral.[13] For the wider chapter as a whole, some 380 clergymen and top civil lawyers served Chichester Cathedral between 1558 and 1700. In calculating who would have numbered amongst the residential elite, however, it seems safer to work with a total of 189 individuals.[14] These include all those who served as dignitaries of the Cathedral – the dean, chancellor, precentor and treasurer – together with all the bishops and archdeacons. They also include all of the Wightring prebendaries, the Highleigh prebendaries and the Wiccamical Prebendaries of Bargham, Bursal, Exceit and Windham who had homes in the Close.[15] To these should be added all those who served as residentiary canons, who by definition were required to keep residence on a quarterly basis. And finally, we should include the number of diocesan chancellors who served in this period, to whom one might ideally add the even more shadowy registrars and other lawyers who would have been active for the cathedral and diocese in the city at any one time.

This working cathedral chapter and wider 'establishment' might have consisted of around eighteen people at any one time, if one includes a registrar, another civil lawyer and a resident chaplain in the episcopal palace. And this would have been very much on a par with Oxford and Cambridge colleges in this period, where such a number would have accounted for the fellowships of the admittedly smaller – but majority – of colleges.[16] Oriel College, Oxford, for example, had exactly eighteen fellows in 1714.[17] In a list of Cambridge colleges compiled around 1672, of fifteen colleges noted with details of fellows, seven

[13]   This matter of effective management of the cathedral was pursued in several articles in *Chichester Cathedral*, Hobbs, ed.

[14]   All listed in an appendix to this chapter.

[15]   The Wiccamical prebends are notable because they were all expected to have been educated either at Winchester College or New College, Oxford – both places associated with Bishop Sherbourne. They might thus have been better educated than average and they were also provided with accommodation in the Close in order to encourage residence: *Fasti Ecclesiae Anglicanae 1541–1857, II, Chichester Diocese*, comp. Joyce Horn (London: University of London, Institute of Historical Research, 1971).

[16]   I am grateful to Professor Kenneth Fincham for discussions on this point.

[17]   J. Ayliffe, *The Antient and Present State of the University of Oxford*, 2 vols, 1714, I, 292; I am grateful to Kenneth Fincham for illuminating discussions about the history of Oriel that is currently in the press.

had fewer than eighteen.[18] What we are talking of here is one of the better cathedral establishments, and a larger number of potentially resident clergy than I surmised in my general account of the dean and chapter for a more limited time period in the collection edited by Dr Mary Hobbs.[19] That should still be read for an idea of how the cathedral was run, but the argument presented here revises the view that Chichester was 'a rather sleepy backwater'.[20] Chichester Cathedral's establishment was possibly the sixth largest in the country, and thanks to Sherbourne's Wiccamicals, may have furnished more scholars with residence – and some preaching and teaching obligations – than almost any other cathedral in the land. As argued before, however, many of the intellectual stars of the cathedral may not always have been resident, and there were many lapses in discipline – as there were in Oxbridge colleges. Nevertheless, a case can be made for Chichester's clergy providing greater intellectual stimulus for their community than hitherto supposed.

This chapter thus aims to explore a variety of questions associated with how this cathedral 'establishment' of well-qualified clergy and lawyers might have acted as a hub for general intellectual activity in the region. This will entail consideration of cathedral library resources, possible use and evidence of attachment, and will extend to discussion of the revolving circles of friendships, patterns of patronage, and evidence of publications that emerged over the period in question. It will touch upon how Chichester was peculiarly fortunate in the size of its establishment, its close links with London and the court, and its continued connections with Oxford and Cambridge colleges, all of which contributed to an interlocking range of intellectual networks. It will pursue the analogy with Oxbridge colleges, showing how in both quantity and quality, the number of scholars resident, their educational qualifications, their publications, combined projects networked with scholars elsewhere, and the library resources upon which they could call – all equal what was to be found in an Oxbridge college at that time.[21]

---

[18] John Groome, *The Dignity and Honour of the Clergy* ... , 1710, pp. 417–45.

[19] Andrew Foster, 'The Dean and Chapter 1570–1660', in *Chichester Cathedral*, Hobbs, ed., pp. 85–100.

[20] Ibid., p. 95.

[21] The range of work on the two old universities and their colleges has grown considerably in recent years, but still useful is Hugh Kearney, *Scholars & Gentlemen Universities & Society in Pre-Industrial Britain 1500–1700*, 1970; *The History of the University of Oxford, IV, Seventeenth-Century Oxford*, N. Tyacke, ed. (London: Faber and Faber, 1997) contains many valuable articles; for Cambridge, see John Twigg, *The University of Cambridge and the English Revolution, 1625–1688* (Woodbridge: Boydell and Cambridge University Library, 1990) and the more recent

Two important points need to be made about the time period chosen for this study. First, in starting with the cathedral of the Elizabethan Settlement, it should be remembered that a strong network of scholars with international connections was broken at that date. Thanks to deaths, deprivations and resignations, over two-thirds of the cathedral establishment had to be replaced between 1558 and 1562.[22] Indeed, this was the case in the entire diocese and must have represented quite a shock to the system. It is little wonder that the Protestant Reformation took time to get going in this region and effectively had to wait for the efforts of Bishop Curteys and his associates after 1570.[23] Amongst the leading Catholic scholars lost at this stage were Bishop John Christopherson who left his library to Trinity College, Cambridge on his death in 1558; William Tresham, the cathedral chancellor and well-known disputant with Peter Martyr; Alban Langdale, the archdeacon who went to live with the Mountague family at Cowdray, and most famous of all – claimed by Anthony Wood to have been 'the most learned Roman Catholic of his time' – Thomas Stapleton, who retired to the Continent to write.[24] It is perhaps a mark of Bishop Sherbourne's achievements that such a group of Roman Catholic intellectuals had become so well established at Chichester, buttressed by his four Wiccamical prebends, all of which changed hands around this time.[25]

Yet there was a second critical juncture in our period, for the process of having to start all over again was experienced by those clergy who arrived at the cathedral between 1660 and 1662. The Civil Wars and Interregnum clearly dislocated many of the intellectual networks established by that date; clergy

---

magnificent work of Victor Morgan, *A History of the University of Cambridge, II, 1546–1750* (Cambridge: Cambridge University Press, 2004).

[22]   See the pioneering article by Tim McCann, 'The Clergy and the Elizabethan Settlement in the Diocese of Chichester', in *Studies in Sussex Church History*, M.J. Kitch, ed., 1981: 99–123, and Peter Wilkinson's visual summary, 'The Struggle for a Protestant Reformation 1553–1564', in *An Historical Atlas of Sussex*, K.C. Leslie and B. Short, eds (Chichester: Phillimore, 1999), pp. 52–3. John Fines covered this period with 'Cathedral and Reformation', in *Chichester Cathedral*, Hobbs, ed., pp. 47–68. Another pioneer in this field was Malcolm Kitch, 'The Chichester Cathedral Chapter at the Time of the Reformation', *Sussex Archaeological Collections*, 116 (1978): 277–92.

[23]   For more on Bishop Curteys and his efforts, see the *ODNB*, and R. Manning, *Religion and Society in Elizabethan Sussex* (Leicester: Leicester University Press, 1969).

[24]   For details of all, see the *ODNB*, inclusion in which is a comment in itself on their status.

[25]   Other key Catholic scholars who were deprived at Chichester included Cathedral Treasurer John Smith, who was also a distinguished Professor of Divinity in Oxford and Provost of Oriel College between 1550 and 1564, about whom I have learned much from Kenneth Fincham; William Devenishe, the Prebendary of Exceit, was likewise Provost of Queen's College, Oxford until his death in 1558.

were forced into hiding, many fled abroad, others suffered deprivations and 'sufferings' later captured in the writings of John Walker.[26] The fellows of Oxford and Cambridge were likewise scattered. Chichester was fortunate in that Bishop Henry King, the poet and scholar, returned to office, but the situation was possibly even worse than that which faced his predecessors in the sixteenth century: he started to rebuild with almost entirely new colleagues, and there was no precentor's post, for his dean had to live in that post-holder's house while a new deanery was built.[27] Significant losses in the early 1660s, either through death, resignation, deprivation, or promotion included Dean Bruno Ryves, the Anglican apologist Henry Hammond, Aquila Cruso, William Paule and Stephen Goffe, the latter of whom had defected to Rome.[28] On the other hand, there were some significant gains in Thomas Ballowe, Professor of Moral Philosophy at Oxford between 1630 and 1634, who became Prebendary of Firle and a canon residentiary in 1660.[29] And Jasper Mayne, the dramatist, became Archdeacon of Chichester.[30]

The period under scrutiny might usefully be split into three sections: those clergy largely active between 1558 and the death of Elizabeth in 1603, those active between 1603 and the death of Charles I in 1649, and those active between 1660 and 1700. Analysis of the educational qualifications of those clergy and lawyers included in the inner core of 189 people suggests that they were an highly qualified elite by contemporary standards, well able to claim the accolade of being equal in many respects to an Oxbridge college. Of 68 people active between 1558 and 1603, over half held higher degrees above that of MA level;

---

[26]   *Walker Revised*, A.G. Matthews (Oxford: Oxford University Press, 1988 edn), pp. 3–4 covers the cathedral clergy, while Sussex in general is covered on pp. 353–62; for discussion of the implications of this, see Walter Simon, *The Restoration Episcopate* (New York: Bookman Associates, 1965), and Ian Green, *The Re-Establishment of the Church of England 1660–1663* (Oxford: Oxford University Press, 1978).

[27]   See *Fasti Ecclesiae Anglicanae, Chichester*, 1971; only six out of 37 positions were held by experienced colleagues – the rest were new appointments; the precentor's position was not filled in its own right until 1688.

[28]   Ryves had been the author of the royalist newsletters *Mercurius Rusticus* during the Civil War – *ODNB*; Henry Hammond was the author of numerous theological works including *Practical Catechism*, 1643, and was a royal chaplain – *ODNB*; for Aquila Cruso see later; William Paule was another royal chaplain who was promoted to be Bishop of Oxford in 1663; Paule apparently tried to copy cathedral archives and create an index that has since been lost to Chichester – *ODNB*; Stephen Goffe was apparently a great loss to the Church of England, another royal chaplain and a friend of Vossius.

[29]   Robert Holtby, 'The Restoration to 1790', in *Chichester Cathedral*, Hobbs, ed., p. 102.

[30]   *ODNB*, Mayne.

this figure jumps to around 70 per cent for the next two periods between 1603 and 1649, and 1660 and 1700. Clergymen of all periods were heavily involved in preaching, disputations, translation work, the writing of theological tracts, and numerous works of a scholarly and practical nature in relation to their chosen profession. Many maintained strong links with their old colleges and acted as patrons and mentors for young scholars coming through from those colleges to serve the cathedral and diocese.

This group of 189 is the total of those who might have been closely associated with the work of the cathedral in this period by dint of their offices. In fact, we know that the figure may be reduced, for a fair number of even those who held eminent positions – such as the deans and treasurers – held posts of importance elsewhere and may seldom have come to Chichester.[31] Two treasurers who held office for a combined period of 44 years – Richard Neile and his half-brother, Robert Newell – are scarcely known to have ever visited Chichester. While Dean Thorne was dutiful in his attendance to Chichester business, his illustrious predecessor Martin Culpepper was Warden of New College, Oxford between 1573 and 1599, and was to be found in Oxford much more than in Chichester. The use of cathedral positions as sinecures for those with many posts elsewhere – and particularly for those with London and court connections – was common. These links were, on the other hand, vital to wider intellectual networks and illustrate close ties with Oxbridge colleges.

As a group, nevertheless – and these caveats aside – this would have constituted an highly educated elite: all of the bishops held Doctorates of Divinity; all of the deans held doctorates, even if one was for medicine and several were Doctors of Civil Law. Out of the 189 as a whole – where qualifications are known – 91, or nearly half, held doctorate-level qualifications.[32] Looked at another way, at least forty are known to have published, to use a criterion familiar to several generations of university scholars in modern times.[33] Virtually all of them held higher degrees of some sort, ranging from MA to BD. This is a group of people who would have been very familiar with the insides of libraries, would have appreciated their value, and would have been involved in

[31] For discussion of this theme, see also, Foster, 'Dean & Chapter 1570–1660', *Chichester Cathedral*, Hobbs, ed., pp. 92–5.

[32] To provide some modern context here, this is a better strike rate for 'staff' holding doctorates than that achieved by many British 'universities' in the twenty-first century.

[33] In keeping with this perhaps over-cynical, modern line of thinking, on the criterion of REF 'impact', Chichester clergy would come out well for 57 of this group have merited inclusion in the *ODNB*! And that too might merit comparison with any Oxbridge college of the day.

establishing the contents of their old college libraries, not to mention assisting in new foundations.[34] Hence, Bishop Samuel Harsnett is famous for the library he founded on his death at his old town of Colchester, while Bishop Peter Gunning gave his collection to his old Cambridge college of Clare in the later seventeenth century.[35]

It looks as if the first decade of Elizabeth's reign was spent getting the cathedral re-established and none of the clergy involved stand out for his intellectual endeavours. The arrival of Dean Curteys in 1567 and his subsequent elevation to the bishopric in 1570 seems to have brought about a renewal of energy, fuelled partly by his use of Cambridge contacts. His Archdeacon of Lewes, Thomas Drant, for example, had been educated at St John's College, Cambridge when Curteys had been a Fellow there. Drant was active in producing anti-Catholic works and translations of Horace.[36] Drant's *Epigrams and Sentences Spiritual in Verse*, published in 1568, was said to have broken new ground with regard to the art of composing epigrams.[37] Drant may have owed his promotion to Curteys and the Cambridge links, but he was also a domestic chaplain to Edmund Grindal when the latter was Bishop of London, and he also held posts at St Paul's Cathedral. A strong Protestant, Drant wrote the dedicatory verse for the second edition of John Foxe's *Acts and Monuments* published in 1570. Yet he is symbolic of many a member of a cathedral chapter who at this date was possibly better known for his general intellectual pursuits than for his theology, and in this case, those pursuits were translations and poetry. Gabriel Harvey referred to him as 'a fat-bellied Archdeacon', but he was active in the literary group known as 'Areopagus' in the 1570s that included in its number the glitterati of English poets: Edmund Spenser, Gabriel Harvey, Philip Sidney, Edward Dyer and Fulke Greville. As his *ODNB* biographer has put it, 'Drant's contribution as poets began to experiment and seek new forms was significant, and awaits fuller appreciation.'[38]

A pupil of Drant at St John's College, Cambridge, and a chaplain to Bishop Curteys, was William Hopkinson, who briefly held the prebend of Bursal and also assisted Drant as Commissary of the Archdeaconry of Lewes in the

---

[34]   These figures accord well with the findings of Stanford Lehmberg for all cathedrals in this period, for which see his works cited above.

[35]   *ODNB* entries for Harsnett and Gunning.

[36]   *ODNB*, Drant.

[37]   Ibid.

[38]   Ibid.; see also Chapter 2, 'Two Sussex Writers: Anthony Copley and Thomas Drant' in this volume.

early 1570s. A strong Protestant, Hopkinson wrote *An Evident Display of Popish Practises, or, Patched Pelagianisme* that was published in 1578. He took to living more at his vicarage in Salehurst, where he continued his studies and wrote *A Preparation into the Waye of Lyfe, with a Direction into the Right Use of the Lord's Supper* published in 1581. A later edition of 1583 was dedicated to Sir Henry Sidney. Hopkinson played a prominent part in Sussex petitions to Archbishop Whitgift in that year, and later returned to West Sussex to live out his years at Warbleton.[39]

Unfortunately, it is difficult to claim that Drant made great use of Chichester Cathedral Library, for he apparently spent the majority of the latter years of his life until his death in 1578 in Cripplegate in London. More home-grown talent, who in turn networked a number of people locally, was Henry Blaxton, who also attended St John's College, Cambridge and was another supporter of Bishop Richard Curteys. He sired a clerical dynasty through his marriage with Joan Nunn, and held various cathedral appointments, including the West Wittering prebend, that of Highleigh very briefly, and died in 1606 as Chichester Cathedral Chancellor. The poet Gerard Peeters married Blaxton's daughter Elizabeth and gained various Chichester diocesan livings presumably by courtesy of his father-in-law.[40] Most intriguingly, however, he was related through marriage to one George Buck who served very briefly as the Prebendary of Highleigh between 1578 and 1581. This post, acquired when he was only 18, has not been picked up in the biography in *ODNB*, for this man went on to be knighted in 1603 and was the famous Sir George Buck, Master of the Revels, Fellow of the Society of Antiquaries, and author of a manuscript history of Richard III which circulated in 1619. Alas, this is also the same George Buck who was declared a lunatic and died at the house of his sister in Broadwater, Sussex in 1622.[41]

Bishop Curteys may have been the first Protestant bishop of Chichester really to make an impact and gather around him men of like mind, but Bishop Bickley, who succeeded him after a brief interregnum, was the first bishop that we can safely record as leaving a book to the cathedral library. He gave a copy of the famous controversy between Bishop John Jewel of Salisbury and the Jesuit Thomas Harding on his arrival in 1585.[42] Bishop Henry King stands out as the chief benefactor, but it is possible that Bishops Andrewes, Harsnett, Mountague

---

[39]   *ODNB*, Hopkinson.

[40]   W.H.Challen, 'Henry Blaxton, DD', *Sussex Notes and Queries*, (14) (1957): 221–5; *ODNB*, Peeters.

[41]   Ibid.; *ODNB*, Buck.

[42]   Mary Hobbs, 'The Cathedral Library', in *Chichester Cathedral*, Hobbs, ed., p. 174.

and Duppa also took an interest, given the quantity of Arminian texts in the library, and there is clear evidence concerning bequests by Bishops Gunning and Williams.[43]

Bishops were not always resident in Chichester, often preferring their nearby palace at Aldingbourne, but they still could play a significant part in acting as a focus for some of the intellectual networks that would have operated in the area. Through their patronage, appointment of chaplains, and ability to offer hospitality, bishops could have used their college connections to create local networks. Mention has already been made of the way in which Curteys used his links with St John's College, Cambridge to provide posts for other 'Johnians'. Mention will be made of the importance of another St John's circuit after the Restoration. But Henry King's era in the mid-seventeenth century also affords a high number of links with Christ Church, Oxford. His predecessor, Brian Duppa, Dean George Aglionby, diocesan Chancellor Richard Chaworth, Treasurer Philip King, and Archdeacons Lawrence Pay and Jasper Mayne were all scholars of 'the House'.[44]

Scholars of St John's College, Cambridge and the above list for Christ Church, Oxford might come in sudden flurries, but it is New College, Oxford that stands out for its unbroken contribution of scholars to Chichester's establishment. Aided of course by the Wiccamical foundation decrees, New College provided a steady flow of Chichester appointments throughout the period and a total of 41 people – almost double that of the next best college, which was St John's College, Cambridge. While the Wiccamical appointments provided a stream of clergymen with sound if unspectacular qualifications, the stars of this college were undoubtedly Dean Martin Culpepper after 1577, and his successor, William Thorne. They served as deans for a combined total of 53 years. Other significant New College alumni included Dean Bruno Ryves, Chancellor Augustine Bradbridge, Precentors Henry Ball and William Cox, Wittering prebendary Francis Cox, and Highleigh prebendaries Barker and Elgar. Just four Oxford colleges provided 66 per cent of all Oxford graduates (where known) who gained posts at Chichester in this period: Christ Church, Magdalen, Merton and New College, and the latter exceeded the other three put together. While Oxford supplied 104 graduates, Cambridge – with St John's College dominant on 22 – only supplied 65.

---

[43]   See Chapter 5, 'This strange conglomerate of books', or 'Hobbs' Leviathan': Bishop Henry King's Library at Chichester Cathedral by Daniel Starza Smith in this volume.

[44]   See the *ODNB* for many of these individuals, a useful indicator of their repute.

Moving into the seventeenth century, Chichester intellectuals included Bishop Lancelot Andrewes and Dean William Thorne, both of whom were involved in the great project to produce a new translation of the Bible.[45] Thorne was a distinguished scholar who had served as Professor of Hebrew in Oxford. Bishop Carleton was one who published anti-Catholic material and had represented the British church at the Synod of Dort.[46] On the other end of the theological spectrum, Bishop Richard Mountague was a scholar with an extensive network that embraced the Durham House set. Chichester Cathedral proudly proclaims in stained glass over his image that he was a 'champion of the English Church', a controversial appellation even to this day. What is not in dispute is that he was a distinguished scholar with many publications to his name. He was educated at Eton and King's College, Cambridge and worked briefly for Henry Saville, the Provost of Eton, on his Greek edition of the works of Chrysostom. His famous and controversial works were *A New Gagg for an Old Goose* published in 1624 and *Appello Caesarem* which came out a year later. As Bishop of Chichester between 1628 and 1638, he was one of Archbishop Laud's most loyal lieutenants and he surrounded himself with like-minded clergymen.[47] His daughter married David Stokes who became Precentor of Chichester in 1629 and he later became a Fellow of Eton and a prebendary of Windsor. His brother-in-law, John Scull, became Chichester Chancellor and published sermons in 1624.[48] Mountague's circle while at Chichester included Christopher Potter, the Provost of Queen's College, Oxford and tutor to Laud's godson, William Chillingworth.[49] It also included Richard Steward,

---

[45]   *ODNB*, Andrewes; the case for William Thorne's involvement is less clear-cut, but as Professor of Hebrew at Oxford between 1598 and 1604, he certainly possessed the right credentials. Thorne is noted as having been a possible contributor in the celebratory *Manifold Greatness The Making of the King James Bible*, Helen Moore and Julian Reid, eds (Oxford: Bodleian Library, 2011), p. 202.

[46]   *ODNB*, George Carleton; typical of his work was *A Thankfull Remembrance of God's Mercy* which had run into three editions by 1627, a book about the defeat of the Spanish Armada in 1588.

[47]   *ODNB*, Richard Mountague; *ODNB*, 'The Durham House group'; Nicholas Tyacke, *Anti-Calvinism The Rise of English Arminianism c.1590–1640* (Oxford: Oxford University Press, 1987), pp. 125–63.

[48]   John Scull, *Two Sermons ...* , 1624; Scull left £100 for re-edifying the cathedral provided that his executrix, his mother 'first see whether the parliament will dissolve Deans and Chapters', showing his awareness of problems as early as 1641: TNA, Prob 11/188; I owe this fascinating reference to Helen Whittle.

[49]   *ODNB*, William Chillingworth; author of the famous tract *The Religion of Protestants A safe way to Salvation*, 1638.

his Dean after 1634 and Clerk of the Closet to Charles I and later Dean of the Chapel Royal.[50]

Chichester was fortunate to have a number of poets in the cloisters in the sixteenth and early seventeenth centuries, and none was more illustrious than Bishop Henry King, whose tenure spanned the Civil War and Interregnum, and who survived to see the Restoration before dying in 1669. It is King who is considered to have been the greatest benefactor to the cathedral library, largely through the bequest left by his surviving son John in 1671. It is his library – estimated at its peak to have numbered some 2,000 books – that was decimated along with the cathedral library after the siege of 1642. And it was the core of what was recovered that was used to rebuild the library after 1671, and which seems to have laid the template for future purchases in an effort to restore the collection.[51] Henry King had been born into a good family, for his father was Bishop John King of London, the famous preacher and royal chaplain. He was on good terms with members of his father's circle, notably Lord Keeper Egerton and the distinguished poet, John Donne, some of whose books he inherited in 1631. He edited a collection of Donne's poems in 1633, published a number of sermons, and his own *Poems, Elegies and Paradoxes* in 1657, which went into a second edition in 1664. Henry King's younger brother John was a canon of Christ Church, Oxford and also of Windsor, before his death in 1639.[52] Henry was a great friend of his predecessor as bishop, Brian Duppa and preached at the latter's funeral in 1662; John Hales served as a domestic chaplain to both King and Duppa. Jasper Mayne, the 'quaint preacher and a noted poet' formed another link with Duppa and became Archdeacon of Chichester in 1660; he also maintained the connection with Donne's family. So a cluster of poets flourished yet again in the cathedral precincts during the mid-seventeenth century.

What stands out for the cathedral after the Restoration is the strengthening of ties to the universities, and St John's College, Cambridge in particular. Henry King was succeeded as bishop by Peter Gunning in 1670, a man who had impeccable scholarly credentials and who had served as Master of Corpus Christi College, Cambridge, acted as Regius Professor of Divinity, and also as Master of St John's. Gunning was the author of numerous theological works

---

[50]   *ODNB*, Richard Steward.

[51]   Mary Hobbs wrote extensively on Henry King; see her 'The Cathedral Library' in *Chichester Cathedral*, Hobbs, ed., pp. 171–88; *The Sermons of Henry King (1592–1669), Bishop of Chichester*, Mary King, ed. (Aldershot: Scolar Press, 1992); see Chapter 5 by Daniel Starza Smith in this volume.

[52]   *ODNB*, John King; *ODNB*, Henry King.

dealing with infant baptism and the meaning of Lent. It is a sign of his closely maintained links with Cambridge that he left his own library on his death to his first college of Clare.[53] His chaplain, William Saywell, also a Fellow of St John's, became cathedral chancellor in 1672 and was another poet. More significant for the colour of Chichester's post-Restoration clergymen, however, he was also an active theologian and author of a number of books such as *The Original of all plots in Christendom*, published in 1680, and followed by *A Serious Enquiry* and *An Apology* in 1681 and 1682.[54] Here was a throwback perhaps to the work of Bishop George Carleton and these publications would have clearly benefited from some of the books to be found in Chichester Cathedral Library.

Another bishop and chaplain combination based on St John's College, Cambridge was formed after 1685, when John Lake became Bishop of Chichester. A great friend of Sheldon and Sancroft, Lake would have become one of the non-jurors had he not died in 1689. He was noteworthy also for his interest in poetry, for he had published a life of John Cleveland in 1677.[55] His chaplain, Robert Jenkin, a Fellow of St John's, became Precentor of Chichester in 1688, the year which also saw publication of his *An Historical Examination of the Authority of General Councils*. A year later he published *A Defence of the Profession*, and in 1696, *The Reasonableness and Certainty of the Christian Religion*. Jenkin completed the circle in his life when he became Master of St John's College, Cambridge in 1711.[56] After an interlude with Simon Patrick as bishop, Robert Grove – another Johnian – was appointed Bishop of Chichester in 1691. His focus was on attacking the dissenters, hence his earlier publications on a *Vindication of the Conforming Clergy* published in 1676, and *A Persuasive to Communion with the Church of England* in 1683.[57] After the poets, there was a distinctly practical tone to the publications and intellectual interests of clergy associated with Chichester, captured also by William Watson, Prebendary of West Wittering between 1673 and 1689, author of *The Clergyman's Law*, a new type of book that became typical of a revival of interest in clergy rights post-Restoration.[58]

Not all members of the cathedral establishment earned their fame through publication. The Highleigh prebendaries in particular were employed to

53   *ODNB*, Gunning.
54   *ODNB*, Saywell.
55   *ODNB*, Lake.
56   *ODNB*, Jenkin.
57   *ODNB*, Grove.
58   *ODNB*, Watson.

teach, and as seen with George Buck, could have been young scholars at the very start of their careers. Yet even in the ranks of those who clearly settled into this post for more than ten years, some notable civil lawyers were to be found. Hugh Barker, who obtained his DCL after his appointment at Chichester in 1590, deserves fame for teaching John Selden, the future lawyer, and William Juxon, a future Archbishop of Canterbury and son of a Chichester Cathedral Registrar. Barker went on to enjoy an illustrious career, becoming Dean of the Arches and Chancellor of Oxford diocese between 1618 and his death in 1632.[59] George Elgar LLB gave notable service to the school and cathedral over two fifteen-year spells between 1604 and his death in 1647. Given the change of status of the post after 1662, it looks as if lengthy service to the school became expected.

The intellectual stars who held the Wightring prebend have been discussed elsewhere, and were clearly those of the Arminian persuasion assembled around Richard Mountague in the 1630s.[60] It is tantalising that we do not know more about their illustrious predecessor, Anthony Corano, whose Chichester appointment in 1570 was missed by the author of his *ODNB* entry under Antonio del Corro.[61] His importance to the Arminian movement has been well documented by Nicholas Tyacke.[62] Jerome Beale, chaplain to Lancelot Andrewes, held the prebend for eleven years before moving to become Master of Pembroke College, Cambridge.[63] The career of William Hicks who succeeded him in 1620 offers a revealing warning, for Bishop Mountague complained that he neglected his preaching duties. Aquila Cruso, on the other hand, was praised as a 'man of almost unequalled learning' and praised for his endeavours to revive preaching at the cathedral.[64]

While it is possible to show connections between people and highlight some distinguished and influential publications, it is less easy to point to how they might have used the cathedral library, if at all. This is where we are back to speculation. Yet it is interesting to see just how active some of the Chichester Cathedral clergy were, and far away from their Oxbridge college libraries. This

---

[59] Brian Levack, *The Civil Lawyers in England 1603–1641 a political study* (Oxford: Clarendon Press, 1973), pp. 208–9.

[60] Foster, 'Dean and Chapter', in *Chichester Cathedral*, Hobbs, ed., p. 98; A. Fletcher, *A County Community in Peace and War: Sussex 1600–1660* (London and New York: Longman, 1975), pp. 76–93.

[61] *ODNB*, Corro.

[62] Tyacke, *Anti-Calvinism*, pp. 58–60.

[63] *ODNB*, Beale.

[64] Foster, 'Dean and Chapter', p. 98.

sense of an intellectually re-equipped and re-vitalised clergy is supported by analysis of probate inventories for the clergy of Sussex. In a work edited for the *Sussex Record Society*, Annabelle Hughes has revealed just how many clergy owned books and had studies that later became 'libraries'. Probate inventories covering the period 1600 to 1750 reveal that 148 out of 181 clergymen possessed books, 57 of whom referred either to a 'study' or even a 'library'.[65] Aquila Cruso, noted above, left books worth over £20 out of a total inventory worth just over £35.[66] The study of Nicholas Garbrande, Prebendary of Sommerley, yielded books worth £50 in 1671.[67] That of Matthew Woodman, ejected from Slinfold in 1662, yielded 400 books in 1683, no mean figure for an ordinary clergyman.[68] These figures suggest a well-educated and interested band of clergymen in the region.

The sources for this kind of enquiry are necessarily scant and circumstantial. We are speculating about often tenuous networks, making assumptions about college and family relationships where they can be uncovered, and building on scraps of information in dean and chapter minute books, library catalogues (usually of the eighteenth-century reading back), and lists of benefactors and their gifts.[69] As another chapter in this volume reveals, there are still many questions abounding about the actual nature and identity of the 'King' collection, said to form the heart of the library that was re-founded in the 1670s.[70] Many questions remain about the range of people – primarily cathedral and local clergy, together with a smattering of city fathers and local gentry – who might have used the library.

As discussed elsewhere, the library was decimated during the Civil Wars and the story of how it was rebuilt after 1660 is complex, entangled as it is with the story of Henry King. What is critical here, however, is the way in which other benefactors come to the fore and there is a sense of more people giving books to the library, and regarding it as a safe repository. Clergy continued to leave books to their college libraries, such as Gunning and

---

[65] 'Sussex Clergy inventories 1600–1750', A. Hughes, ed., *Sussex Record Society*, 91 (2009); this recording of books was fairly evenly spread over the whole period

[66] Ibid., pp. 206–7.

[67] Ibid., pp. 228–30.

[68] Ibid., pp. 111–12.

[69] Francis Steer, 'Chichester Cathedral Library', *The Chichester Papers*, 44, 1964 and Mary Hobbs, 'The Cathedral Library', in *Chichester Cathedral*, Hobbs, ed., pp. 171–88, confirm the impression given by those writing of cathedral libraries in general that we have scant evidence about many of the practicalities concerning libraries before the eighteenth century.

[70] See Starza Smith, Chapter 5, this volume.

Maurice, or to Lambeth, like Zachary Cradock, but Gunning also left a book for Chichester, and ordinary canons like John Sefton and George Heath felt impelled to do so, as well as the more illustrious and wealthy Dean Hayley or Bishop Williams.[71] John Sefton, one of the residentiary canons, left a hundred books to the library on his death in 1679 with the proviso that the chapter might store them in the Vicars' Hall and turn it into a public library.[72] George Heath's bequest of a Polyglot Bible in 1672 had also been made 'to begin a new library withal for that the Church which hath been spoiled in these ill times'.[73]

The library would have been stocked with a standard range of books covering the works of the Fathers in Latin, Greek and Hebrew, commentaries, dictionaries, concordances, bibles, liturgical works, sermon collections, tracts on civil law, ancient histories and tracts produced on all sides in the various controversies of the day. At around a thousand books, it would have also been reasonably comparable with the smaller college libraries that only really got established in the seventeenth century. Moreover, a good cathedral library would have been one place outside of Oxford, Cambridge and London where it would have been possible – and legal – to find Catholic writers as well as Protestant.[74] Hence for Chichester, there is the copy of Cardinal Bellarmine's works that was used by John Donne when assisting in responses, a thankless task performed by many in the reign of King James I.[75] There would also have been books used presumably by the teachers at the school, and possibly even the pupils. Apart from serving the day-to-day needs of cathedral clergy in producing sermons for services, producing music for the organist and the choir, and supplying the liturgical books in common use, the library might have been the source of real treasures for intellectuals now stranded from London or Oxbridge.

---

[71]   These bequests are captured in the relevant *ODNB* entries, noted in the articles by Hobbs, and also by Starza Smith, Chapter 5, this volume.

[72]   M. Hobbs, 'Cathedral Library', in *Chichester Cathedral*, Hobbs, ed., p. 177.

[73]   W. Peckham, 'Chichester in the Civil War', *Sussex Notes and Queries*, 13 (1950): 14.

[74]   I.G. Philip and Paul Morgan, 'Libraries, Books, and Printing', in *History of Oxford University*, III, N. Tyacke, ed. (Oxford: Oxford University Press, 1997), pp. 659–85, confirms this general picture of the size of college libraries and their development and provides a useful reminder that the now famous Bodleian Library only had around 2,000 books when it was officially opened in 1602; this soon rose to some 16,000 printed books and manuscripts by 1620 (p. 661), by which date New College Library apparently contained some 3,300 printed books (p. 677). I am grateful to Kenneth Fincham for this reference.

[75]   Cardinal Bellarmine, *Disputations*, 1603; see Daniel Starza Smith's Chapter 5 in this volume and the previously cited work of Mary Hobbs and Francis Steer.

One final group of people deserves special mention. The diocesan chancellors represented a significant group of highly qualified intellectuals, as well qualified, probably better socially connected than the bishops whom they served. Robert Taylor, one of those deprived in 1559, had been Principal of St Alban's Hall before his Sussex appointments. Anthony Blincow, diocesan chancellor between 1590 and 1607, was Provost of Oriel for all of that time, and later served as diocesan Chancellor of Oxford.[76] Several of these diocesan chancellors served for more than one diocese, thus establishing a critical network for the band of civil lawyers that surrounded them. John Beacon was connected with the dioceses of Norwich and Lichfield and Coventry.[77] Clement Corbett followed Bishop Harsnett to Norwich in 1625, having been Professor of Law at Gresham College, London before his appointment to Chichester in 1614.[78] Richard Chaworth was at the heart of the Restoration settlement, serving as diocesan Chancellor of Canterbury, Chichester and London in the early 1660s.[79]

These examples reveal a problem, however, for such high-flying officials may often have had recourse to the use of suffragans. Yet they still provided the glue to another interlocking network. They linked civil lawyers across the country; through their work as members of High Commission or in Chancery, or membership of Doctors' Commons, their own club near St Paul's Cathedral, they networked in the capital.[80] These chancellors were consummate professionals by the end of the period. Until Drury's death in 1614, all of the chancellors had been clergymen, those at the outset of the period often serving in the linked disciplinarian role of an archdeacon. Yet all moved in high social circles, Fletcher and Chaworth serving as Members of Parliament, and four others serving as Justices of the Peace. They were all men of letters, several were heads of colleges, Blincow gave his books to Oriel, and they included a one-time Professor of Law and a diplomat who wrote about his expedition to Russia.[81] These were well-networked people in more senses than one.

---

[76] Levack, *The Civil Lawyers in England 1603–1641*, p. 212.

[77] *ODNB*, Becon.

[78] *ODNB*, Corbett; Levack, *The Civil Lawyers in England 1603–1641*, pp. 220–21.

[79] Levack, *The Civil Lawyers in England 1603–1641*, pp. 217–18; Ian Green, *The Re-Establishment of the Church of England 1660–1663* (Oxford: Oxford University Press, 1978), pp. 72, 118–19.

[80] Levack, *The Civil Lawyers in England 1603–1641*, provides excellent material on the work of these civil lawyers.

[81] Clement Corbett was Professor of Law at Gresham College, London 1607–13; Giles Fletcher was the ambassador who went to Russia.

This chapter has only scratched the surface of this line of enquiry. More remains to be done to track all the clergy involved and their publications. More might yet be made of connections through marriage. Further analysis of publications, prefaces and dedications might throw more light on how these scholars worked as groups, for writing is rarely a completely individual endeavour. Establishing chaplaincies is always difficult, but always revealing – and many of these clergymen had served as chaplains for members of the local aristocracy and thus had homes in other grand libraries such as those at Petworth or Arundel. While connections have been revealed between members of the chapter, more needs to be investigated regarding possible connections between the clergy and the lay communities around them – that is, the civic fathers of Chichester, the gentry and aristocracy of the surrounding Sussex countryside. It is one thing to reveal some of the networks and to outline the contribution of clergy as published scholars of some repute – more than has been supposed hitherto – it is quite another to establish exactly what significance all this had for the clergy of the diocese – or indeed, for the wider community. Yet the evidence of probate inventories and wills could lead to more evidence of a growing reading public, and analysis of all the scholars attending a growing numbers of schools might point to a cultural renaissance in the provinces, and one in which cathedrals may have played a significant part.

One final point of note is that this line of argument accords very well with a contemporary defence made of cathedrals when facing calls in Parliament for their abolition in 1641. John Hacket, who became a bishop on the Restoration, faced down his critics with a powerful defence of cathedrals and their deans and chapters. He noted that 'the divines for the most part are studied and able men' and that 'cathedrals are usually supplied with large and copious libraries ... Our principal Grammar Schools in the kingdom are maintained by the charity of those churches.' The cathedral clergy were 'champions of Christ's cause against the adversary by their learned pens' and performed a vital part in supplying students for Oxford and Cambridge. Most critically for the argument advanced in this chapter, Hacket noted that 'as in universities the society of learned men may be had for advice and discourse; so when we depart from them to live abroad, we find small academies in the company of many grounded scholars in these foundations.'[82]

---

[82]   John Hacket, *A Century of Sermons*, 1675 – the preface providing a life of Hacket was supplied by his friend Thomas Plume; I am grateful to Ken Fincham for reminding me of where I could locate this famous speech.

Appendix: List of clergy and civil lawyers associated with Chichester Cathedral between 1558 and 1700, comprising those post-holders who might have been expected to maintain close contact and residence. This list comprises what might effectively be referred to as the 'Chichester Cathedral establishment'.

Bishops:

William Barlow	DD	Oxford
Richard Curteys	DD	Cambridge
Thomas Bickley	DD	Oxford
Anthony Watson	DD	Cambridge
Lancelot Andrewes	DD	Cambridge
Samuel Harsnett	DD	Cambridge
George Carleton	DD	Oxford
Richard Mountague	DD	Cambridge
Brian Duppa	DD	Oxford
Henry King	DD	Oxford
Peter Gunning	DD	Cambridge
Ralph Brideoak	DD	Oxford
Guy Carleton	DD	Oxford
John Lake	DD	Cambridge
Samuel Patrick	DD	Cambridge
Robert Grove	DD	Cambridge
John Williams	DD	Oxford

Deans:

Henry Turnbull	DD	Oxford
Richard Curteys	DD	Cambridge
Anthony Rushe	DD	Oxford
Martin Culpepper	MD	Oxford
William Thorne	BD	Oxford
Francis Dee	DD	Cambridge
Richard Steward	DCL	Oxford
George Aglionby	DD	Oxford
Bruno Ryves	DD	Oxford
Joseph Henshaw	DD	Oxford
Joseph Gulston	DD	Cambridge
Nathaniel Crew	DCL	Oxford
Lambrook Thomas	DD	incorp. Cam
George Stradling	DD	Oxford
Francis Hawkins	DD	Cambridge
William Hayley	DD	Oxford

Precentors:

Thomas Day	BCL	Oxford
Thomas Willoughby	MA	Oxford?
John Beacon	DCL	Cambridge
John Reynolds	DD	Oxford
Henry Ball	MA	Oxford
John Mattock	BD	Cambridge
Thomas Murriell	MA	Cambridge
David Stokes	DD	Cambridge
Christopher Potter	DD	Oxford
William Cox	DD	Oxford
Joseph Henshaw*	DD	Oxford
Joseph Gulston*	DD	Cambridge
Nathaniel Crew*	DCL	Oxford
George Stradling*	DD	Oxford
Robert Jenkin	MA	Cambridge
John Patrick	MA	Cambridge
Henry Edes	DD	Oxford

Cathedral Chancellors:

William Tresham	DD	Oxford
Augustine Bradbridge	BA	Oxford
William Bradbridge	BD	Oxford
John Chaunter	MA	Oxford
Henry Blaxton	DD	Cambridge
Roger Andrewes	BD	Cambridge
John Scull	MA	Oxford
James Marsh	DD	Oxford
Lambrook Thomas	DD	incorp. Cam.
William Saywell	DD	Cambridge

Treasurers:

John Smith	MA	Oxford
Augustine Bradbridge	MA	Oxford
William Overton	DD	Oxford
Stephen Chatfield	MA	Oxford
Richard Neile	DD	Cambridge
Robert Newell	DD	Cambridge
Philip King	DD	Oxford
Walter Jones	DD	Oxford
Toby Henshaw	BD	Cambridge

Treasurers *(cont.)*:

Henry Maurice	DD	Oxford
William Barcroft	MA	Cambridge

Archdeacons of Chichester:

Thomas Spencer	DD	Oxford
John Coldwell	MD	Cambridge
Thomas Gillingham	MA	Oxford
John Langworth	DD	Cambridge
William Stone	BD	Cambridge
Henry Ball	DD	Oxford
Thomas Pattenson	BD	Cambridge
Roger Andrewes	BD	Cambridge
Laurence Pay	MA	Oxford
James Marsh	DD	Oxford
Henry Hammond	DD	Oxford
Jasper Mayne	DD	Oxford
Oliver Whitby	BD	Oxford
Josiah Pleydell	MA	Cambridge

Archdeacons of Lewes:

Edmund Weston	LLB	Peckwater Inn
Thomas Drante	BD	Cambridge
William Coell	MA	Cambridge
William Cotton	MA	Cambridge
John Mattock	MA	Cambridge
Richard Buckenham	BD	Cambridge
William Hutchinson	MA	Oxford
Thomas Hook	DD	Oxford
Philip King	DD	Oxford
Nathaniel Hardy	DD	Oxford
Toby Henshaw	BD	Cambridge
Joseph Sayer	BD	Oxford
Richard Bowchier	BD	Oxford

Prebendaries of Highleigh:

Robert Okinge	LLD	Cambridge
Matthew Myers	BA	Oxford
Henry Blaxton	DD	Cambridge
John Penven	BA	Cambridge

John Beeching		
George Buck		
John Sanford		
Edward Bragge	MA	Oxford
Hugh Barker	DCL (later)	Oxford
George Elgar	LLB	Oxford
John Woodhouse		
Thomas Barter	BA (BD later)	Cambridge
Daniel Barnes	BA	Cambridge
John Baguley	MA	Cambridge
Francis Bacon	MA	Oxford
Robert Topp	MA	Cambridge

Holders of the above post did not have to be ordained before the Act of Uniformity of 1662. This helps to explain the lack of educational qualifications noted above for several appear to have been young people working a 'gap year' before going to university.

Prebendaries of 'Wightring' (West Wittering):

George Beaumont	DD	Cambridge
Augustine Bradbridge	BA	Oxford
Francis Cox	DD	Oxford
Anthony Corano	DD	Abroad
Henry Blaxton	DD	Cambridge
Roger Andrewes	BD	Cambridge
Jerome Beale	DD	Cambridge
William Hickes	MA	Cambridge
Aquila Cruso	BD	Cambridge
Daniel Whitby	MA	Oxford
James Herring	MA	Cambridge
Giles Collier	MA	Oxford
William Watson	LLD	Cambridge
Conyers Richardson	MA	Oxford

The Wiccamical Prebendaries:
Bargham:

George Sutton		
Thomas Packard	BCL	Oxford
John Satwell		
John Richardson	BA	Cambridge
Laurence Alcocke	MA	Oxford
Christopher Tesdall	MA	Oxford
John Richards	MA	Oxford

The Wiccamical Prebendaries *(cont.)*:

Mountjoy Cradock	MA	Oxford
Richard Glyd	BCL	Oxford
Samuel Palmer	BCL	Oxford
Bursal:		
William Harwarde	MA	Oxford?
William Longford	MA	Oxford
John Bachter	MA	Oxford
William Hopkinson	BA	Cambridge
Daniel Gardiner	MA	Cambridge
Henry Ball	BD	Oxford
William Thorne	DD	Oxford
Ambrose Sacheverell	BCL	Oxford
William Parsons	DCL	Oxford
Edmund Coles	MA	Oxford
Weeley Cale	MA	Oxford
Exceit:		
William Devonishe	MA	Oxford
Arnold Goldsmith	BA	Oxford?
Richard Roberts	BCL?	Oxford?
Ralph Dowell		
Thomas Makinge		
William Skelton		
Thomas Dennys	MA	
Robert Beeching		
Edmund Culpepper	MA	Oxford
George Scott	MA	Cambridge
Robert Moore	MA	Oxford
Edward Stanley	DD	Oxford
Leonard Alexander	BCL	Oxford
Robert Matthew	DCL	Oxford
William Eames	MA	Oxford
John Thistlewaite	MA	Oxford
Windham:		
Laurence Woodcock	BCL	Oxford
Miles Man		
Richard Hicks		
Ralph Earle		
Gabriel Teynter	MA	Oxford
Nathaniel Field	MA	Oxford
Henry Complen	MA	Oxford
Jonathan Cooke	BCL	Oxford
John Cocke	MA	Cambridge?

John Harrison	DCL	Oxford
John Reynell	MA	Oxford

Residentiary Canons (only those clergy not already noted above):

Henry Worley	LLD	Oxford
William Clarke	BD	Cambridge
Richard Kitson	MA	
Garrett Peters	MA	Cambridge
Garrett Williamson	BD	Oxford
Richard Man	MA	Cambridge
Miles Hodgson	BD	Oxford
Humphrey Booth	MA	Oxford
John Cradock	BCL	Oxford
William Coxe	MA	Oxford
Thomas Searle	MA	Oxford
Thomas Emerson	MA	Oxford
Owen Stockton	MA	Cambridge
George Benson	BD	Oxford
Robert Bostock	DD	Oxford
Adrian Dee	MA	Cambridge
William Paule	DD	Oxford
Stephen Goffe	DD	Oxford
Samuel Wilkinson	DD	Oxford
Thomas Ballowe	MA	Oxford
Nicholas Garbrande	BD	Oxford
Zachary Cradock	DD	Cambridge
John Sefton	MA	Oxford
George May	MA	Cambridge
Francis Hall	DD	Cambridge
Thomas Woodward	MA	Oxford
John Saywell	MA	Cambridge

Diocesan Chancellors (only those not already cited above):

Giles Fletcher	LLD	Cambridge
Anthony Blincowe	DCL	Oxford
John Drury	DCL	Oxford
Clement Corbett	LLD	Cambridge
William Neville	DCL	Oxford
Richard Chaworth	DCL	Oxford
Thomas Croft	LLD	Oxford
Thomas Briggs	LLD	Cambridge

Chapter 5

'This strange conglomerate of books', or 'Hobbs' Leviathan': Bishop Henry King's Library at Chichester Cathedral

Daniel Starza Smith

This chapter sets out new evidence about the library of Henry King (1592–1669), Bishop of Chichester. The library has the potential to illuminate not only King's own biography, sermons and poetry, but also mid-century episcopal scholarship, politics, law and theology. In order to use this important resource, it is vital first to understand what exactly is represented by the 300 volumes surviving at Chichester and designated the 'Bishop Henry King Library'. This group of books, a more porous collection than we might expect, appears to have been collected, confiscated, dispersed, partially re-collected and partially re-dispersed. Identifying many of the people other than Bishop King who owned these books, this chapter uses previously unrecorded provenance evidence to reconstruct the routes by which they passed into and out of his collection.[1]

Any research into Bishop King or Chichester Cathedral necessarily builds on Mary Hobbs's thorough analyses of these subjects. As cathedral librarian, Hobbs sought to establish how King's original collection related to the books that remained at the library. It is thus fitting, in a book on early modern Sussex, to draw attention to seven boxes of Hobbs's unpublished notes, which the present cathedral librarian Charlotte Hansen and I discovered in 2012 while exploring a dusty architrave. A further box of Hobbs's papers was kindly made available

[1]   I would like to thank the Bibliographical Society for providing me with funding to visit Chichester in Spring 2012, and Hugh Adlington, Charlotte Hansen and Henry Woudhuysen for their help and advice. Andrew Foster has been particularly generous with his knowledge and hospitality, and kindly shared with me advance versions of his chapter in this book. I am grateful for the opportunity to access a draft version of Peter Beal's forthcoming online *Catalogue of English Literary Manuscripts* (*CELM*), and especially to Chichester Cathedral Library for permission to include the images in this chapter.

to me by Peter Beal, their current custodian.[2] Among these papers, Chichester's indefatigable librarian corrects a student's mis-spelling of her surname, adding the wry note 'Tho I may in my time have been referred to as Hobbs' Leviathan!' Hobbs remains the Leviathan of Henry King studies, and this essay relies throughout on the extensive work that she carried out on his library and sermons.

Nevertheless, King himself still makes only a modest mark on current scholarship, despite the rapid recent expansion of work on early modern sermons and on John Donne, King's friend. Less influential in the Church, less learned a scholar and less compelling a preacher than Donne or Lancelot Andrewes, he receives just a handful of index entries in the *Oxford Handbook of the Early Modern Sermon* (2011). Karen Armstrong cites John Chamberlain's astonishment that King's first sermon should be a high-profile one at Paul's Cross.[3] (He 'did reasonablie well but nothing extraordinarie, nor neere his father'.) Jeanne Shami notes that a portrait of Lady Anne Clifford uses Clifford's book collection as a background, and that among 48 identifiable books on display we can discern King's sermons.[4] Tom Webster, in his analysis of preaching and Parliament between 1640 and 1659, does not discuss King, whose Interregnum sermons, if there were any, do not survive.[5] Elsewhere, Mary Morrissey has made a useful short analysis of King's loyalist sermon of 27 March 1640.[6] King is not in the index to Arnold Hunt's *The Art of Hearing* (2010), which focuses on the pre-Civil War era; he is only briefly discussed in Shami's 2003 monograph on Donne and conformity in the later Jacobean era.[7]

---

[2]   The boxes at Chichester include several lectures Hobbs gave on the library, and an unpublished Master's degree essay by a student in the Department of Library, Archive and Information Studies at University College London in 1995: Mark Purcell, 'The Library of Chichester Cathedral' (CCL, Box 1/3). This existing research helped me assemble references and reconstruct the story of the siege of Chichester, but the following investigation of alternative provenances is new.

[3]   Karen Armstrong, 'Sermons in Performance', in *The Oxford Handbook of the Early Modern Sermon*, Peter McCullough, Hugh Adlington and Emma Rhatigan (eds) (Oxford: OUP, 2011), pp. 120–36.

[4]   Jeanne Shami, 'Women and Sermons', in ibid., pp. 155–77.

[5]   Tom Webster, 'Preaching and Parliament, 1640–1659', in ibid., pp. 404–20. On the apparent twenty-year pulpit silence from King during the war, see Barbara Donagan, review of *The Sermons of Henry King (1592–1669), Bishop of Chichester*, Mary Hobbs (ed.) (Cranbury, NJ: Associated University Presses, 1992), in *Huntington Library Quarterly*, 57 (1994): 204–08, at p. 208. Donagan suggests that King had not done enough during the Interregnum to earn the Archbishopric of York.

[6]   Mary Morrissey, *Politics and the Paul's Cross Sermons, 1558–1642* (Oxford: Oxford University Press, 2011), p. 156

[7]   Arnold Hunt, *The Art of Hearing: English Preachers and Their Audiences, 1590–1640* (Cambridge: Cambridge University Press, 2010); Jeanne Shami, *John Donne and Conformity in*

This chapter does not make any fresh claims about King's preaching, or his role, political or ecclesiastical, in the Civil War. Instead, it presents extensive unpublished manuscript evidence about the collection designated the 'Bishop Henry King Library' at Chichester Cathedral, and enquires into the nature of this 'strange conglomerate of books', as Hobbs called it.[8] The library was once a principal repository of knowledge in early modern Sussex, and its history is intimately tied to mid-seventeenth-century disputes in the county. However, scholarly understanding of this collection is far from complete. Looking afresh at the story of King's library, it becomes necessary to involve a cast of often unexpected supporting characters – not only several generations of Chichester clergy, but such disparate individuals as Archbishop Thomas Cranmer, Pocahontas, the polar explorer Apsley Cherry-Garrard and Mrs E.J. Rolls of Bognor Regis.

The Siege of Chichester, 1642, and Confiscation of King's Library

A moderate Calvinist, King was not highly favoured by Laud, but his devotion to the monarchy helped him become Dean of Rochester in 1638. However, he was to suffer the consequences of the Roots and Branches Petition of 1640, which called for the eradication of episcopacy. King was consecrated at Chichester on 6 February 1642 but, as Hobbs notes, 'the very next day, Parliament brought in a Bill to abolish bishops.'[9] King took up the bishopric in October, but within two months Sir William Waller's forces were advancing through Sussex taking important towns loyal to the Royal cause. Arundel's castle stronghold fell easily in December 1642, and Chichester, strategically placed on naval supply routes, was taken by Waller soon after, surrendering on the 29th.[10] The story of the siege of Chichester has been told several times so I shall not repeat all the details: the key point for this study is that the cathedral was despoiled.[11] Bishop King, like many

---

Crisis in the Late Jacobean Pulpit, Studies in Renaissance Literature, vol. 13 (Cambridge: D.S. Brewer, 2003).

[8]   Mary Hobbs, 'Henry King, John Donne and the Refounding of Chichester Cathedral Library: Unfamiliar Libraries XXV', *Book Collector*, 33 (1984): 189–205, at p. 202.

[9]   Mary Hobbs, 'The Restoration Correspondence of Bishop Henry King', *Sussex Archaeological Collections*, (125) (1987): 139–53, at p. 139.

[10]   Chichester's Mayor Robert Exton had read the King's proclamation of June 1642, but a group of influential local men led by Willam Cawley declared for Parliament in August.

[11]   There are several useful accounts, although ultimately a degree of confusion still persists. See *Victoria County History of the County of Sussex*, 6 vols (1905–2005), 1.521–3, 3.87–8, 3.112. For other accounts, see C.L. Prince, 'The attack of the Parliamentarians upon Chichester Cathedral', *Sussex Archaeological Collections*, (31) (1881): 205–08; Charles Thomas-

in Chichester, remained loyal to the crown, and at some point after April 1643, much of his property was confiscated by William Cawley, later a regicide and distinguished even in his own time by 'his zeal for seizing and selling the lands of delinquents'.[12] King later referred to the episode as 'the barbarous vsage of a wretched Committee at Chichester', complaining that he had been deprived not only of 'seuerall collections of higher moment' (that is, books) but also his private papers, 'the moniments of my course in Study through all my Life'.[13]

King was forced to flee the city until the Restoration, but it was only in 1651 that the County Committee for Sussex wrote to the Committee for Compounding about his books: 'If you approve, a waggon should be hired to bring them up to London, so as to have them appraised and sold for the use of the state, as they have received much damage, and will do still more by lying where they are.'[14]

The transportation of the books to London in 1651 may have been intended to coincide with large-scale sales of confiscated land and property that year and the next. There is no record of a sale, and only a few references to King's recovery of his goods, but he probably compounded for unsold goods within a few years. As C.H. Firth explains:

> In 1652 ... the Act of Indemnity alleviated [delinquent Royalists'] condition and partially ended the system of sequestration, and in 1654 and 1655 the limitations imposed by the Protector's government upon the operations of the Committee for Compounding practically terminated its activity.[15]

Stanford, *Sussex in the Great Civil War and the Interregnum, 1642–1660* (London: Chiswick Press, 1910), pp. 50ff; Andrew Foster, 'The Dean and Chapter 1570–1660', in *Chichester Cathedral*, Mary Hobbs (ed.), pp. 85–100, at pp. 88–9; Margaret Crum, *The Poems of Henry King, Bishop of Chichester* (Oxford: Clarendon Press, 1965), p. 19; Peter Beal, 'Henry King', in Beal (ed.), *Catalogue of English Literary Manuscripts 1450–1700* (Institute of English Studies, www.celms-ms.org.uk). However, there is no mention of King or Chichester in Waller's own *Vindication of the Character and Conduct of Sir William Waller, Knight* (London: J. Debrett, 1793), nor in more recent accounts of his life such as John Eric Adair's *Roundhead General: the Campaigns of Sir William Waller* (Stroud: Sutton, 1997).

[12] J.T. Peacey, 'William Cawley', *ODNB*. For King's petition for compensation after the Restoration, see National Archives, Kew, SP 29/17/24.

[13] Henry King to Edward Bysshe, 22 January 1657 (*CELM*, KiH 808).

[14] Cited in Hobbs, 'Henry King, John Donne', p. 189.

[15] C.H. Firth, 'The Royalists Under the Protectorate', *The English Historical Review*, 52 (1937): 634–48, at pp. 639–40.

Certainly he was able to retrieve some of his books, but what that small remainder might have included, and how it relates to the books currently in Chichester Cathedral Library, is the subject of the rest of this chapter.

Re-assembling the 'Bishop Henry King Library'

David Pearson notes that, as book collectors, bishops are 'a select group, set apart both by their wealth and by the scholarly attainments expected of them':[16]

> The episcopal bench in the first half of the seventeenth century included some of the most noteworthy scholars and theological controversialists of the day ... As leaders of the Church, they were expected to play a prominent part in protecting Anglicanism against a constant flow of highly learned attacks from Roman Catholics and Puritans; defence required an equally profound knowledge of a wide range of texts.[17]

Pearson's estimates of the sizes of bishops' libraries suggest that Andrewes had 600–1,000 books, Francis Dee 200, Richard Howland 270, and Arthur Lake 500; archbishops tended to have many more, such as Richard Bancroft, with over 6,000. Sizes of cathedral libraries were largely commensurate with income: by the Restoration, the Archbishop of Canterbury's annual income was roughly £4,500, the Bishop of Bristol's about £340; Chichester, as a middle-ranking institution, probably made around £1,000. The collection associated with Henry King, however, contained at least 1,000 books, and maybe as many as 2,000, denoting a collection larger than we might expect.[18]

However, any attempt to tell the story of Chichester Cathedral Library, and to specify a discrete 'Henry King collection' within it, soon runs into problems. By the early seventeenth century, the cathedral had a library, built up over many years, but no early catalogue survives to tell us how many or which books it owned. On King's arrival as bishop, he presumably brought some of his own

---

[16]   David Pearson, 'The Libraries of English Bishops, 1600–40', *The Library*, 6th ser., 14 (1992): 221–57, at p. 222. Pearson's article covers the period before the Civil War, so does not discuss King. Beriah Botfield discusses Chichester but does not record details of provenance or, for that matter, Henry King, in *Notes on the Cathedral Libraries of England* (London: Charles Wittingham, 1849), pp. 74–88. Cf. Andrew Foster's analysis of income and educational attainment among Chichester clergy between 1570 and 1660; 'Dean and Chapter', pp. 92–3.

[17]   Pearson, 'Libraries of English Bishops', p. 223.

[18]   The number of 2,000 is an estimate derived from discussions with Andrew Foster. Three thousand seems far too large, yet King certainly seems to gesture to a collection larger than 1,000.

books, including gifts from others, plus books he had inherited from his friend John Donne (d. 1631) and his (Henry's) father John King (d. 1621). While at Chichester, he acquired more books, though no records attest to his purchasing habits, and we know of no contemporary catalogue or estimated number of books. When Waller took Chichester in 1642, King fled, and may have taken some books with him. The confiscated library was not removed immediately by the Parliamentarian victors, but some books were put aside in a damp building.

It is not clear whether all the books were sequestered but, as noted above, those which were taken were not sold until 1651. There is no known sale of this collection, and no subsequent mentions in the *Calendar of the Committee for Compounding*. External provenance information from this point onward is limited to a few mentions in King family wills.[19] However, despite the fact these books were supposedly taken to London, a collection apparently descending from Henry King does now exist at the cathedral library. At some point, therefore, certain King-related books must have been returned. Some books may have been re-incorporated at King's own return to the cathedral after the Restoration (thus, after 1660), which would mean he had re-acquired them in the meantime.

In his will, King bequeathed his sons the majority of his books, but noted that these were but 'a small remainder of a large Library taken from me at Chichester contrary to the condicion and contracte of the Generall and Counsell of Warre'.[20] King bequeathed some books to his son, John, 'excepting only such English bookes which may be fit for my sonne Henryes use'. To John Millington he gave 'fower volumes fairely bound, being a description of the world in French, written by Pierre Avity'; Sir Richard Hubert was to receive 'Camdens Brittannia with mapps, K. James his works, and history of the Irish warres, all three in folio'; while King's sister Anne was left 'my great french Bible with prints, which once belonged to my honored Friend Doctor Donne'. Walter Jones was left 'the workes of Barradius in three Vol. in folio, and the last concordance in Latine by Stephanus'. Henry's brother Philip was to be given 'that parcel of books which once belonged to my deceased brother Mr William King, which I redeemed in Oxford', although Philip actually pre-deceased Henry, as did Francis Tryon, who left 'the workes of Mr. Samuell Purchas in folio, and Stowes Chronicle, and the History of the Church of Scotland by Io. Spotswood'.[21]

Two of Henry King's sons pre-deceased him so most books descended to his son John. When John died in 1671, he left his father's books to the cathedral as

---

[19]   See Hobbs, 'Henry King, John Donne', pp. 189–90.

[20]   Quoted in Hobbs, 'Henry King', *ODNB*.

[21]   This information is usefully summarised by Peter Beal in *CELM*.

a philanthropic gesture designed to provoke further giving and found a site of learning: 'All my Latine books wth some others I shall choose out I give to the use of Schollers in this Diocese of Chichester hopeing this example will move others to do the same so yt ye Deane and Chapter will assigne a place to dispose them in[.]'[22]

Hobbs's investigations imply that a (now-lost) catalogue was drawn up in 1684, of certain books then in the library, but not all of them. Hobbs suggested that the 1684 list was therefore a catalogue of a discrete collection within the library, and because so many books owned by King and Donne can be identified in it, there is a strong likelihood of a King connection. A surviving copy of the 1684 catalogue, with some additions, called *Old Catalogue of books before 1735*, was drawn up at an unknown date (but 1735 seems like a reasonable guess).[23] This listed about a thousand volumes. In the 1990s, Hobbs compared the contents of the *Old Catalogue* with existing books in the cathedral, and drew up 'Appendix 9' to the library's printed catalogue, which she called the 'Bishop Henry King Library'. This contains about three hundred volumes.

The narrative to this point, as summarised by the former cathedral library clerk Tony Savill, makes sense:

> The Bishop at the time [of Waller's assault on Chichester], Henry King, did have a considerable library, which was ... looted and sold off in London. Bishop King managed to buy some of his own books back, and, after the King's (and his own) restoration left his books to the Cathedral to form the nucleus of a new library.[24]

However, based on an examination of ownership inscriptions and bookplates, it seems clear that many of the books in the 'Bishop Henry King Library' *must* have come into the cathedral collection a) after 1684, and b) after 1775. This rather confusing conundrum has not been addressed by Hobbs or previous scholars of the library.[25] In order to advance a solution, one needs to re-arrange

---

[22]   The National Archives, Kew, PRO, PROB 11/133, sig. 136, 16 November 1669; cited by Hobbs, *ODNB*. Chichester Cathedral Library was not properly established until the eighteenth century, when it received its own dedicated space. It is not clear where the books were stored before this time, but see Mary Hobbs 'The Cathedral Library', in *Chichester Cathedral: An Historical Survey*, Hobbs (ed.) (Chichester: Phillimore, 1994), pp. 171–88.

[23]   See Hobbs, 'The Cathedral Library', p. 175.

[24]   Tony Savill, 'Introduction', *Chichester Cathedral Library Catalogue*, 2 vols (Chichester, 2001), 1.1–3, at 1.3.

[25]   I also found that a large number of books in this collection had been bound or rebound using strips or whole pages of other books and manuscripts, some medieval. I have deposited digital images of these with the cathedral librarian in case they may be of use to future scholars.

the books conceptually from their shelf or catalogue order into several distinct groups: 1) books that may have been owned by Henry King, but contain marks of ownership unrelated to him, his family, or friends; 2) books certainly owned by Henry King, his family, or friends; 3) books certainly once held at Chichester but which are known to have left the collection; 4) books whose owners inscribed them before King owned them; 5) books with owners who post-date King.

Books with Ownership Marks not made by Henry King or his Known Associates

The principal evidence for ownership by collectors other than King can be gathered from handwritten inscriptions and marginalia and pasted-in bookplates. Books which offer provenance information that cannot be identified or dated will be dealt with first. Several inscriptions demonstrate that some of the books, if they were owned by King, had previously been someone else's (see, for example, Figures 5.2, 5.3 and 5.4). Vives's *Exercitationes animi in Deum* (Lyons, 1558; CLC V747; KB.02.04) carries anonymous manuscript marks on the inside upper cover that date to 1579. The inscription in Hieronymus Weller's *In Epistolam diui Paulis as Ephesios* (Nuremberg, 1559; CLC W218; KA.01.07), helps identify two owners before King: 'Liber John Howseman ex dono magistri Cooper 19. die maij: 1592' (see Figure 5.1).[26] Howseman matriculated from Brasenose College, Oxford, in 1578, receiving his BA in 1582 and his MA in 1584, and was appointed rector of Stratfieldsaye, Hampshire, in 1587. He was probably given the book by his contemporary at Brasenose, William Cooper, who gained his MA in the same year.[27]

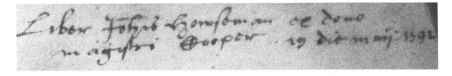

Figure 5.1   The inscription in Hieronymus Weller's *In Epistolam diui Paulis as Ephesios* (Nuremberg, 1559; CLC W218; KA.01.07).

---

[26]   Images reproduced in this chapter are not actual size.

[27]   Another Cooper, Edward, was awarded an Oxford MA in 1584, but from Trinity College.

Henry Cornelius Agrippa's *De incertitudine et vanitate* (Lyons, 1564; CLC A211; KD.02.07) was inscribed by 'Gul: Zouche', who cannot be identified with any of the *ODNB*'s William Zouches (see Figure 5.2).

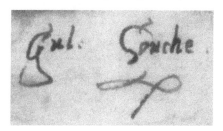

Figure 5.2   Henry Cornelius Agrippa's *De incertitudine et vanitate* (Lyons, 1564; CLC A211; KD.02.07), inscribed by 'Gul: Zouche'.

A volume of manuscript sermons by Edward Burton (KD.05.20) was at some stage owned by John, Elyzabeth and Thomas Large, who wrote their names in it several times (see Figure 5.3).

Figure 5.3   A volume of manuscript sermons by Edward Burton (KD.05.20), inscribed by John, Elyzabeth and Thomas Large.

'Sam: Bernard Magistri. Oxon' – probably Samuel Barnard (1590/1–1657), vicar of Croydon, a graduate of Magdalen College[28] – wrote his name in all three volumes of St Ambrose's *Omnia quotquot extant opera* (Basle, 1567; CLC A594; KA:04:10–12), deleting a previous mark of ownership, 'Num Johis Revij

---

[28]   Samuel Bernard's 1657 will, in which he bequeaths books to his sons, survives at The National Archives, Kew, PRO, PROB 11/269, sig. 446. One of Barnard's sons, Francis (1628–98), owned a large library and lived in Little Britain, at the heart of the London booktrade. His 1698 will is at TNA, PRO, PROB 11/443, sig. 31; Juanita Burnby, 'Francis Barnard', *ODNB*.

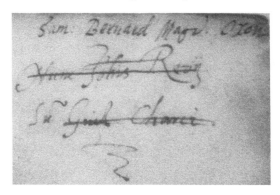

Figure 5.4   'Sam: Bernard Magistri. Oxon' – probably Samuel Barnard
               (1590/1–1657) – in St Ambrose's *Omnia quotquot extant opera*
               (Basle, 1567; CLC A594; KA:04:10–12).

Sum Guil. Charci.'. The inscription in Figure 5.4 may indicate former ownership
by William Charke (d. 1617) the religious controversialist expelled from
Cambridge who sparred in print with Campion and Persons.[29]

The King library contains five books by Erasmus, several of which derived
from other collections. The *Constructione Libellus* (Antwerp, 1535; CLC E 396;
KD.04.17d) clearly meant a lot to its owner: 'Gulielmus Renoldus est Verus
possessor Huius libri testibus.' The charming possessiveness of this phrasing
may indicate a schoolboy owner and the name appears again as part of a list of
names, probably the owner's classmates, in a school book printed for Cardinal
Wolsey's grammar school at Ipswich (see KD.04.17a–f); suggestively, one of the
other names written there is 'Kynge'.[30] Erasmus's *Tomus secondus* (Basle, 1539;
CLC E458; KA.01.13) was owned by 'Richard Burton', who scored through
the name of the previous owner, making it only partially legible as 'Johannes
[—]'; Foster lists two Richard Burtons, but we do not know if this man was an
Oxford student. The *Lingua* (Basle, 1526; CLC E431; KD.04.09) is covered in
manuscript notes in three or four hands, including one name struck through,
now illegible, and the year 'Anno 1570', meaning it was owned before it came
to King's hands. Sig. A2r is marked 'Sum Johannis Bust ex aede Christi', helping
to identify this owner as John Buste, a student at Christ Church, Oxford
before 1561.[31] The same page carries a similar mark of ownership that may read

---

29   Richard L. Greaves, 'William Charke', *ODNB*.
30   See Hobbs, 'Cathedral Library', pp. 175, 177.
31   He was later ordained, in 1568: Foster, *Alumni Oxoniensis*.

'Guilisti Late'; sig. &8v features the same illegible last name mentioned above, and Buste's name again.

The *Liturgies Breviaries* of Pius V (Salamanca, 1589; CLC L1237; KD.02.04) were owned by one 'Thomas Cornwaleis', though it is unclear whether this was the seventeenth-century colonial administrator Thomas Cornwallis (c. 1605–75) who served in Maryland, or one of the Cornwallises from the large recusant family of that name, or an unconnected individual (see Figure 5.5).

Figure 5.5   The *Liturgies Breviaries* of Pius V (Salamanca, 1589; CLC L1237; KD.02.04), signed by 'Thomas Cornwaleis'.

Chichester's copy of St Gregory's *In Julianum invectivae Duae* (Eton, 1610; STC 12346; KA.01.15a) features several drawings of human faces on the title page and throughout the margins (See Figures 5.6 and 5.7; the chin of the one in Figure 5.7 also seems to double as a manicule). The book also carries the words 'John Smith booke' on the title page (probably the cathedral librarian of this name around 1761);[32] 'Puritan ownes this book' (?) on sig. 2r (struck through); and, on sig. L1v, 'formas Douglas notæ'.

Figures 5.6 and 5.7
Faces drawn in Chichester's
copy of St Gregory's *In Julianum
invectivae Duae* (Eton, 1610;
STC 12346; KA.01.15a).

---

[32]   Hobbs, 'Cathedral Library', p. 178.

'W. Morton' at some point owned King's copy of *De formandis concionibus sacris* by Andreas Gerhard Hyperius (Basle, 1579; CLC H1244; KB.02.17b). The likely candidate for this owner is Sir William Morton (1605–72), an extremely loyal supporter of the king, who was forced to surrender Sudely Castle, Gloucester, to Sir William Waller in 1644.[33] Chichester's *Dialogus quo patrum sententiam de Coena Domini bona fide explanat*, jointly written by Oecolampadius, Zwingler and Melanchthon (Basle, 1590; CLC O54L; KD.02.05a), came from the library of 'Jacobi Medousii'; some writing has been erased decisively (see Figure 5.8).

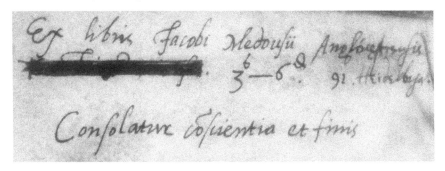

Figure 5.8 From the library of 'Jacobi Medousii': *Dialogus quo patrum sententiam de Coena Domini bona fide explanat*, jointly written by Oecolampadius, Zwingler and Melanchthon (Basle, 1590; CLC O54L; KD.02.05a).

Finally, in this grouping, Thomas More's attacks on Luther (published under the pseudonym Guilelmus Rosseus) of 1523 (STC 18089; KC.01.08) features underlining in lead and some brief marginal markings including, on the title page, 'Ex dono baccalarij bower porit', that is, 'given by Bower, Bachelor [of Arts]', although it is not clear who this was (see Figure 5.9).[34]

Figure 5.9 Thomas More's attacks on Luther (published under the pseudonym 'Guilelmus Rosseus') of 1523 (STC 18089; KC.01.08).

---

[33] Mary S. Redd Magnotta, 'Sir William Morton', *ODNB*.
[34] Foster lists eight Bowers awarded their BA from Oxford after this book was published.

Books that Certainly Belonged to King, his Family, or his Friends

Books in the 'Bishop Henry King Library' which had owners before King was collecting, or were owned by individuals who are not identifiable, are instructive, as they warn us not to define the collection too strictly as King's alone. Nevertheless, a number of books at Chichester do offer reliable provenance information which confirms that several items definitely belonged to Henry King. Peter Beal notes 'at least twenty-four volumes (or sets of volumes)' at Chichester which feature King's own hand.[35] These include three books from his time at Christ Church, Oxford: Cato, *De re rustica* (Cologne, 1536; CLC C766; KD.03.13); John of Salisbury, *Policritacus sive de nugis Curialium* (Leiden, 1595; CLC J300; KB.01.05), and Hieronymus Zanchius, *De incarnatione Filii Dei* (Neustadt, 1601; CLC Z37; KD.02.02). Editions at Chichester of St Gregory (Paris, 1615; CLC G901; KB.01.08–09) and St Augustine's *Omnia Opera* (ten books in seven volumes, Paris, 1555; CLC A1371; KB.04.01–07) are also clearly King's. King's sermons quote Augustine more than any other author; fittingly, the volume of the *Opera* containing Augustine's letters is the most heavily annotated.[36] Some books carry King's graphite marginal notes, such as George Buchanan, *De Iure Regni apud Scotos* (Edinburgh, 1583; CLC B2583; KD.05.09), which King quoted in three surviving sermons (1640, 1661 and 1664).

One of most heavily annotated volumes among King's surviving books is the *Summa conciliorum et pontificum* of Bartolome Miranda Carranza, Archbishop of Toledo (Geneva, 1600; CLC C1988; KD.03.18). *De Republica Ecclesiastica*, by Marcus Antonius de Dominis, Archbishop of Spoleto (Hanover, 1622; CLC D727, vol. 3; KC.02.07), is marked up on pp. 323–4, a passage quoted in King's 1640 sermon.[37] Another volume King clearly used in his sermons was Martin Bucer, *Gratulatio Martino Buceri ad Ecclesiam Anglicanum* (Strasbourg, 1549; CLC B2569; KB.02.07a). Although we can be sure that these books were in King's possession, the means by which he acquired them is not clear. Other books, however, do give some clues, since they are readily identifiable as gifts.

---

[35]   *CELM*. We can be certain that one volume in 'Appendix 9', William Beveridge's *Codex canonum ecclesiæ primitivæ vindicatus ac illustratus* (London: Robert Scott, 1678; Wing B2090: KA. 01.16), published nine years after King's death was not ever owned by him, although Hobbs used it as evidence that a bequest was made shortly after King's death: 'Henry King, John Donne', pp. 190–91.

[36]   The Augustine had had a previous owner, 'D. Guilelmus Chester M.L.', who inscribed his name in 1561. I.A. Shapiro suggested this was Sir William Chester, [Lord] M.[ayor of] L.[ondon] (and also 'M.[ercator] L.[ondiniensis]'). Cited in Hobbs, 'Henry King, John Donne', p. 194.

[37]   See *The Sermons of Henry King (1592–1669), Bishop of Chichester*, Mary Hobbs (ed.) (Cranbury, NJ: Associated University Presses, 1992), p. 229.

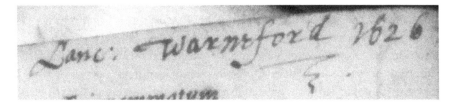

Figure 5.10   John Owen's *Epigrammatum* (London, 1612; STC 18987;
               KD.03.15a), inscribed by 'Lanc: Warneford 1626'

For example, John Owen's *Epigrammatum* (London, 1612; STC 18987;
KD.03.15a), was inscribed by 'Lanc: Warneford 1626' (see Figure 5.10).

One of three Launcelot Warnefords listed by Joseph Foster was an
undergraduate contemporary of Henry King and his brother John at Oxford –
matriculating in 1607 from St Edmund Hall, then receiving his Bachelor of Civil
Law from New College in 1614 – so it was possibly given from this Warneford
to one of the King brothers, his old university friends.[38] A leaflet among Hobbs's
private papers speculates that Launcelot was a relative of William King's wife's
sister, Penelope Warneford.

We can be more certain that other volumes were gifts, especially those
given either to Henry King or his father by Henry Mason, the elder John
King's chaplain, who became a prebendary of St Paul's at the same time as
Henry King. Marquard Freher's *Rerum Bohemicarum antiqui scriptores aliquot
insignes* (Hanover, 1602; CLC F709; KC.04.07a&b), notes it was 'Ex dono
amicissimi m^tri Henrici Mason 162i', the year of Bishop John King's death (see
Figure 5.11).

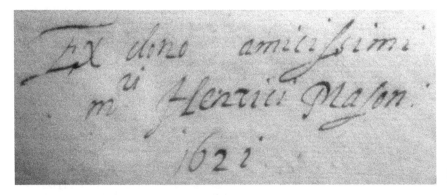

Figure 5.11   Marquard Freher's *Rerum Bohemicarum antiqui scriptores aliquot
               insignes* (Hanover, 1602; CLC F709; KC.04.07a&b).

---

[38]   Foster, *Alumni Oxoniensis*.

Petro Ribandeneira, *Flos sanctorum sive vitae sanctorum ex probatis scriptoribus selectae* (Cologne, 1630; CLC R365; KC.04.09), was given to Henry by Mason in 1631.[39] Mason also gave books to Henry's brother William King, now at Senate House and the University of Bristol (see below). The title page of Sir Henry Spelman's archaeological glossary (London, 1626; STC 23065.5; KD.05.07), which carries King's signature, also notes '20 June 1628, ex dono authoris'. King and Spelman were both shareholders in the Guiana Company in this year, and appear as co-signatories on some company documents.[40] The origin of this book thus appears clear – but its subsequent provenance immediately causes some confusion. Spelman's book carries a manuscript inscription facing the title page which reads 'Guil. Moria' (?), with a date of 30 June 1663. This is probably not an ownership inscription but a manuscript licence for the 1664 edition, suggesting that the name is William Montagu.[41] Between its arrival into King's collection and his death, this book was therefore owned by someone else and used in an official capacity by the licensers. Might it have been one of the books confiscated and later sold?

There are a number of books whose inscriptions link them directly to King through his family members. Several evidently derive from Henry's father. An inscription in William Tooker's *Duellum sive singulare certamen cum Martino Becano Jesuita* (London, 1611; STC 24119; KB.02.12), for example, shows that the author presented it to John King when he was consecrated as Bishop of London. Three books feature the initials ('G.K.') of William, one of Henry's brothers: Thomas Bozius, *De imperio virtutis, sive imperia* (Cologne, 1594; CLC B2217; KD.04.07+1); Nichol Bellus (that is, Michael Lundorp), *Politicarum dissertationum de statu imperiorum* (Frankfurt, 1615; CLC L1956; KD.04.10), and Johannes Philippson (Johannes Sleidanus), *De statu religionis et reipublicae* (Strasbourg, 1558; CLC P828; KD.03.05) (see Figure 5.12). The latter, which William King possessed while at Oxford, was also owned by 'W. Patten' in 1563, possibly the historian William Patten (c. 1510–98).[42]

---

[39]   Henry Mason dedicated his book *Christian Humilities* (London, 1625), to Henry King. See no. 80 in Geoffrey Keynes, *A Bibliography of Henry King, D.D., Bishop of Chichester* (Godalming: St Paul's Bibliographies, 1977), p. 109. Keynes does not in this work list books owned by King, as he does in his bibliography of Donne.

[40]   Hobbs, 'Cathedral Library', p. 175.

[41]   This example is not listed in J.K. Moore, *Primary Materials Relating to Copy and Print in English Books of the Sixteenth and Seventeenth Centuries* (Oxford: Oxford Bibliographical Society, 1992), which discusses the 1626 and 1664 editions of Spelman's book on pp. 24 and 32.

[42]   Peter Sherlock, 'William Patten', *ODNB*.

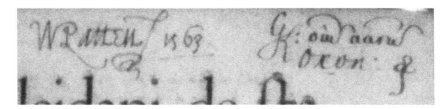

Figure 5.12   Johannes Philippson (Johannes Sleidanus), *De statu religionis et reipublicae* (Strasbourg, 1558; CLC P828; KD.03.05).

William King's Lundorp was also inscribed by 'Josua de Tam', though it is not clear if this individual, who I have not identified, was an earlier or later owner. Papirus Masson, *De episcopis urbis* (Paris, 1586; CLC M605; KC.01.15) (see Figure 5.13) features a distinctive monogram in the upper-right corner (a backwards R attached to a K, see Figure 5.14), and may have belonged to Robert, another King brother.

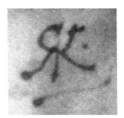

Figure 5.13   Papirus Masson, *De episcopis urbis* (Paris, 1586; CLC M605; KC.01.15).

Hieronimus Osorius's five-volume *De Gloria* (Basle, 1590; CLC O54; KD.02.05a) was inscribed by Henry's brother Philip during his own period of study at Christ Church.

Philip King's wife Mary may be another fruitful line of enquiry in the search for Henry's books.[43] She donated some volumes to the library of Archbishop Thomas Tenison (1636–1715) at St Martin-in-the-Fields, many of which were sold at Sotheby's in 1861 and subsequently dispersed. A number of items in the 1861 sale catalogue are directly relevant, including pre-eminently Bishop John King's theological notebook, with Mary King's signature, now in the Folger (MS V.a.328). Peter Hoare thought that Mary also gave several other books sold in the 1861 sale but not listed in the Tenison Library benefactors' book. These included two books by John Gregory, *Notes and observations upon some passages*

---

[43]   The following information comes from CCL, Mary Hobbs Archive, Box 1/16, letter from Peter A. Hoare to Mary Hobbs, 25 June 1984.

of Scripture (1650) and *Gregoris postuma* (1650), which were presentation copies to Philip King, the first also bearing Mary's signature.[44]

A more certain sub-group contains books at Chichester once owned by John Donne, the poet and Dean of St Paul's Cathedral. King was executor of Donne's will, and may have edited the first edition of his poems (1633).[45] Donne left his friend an unspecified number of books from his own collection, some of which can be identified in the cathedral library, carrying Donne's signature and motto on the title page, or his light marginal annotations.[46] They include Fridericus Balduinus, *Passio Typica* (Wittenberg, 1614; CLC B152; KA.01.06; Keynes, L15); Rudolphus Cupers, *Tractatus de sacrosanctus* (Venice, 1588; CLC C1766; KC.04.07c; Keynes, L57), and ten tracts bound together. Thomas Erpenius (also known as Locman), *Fabulæ et selecta quædem Arabum adagia* (Leiden, 1615; CLC E517pt2; KD.04.03c; Keynes, L112) and Christopher Binder, *De Bonis Ecclesiae ante legem* (Tübingen, 1615; KD.04.03b; Keynes, L23) do not carry the signature or motto, but are bound with Jeremy Wilde's *De Formica* (Hamburg, 1615; KD.04.03a; Keynes, L192), which does.

Keynes notes that Joannes Creccelius's *Collectanea ex historiis* (Frankfurt, 1614; Keynes, L55) was in the private collection of J.H.P. Pafford, but that it carried a shelfmark on the spine which indicates it was once stored at Chichester.[47] This volume, which carries the motto and signature, is bound with David Paré, *Irenicum* (Heidelberg and Frankfurt, 1614; Keynes, L136). Chichester's copy of Alphonsus Vilagut, *Tractatus de Rebus Ecclesiae non Rite alienatis* (Bologna, 1606; Keynes, L188), contains Donne's signature and motto. It was apparently part of the Sotheby's sale of November 1947, and was sold to 'Clark Canon' for £68, but is now back in Chichester (see below for more on this sale). Ten tracts, mostly printed abroad between 1608 and 1610 and now bound together in a composite quarto volume were not listed by Keynes because

---

[44] Another library that may be worth pursuing is that of Edward Waddington (1670–1732), a later Bishop of Chichester, who bequeathed his book collection to Eton. Given the apparent porousness of the King library, one wonders whether some King-related books might have ended up at Eton among this bequest. However, establishing this would require a volume-by-volume investigation of the c. 2,800 Waddington books, a task beyond the limits of the present chapter. Thanks to Rachel Bond at Eton College Library for answering my queries on this matter.

[45] For evidence from Donne's will, see Geoffrey Keynes, *A Bibliography of Dr. John Donne*, 4th edn (1973), pp. 258–79, esp. p. 261. Hugh Adlington is preparing an updated account of Donne's library, provisionally entitled *John Donne's Books: Reading, Writing and the Uses of Knowledge*.

[46] Keynes, *Bibliography of Dr. John Donne*, Appendix IV.

[47] Pafford died in 1996 and the book was sold at Bloomsbury Book Auctions on 19 June 1997, item 179, for £5,500 to Swales. Cf. *American Book Prices Current*, 103 (1996–97): 500.

they do not include Donne's signature, but Hobbs identified them as Donne's on the strength of his characteristic marginalia.[48]

Donne also left King his three-volume copy of Bellarmine's *Disputationes*. Keynes knew of this gift, and cited Izaac Walton's belief that these were the editions of 1586, 1588 and 1593, specifically exempted from the posthumous sale of his goods, so that it could be reserved 'as a Legacy to a most dear friend'.[49] He did not record, however, that one of these volumes, actually published in 1603, survives at Chichester (CLC B482; KB.03.05–07). The binding features the book-stamp of Sir Thomas Roe; it was probably a gift from Roe to Donne.[50]

Chichester Books Known to have left the Collection

In the mid-twentieth century, a bibliographical scandal hit Chichester when the dean and chapter attempted to sell some books from the library through Sotheby's in 1947 and 1949.[51] Fifty of these were printed before Henry King's death and could therefore have been owned by him; buyers at the sale included Apsley Cherry-Garrard, Francis Edwards, E.P. Goldschmidt, Maggs, Harry Mushlin and Winifred Myers.[52] Some books – including King's Cato, Spelman and John of Salisbury, discussed above – were withdrawn in time from the 1947 sale at the insistence of Bishop George Bell. However, Donne's copy of Vilagut was sold to 'Clark Canon' for £68 in the 1947 sale, and King's copy of St Ambrose's *Opera* (Paris, 1549), which he inscribed with his name in 1617, was sold for £4 to Myers in 1949. The Vilagut is now back in Chichester, so was either bought back or returned by 'Clark Canon' soon after his purchase was made. I suspect this man is none other than Rev. Canon Lowther Clarke, the cathedral communar and librarian who sent the books to Sotheby's in the first place; having been unable to withdraw this item from sale, maybe he was sent to buy it back.

This acrimonious high-profile sale has gained a degree of infamy; less well-known is the contemporary private sale of books from the

---

48   Hobbs, 'More Books from the Library of John Donne', *Book Collector*, 29 (1980): 590–92.

49   Walton, *Lives*, 1670, pp. 14–16; Keynes, *Bibliography of Dr. John Donne*, p. 262.

50   See Hobbs, '"To a most dear Friend" – Donne's Bellarmine', *RES*, n.s., 32 (1981): 435–8, at p. 436.

51   Money from this sale paid for restoration of the cathedral's windows, which suffered bomb damage during the war.

52   See marked-up Sotheby's catalogues in the British Library (shelfmark S.C. Sotheby) for sales on 24 November 1947 and 25 October 1949. I have not traced the subsequent provenance of these fifty books.

cathedral.[53] In February 1947, Lowther Clarke placed a notice in *The Times* announcing that the books in his care were being stacked on the floor because of lack of space. The University of London's librarian J.H.P. Pafford wrote to Lowther Clarke, to enquire about buying these books.[54] Lowther Clarke replied: 'We have a number of old books (e.g. prior to 1750) of no possible interest to us, notably in the field of classical texts and law books.' Lowther Clarke sent a copy of the Chichester Library catalogue with the relevant books marked up, and Pafford selected 121 books, which changed hands in 1948 for £50. The 'Chichester Cathedral Library Collection' at the University of London Library (now Senate House Library) currently contains 82 works in 106 volumes, mostly from the seventeenth and eighteenth centuries. Forty-eight of these were printed before Henry King's death and might therefore have been among his collection.[55] I have not listed them all here, but at least one book, Johann Wilhelm Stucki's *Antiquitatum convivialium* (1597) very likely derived from King's books, since an inscription notes it was a 1620 gift from Henry Mason, discussed above.

In response to *The Times* notice, two other institutions made substantial purchases from the cathedral at this time. Reading University Library owns eleven volumes formerly at Chichester, two of which could conceivably have been owned by King: Titus Maccius Plautus, *M. Accii Plauti Comoediae viginti* (Lugduni, 1581) and Suetonius, *C. Suetonii Tranquilli XII. Caesares* (Lugduni, 1539), which contains autograph inscriptions on the title page by Hugo Baskafilde and 'Johis Barunelli' (?). One book was certainly King's, Seneca's *L. Annæi Senecæ philosophi* (Basle, 1590; Reserve 878.5), inscribed by King ('aedis Chri Oxon') in 1610, and heavily annotated by him. Ninety books at Bristol University Library were purchased from Chichester in 1949, 42 of which were printed before Henry King's death, and a considerable number of which bear inscriptions and bookplates not directly connected to the cathedral.[56] For reasons of space I shall not enumerate

---

[53] For an account of this sale, see Jonathan Harrison, 'The Chichester Cathedral Library Collection: Tale of a Sale', *SHeLF Newsletter* (January 2012): 6–7 <www.ull.ac.uk/specialcollections/chichester.shtml> (accessed 2 August 2012). Further information has been taken from Senate House Library, UoL/UL/4/18/12. My thanks to Karen Attar for her help with this enquiry.

[54] 'The University of London Library is comparatively modern and naturally is not strong in older books as compared with its counterparts at Oxford and Cambridge. We are anxious to develop that side of the Library', Pafford to Lowther Clarke, 26 February 1947.

[55] They can be identified by performing a mixed classmarks search for '[Chichester]' here: <http://catalogue.ulrls.lon.ac.uk/search~S1/l>, and arranging the results by date. Hobbs claimed that 14 of these books certainly derived from King's collection, 'Henry King, John Donne', p. 192.

[56] My thanks to Michael Richardson at Bristol and Lucy Evans at Reading for answering my queries.

them all, but several were certainly once part of the King family collections. Bristol's copy of Martial's *Epigrammatum libri XV* (Paris, 1607; Restricted PA6501.A2) bears marginalia in Henry King's hand, and others were owned by his brothers. William King owned two books now at Bristol: Pliny the Elder's *Secundi Historiae mundi libri XXXVII* (Geneva, 1606) (given to him by Mason in 1618), and Stephanus Vinandus Pighius, *Annales magistratuum* (Antwerp, 1599). Bristol's *Claudii Claudiani poetæ prægloriosissimi quæ exstant* (Hanover, 1612), is inscribed 'Philip King his booke'.

Chichester Books Acquired *after* King's Death

The history of books with ownership histories that pre-date King's possession is relatively straightforward to explain: King could simply have acquired books that had already been owned, whether directly from the previous owners or via intermediaries. Initially, it seems just as easy to explain why so many books in the 'King Library' display ownership marks that date after King's death: surely they were set aside by Waller's troops and then sold in the 1650s, only making their way back into the collection at a later date – perhaps after being bought back by King or one of his sons. This explanation will not do, however. Many of the books in Chichester bear ownership marks that post-date both King's death and the creation of the *Old Catalogue*. If the *Old Catalogue* records a bequest of books formerly associated with Henry King and made soon after his death, as Hobbs has suggested, how can so many books identified within it have *entered* the cathedral collection so much later – even after the *Old Catalogue* was created in 1735?

Hermann V's *Simplex ac pia deliberatio* (Bonn, 1545; CLC H446; KD.05.12), for example, was owned by John Williams (c. 1636–1709), Bishop of Chichester between 1696 and 1709, and given to the library by him in 1707.[57]

Figure 5.14   Jacobus Verheiden, *Praestantium aliquot Theologorum* (The Hague, 1602; CLC V367; KD.05.18).

---

[57] This interesting volume was originally part of Archbishop Thomas Cranmer's library, and bears Cranmer's name, in his secretary's hand, on the title page. It is number 147 in David G.

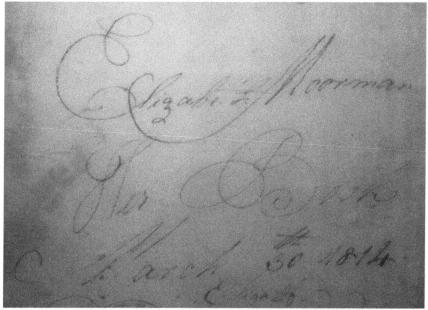

Figures 5.15 and 5.16   Thomas Gataker's sermon *David's Instructor*
(London, 1637; STC 11652; KD.05.19).

Williams's signature in the top-right corner of the title page suggests that
he also gave Jacobus Verheiden, *Praestantium aliquot Theologorum* (The
Hague, 1602; CLC V367; KD.05.18) (see Figure 5.14). Thomas Gataker's
sermon *David's Instructor* (London, 1637; STC 11652; KD.05.19) was inscribed
by several individuals after King's death: 'Martha Herbert Novemb: 6th 1681';
'Elizabeth Moorman Her Book March 30th 1814' (written very extravagantly),
'John Moorman His Book', and 'John Head 1827' (see Figures 5.15 and 5.16).

Selwyn, *The Library of Thomas Cranmer* (Oxford: Oxford Bibliographical Society, 1996), which
does not mention Henry King.

John Moorman is almost certainly identical with the man of this name (1905–89) who was chancellor of Chichester Cathedral, and who was responsible for Chichester Theological College from 1946; Elizabeth, not mentioned in his *ODNB* entry, must have been an older relative.[58] A John Head certainly lived in Chichester in the early nineteenth century.

Perhaps the most intriguing of the books which travelled after King's death is a volume of homilies (Figure 5.17) (incomplete and with no title; London, 1547–62; STC 13650; KD.05.21) which carries the following inscription:

> Thomas Rolfe his Boo<.>
> Rich Lett them be and Who can hurt him then
> Knaues Ropt in Weleth are Counted honest men
> Thomas Rolfe his Booke
> ffebruary 21:th <u>1677:</u>

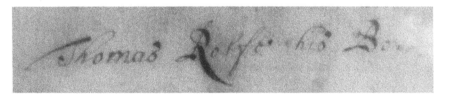

Figure 5.17		Volume of homilies (incomplete and with no title; London, 1547–62; STC 13650; KD.05.21), with verse inscription by Thomas Rolfe, dated 1677.

It seems possible that this man can be identified as Thomas Rolfe (1615–80), the son of Pocahontas (c. 1596–1617), the Virginian Indian who became Rebecca Rolfe on her marriage to a colonial tobacco planter, John Rolfe, in 1614.[59] John King, Henry's father, entertained Pocahontas shortly before her death in 1617, and it seems possible that a book from the King family libraries was given to the Rolfes either by John King or one of his sons to commemorate the friendship.[60] This provenance might explain how it left King's library, but not how it came to be in the collection of Richard Woodman, another inscriber, by 1741 – especially since it was recorded in the *Old Catalogue* as being in the cathedral only six years earlier – or that of James Fraser, a Chichester cleric

---

[58]   Michael Manktelow, 'John Richard Humpidge Moorman', *ODNB*.
[59]   Alden T. Vaughan, 'Pocahontas', *ODNB*.
[60]   Samuel Purchas, *Hakluytus Posthumus*, Vol. 19, p. 118.

whose prebendial bookplate is also evident, who was appointed deputy librarian in 1878, and who donated the book to the cathedral in November 1914.[61] Nor is it obvious how Bartolomeo Platina, *Historia de vitis pontificum Romanorum ad Sixtum IV* (Nuremburg, 1481; CLC P1095; KD.05.13) came into the possession of 'Mrs E.J. Rolls, 64, Marshall Avenue, Bognor Regis', though we know she presented it to the library in 1981.

Chichester's copy of *De antiquitate Britannicae ecclesia* by Matthew Parker, Archbishop of Canterbury (Hanover, 1605; CLC P278; KA.05.08) carries two significant ownership marks. The earlier signifies its possession by Peter Gunning, who donated it in 1684. Gunning was bishop immediately after King (1670–75), after which he moved to Ely. The second inscription in *De antiquitate*, made in 1745, is by John Frankland (d. 1777), prebendary of Chichester, who also owned Chichester's copy of Joannes Meursus the Elder, *Athenae Batavae* (Leiden, 1625; CLC M1156; KD.05.17). He seems to have bequeathed both books to the cathedral among a large number of volumes, many of which have now made their way into Senate House Library. Does the presence of his name mean that he 'assumed ownership' of them during his time in Chichester – or that he removed the book from the main collection into his own private library, only to return it later in life? Alternately, some time after Gunning wrote his name in it, the book was removed from the library, and Frankland purchased it at a later date in order to reunite it with the collection. Hobbs herself speculated on this matter:

> A later 'gift' may be returning what was originally Library property: Archbishop Parker's *De Antiquitate* ... admittedly frequently found, was presented to Chichester in 1745 by a great benefactor, Canon John Frankland. It carries the printed bookplate of Bishop Gunning's bequest of his books to St. John's College, Cambridge, in 1684. ... The book, catalogued among the King Library, is not otherwise present – coincidence? Or a rescue operation by Frankland?[62]

Are these the actual books that belonged to King, which were then dispersed but collected together again over the subsequent centuries? Without any mark of his ownership, or sales history of their provenance, it remains a moot point.

A possible answer to this perplexing puzzle emerges when one notes how many books carrying ownership dates after King's death were owned by cathedral administrators and Sussex residents. What seems most likely is that, working from lists of books known to have been lost, subsequent librarians, clergy and

---

[61] For more on the sixteenth-century man of this name, see Paul Quinn's chapter in this volume.
[62] Hobbs, 'Henry King, John Donne', p. 192, n. 2

members of the communion sought out, bought, or found themselves with individual volumes, and donated them to their cathedral. If it was known locally that the cathedral was trying to recreate its depleted library using an old booklist, then local collectors may have kept an eye on volumes they were buying, enjoying possession of them in their own lifetime then bequeathing them to the cathedral on their death or in later life. Indeed, one librarian noted bequests 'by the widows of clergymen of the rest of their deceased husbands' books after booksellers had already taken the more valuable items'.[63] This would explain the frequency among the names listed above of Chichester men – Frankland, Gunning, Head, Moorman, Williams – and Sussex inhabitants like Mrs Rolls. Hobbs suggests that Cecil Deedes, canon librarian from 1918, independently figured out the connection between the *Old Catalogue* and John King's bequest, and actively sought out many of the original gifts that had gone astray.[64] I find this a persuasive suggestion. Many of the books now at Senate House Library were donated by Frankland and Matthias Mawson (1683–1770), Bishop of Chichester, further evidence, perhaps, of a local drive to stock the cathedral library.

Conclusion

No record survives of the rationale behind Waller's ransacking of Chichester Cathedral Library. His troops, spurred on by anti-Laudian propaganda, were allowed to mutilate the cathedral itself, smashing its altar rails, symbols of the archbishop's unpopular reforms. The attack on the library, however, seems to have been less overtly destructive; a collection containing many hundreds of books was and remains a valuable financial asset. Resold in London, or released for a fine by the Committee for Compounding, the books could raise significant money for the Parliamentary cause. But the confiscation of this major Sussex library also symbolised a victory over one of the best-equipped sources of pro-Royalist policy and rhetoric in the south of England. What is now a site of primarily historical interest was once a repository of both ancient learning and innovative contemporary thought. As Andrew Foster shows in Chapter 4 of this volume, cathedrals had the potential to be 'beacons of light and learning in the provinces', and the parallels Foster draws between Chichester and Oxbridge colleges are suggestive about the kinds of intellectual activity encouraged among the clergy. Little anecdotal evidence testifies to what a cathedral library 'meant'

---

63   Cited in Hobbs, 'Cathedral Library', p. 182.
64   Ibid., pp. 182–3.

to the local community in the early modern period, but the record of publication among Chichester's clergy demonstrates their active use of the library's scholarly resources. Suppressing Bishop King's library silenced a source of intellectual firepower, an ammunition store in the war of ideologies.

King's original collection probably held about 2,000 books, but only around 1,000 are recorded in the 1735 *Old Catalogue*. The fact that only 300 of these latter books remain today suggests that the majority of the King library, as reconstituted and bequeathed shortly after his death and the death of his son John, was removed from the cathedral in the intervening years. Two-thirds of the original collection was thus lost after the 1642 siege; perhaps another 70–100 books were sold in the 1940s. The remaining 600-or-so missing books must have been taken by private individuals, or so damaged by their negligent storage conditions that they were deemed unsalvageable. It seems likely that many books were taken from the cathedral library into private collections (like those of Frankland and Gunning) but later returned by them; indeed, the complex efforts of Sussex residents over the centuries to reconstruct the Henry King collection testifies to the continuing importance of the library both within the cathedral and to the local community. By tracing ownership marks similar to those detailed in this article, perhaps further volumes from the 'Bishop Henry King Library' can be identified. Indeed, as this book went to press, I was made aware of a copy of Donne's *LXXX Sermons* (1640) in the private collection of Dr Mark Byford, which bears the signature of Anne King, Henry's sister, on the title page. More uncatalogued books may therefore yet be found.

Chapter 6

'Your daughter, most devoted': The Sententious Writings of Mary Arundel, Duchess of Norfolk, Given to the Twelfth Earl of Arundel

Elizabeth McCutcheon

In 1548, Nicholas Udall claimed that 'It is nowe a common thynge to see younge virgins so nouzled and trayned in the studie of lettres, that they wyllyngly set all other vayne pastimes at naught for learnynges sake.' And, he continued:

> It is now no newes at al to see Quenes and Ladies of moste high estate and progenie, in stede of Courtely daliaunce, enbrace vertuous exercises of readyng and wrytyng, and wyth most earneste studie both erelye and late to applye theymselues to the acquirynge of knowelage aswel in al other liberall artes and dyscyplynes ... .[1]

Udall exaggerates, but his encomium suggests how the idea and practice of a humanist education for women, based on a knowledge of Latin and Greek, had spread by the middle of the sixteenth century in England. Only twenty some years after Thomas More, Erasmus, Juan Luis Vives and other humanists had promoted it – and More's eldest daughter, Margaret, the prototype for the 'learned lady' in Tudor England, had published her English translation of a Latin devotional work by Erasmus, the *Precatio Dominica* – such an education was becoming something of a fashion for girls and young women in royal, noble and some gentry households.[2]

---

[1]   Nicholas Udall, letter to Katherine Parr preceding 'The Paraphrase of Erasmus vpon the Gospell of Sainct John', sig. A1v, in *The First Tome or Volume of the Paraphrase of Erasmus vpon the Newe Testament* (London, 1548).

[2]   *Vives and the Renascence Education of Women*, Foster Watson, ed. (New York: Longmans, Green & Co., 1912), remains a useful collection of important primary works. See, too, Alice T. Friedman, 'The Influence of Humanism on the Education of Girls and

This chapter is concerned with the education and writings of a less familiar 'learned lady', Mary Arundel, who was the younger daughter of Henry Fitzalan, the twelfth Earl of Arundel, and the youngest member of an extraordinarily privileged noble family. It is through Mary Arundel that the Howards entered Sussex as a political and dynastic force. She was connected through birth and marriage to a number of the important Sussex Catholic families including the Lumleys. Although perhaps best known as the mother of Philip Howard, Mary Arundel is also tied to the political agitations of her husband, Thomas Howard, fourth Duke of Norfolk, and to the long national and county career of her father. However, thanks to her literary exercises, we have a record of her schooling and her academic progress over a five- or six-year period in the 1550s, an important period, both politically and personally, for the entire Arundel household. They serve as a reminder of the cultural role performed by members of the Arundel and Howard families across the early modern period, both nationally and regionally. Mary Arundel's writing is interesting because of the way that it both conforms to and departs from the norm or fashion as Udall pictures it and as women like Margaret Roper, Katherine Parr, the daughters of Henry VIII, Lady Jane Grey, and the daughters of Sir Anthony Cooke came to exemplify it. Mary's education, like her older sister's and her brother's, was certainly steeped in the liberal arts, and she was tutored in Latin and Greek, as well as English. But her education seems to have been almost completely based on Greek and Latin secular classics and contemporary humanist works. Though the Arundels were a distinguished Catholic family, there is no evidence that Mary studied the Church Fathers, for example, and her reading was focused on what the Renaissance would have called 'moral philosophy' – a mixture of ethics, psychology and politics, or governance. At least as striking, her education relied on varieties of the sententious, in this way capitalising on a habit of mind that the other members of her family shared. Moreover, unlike other learned women, neither she nor her older sister turned to print.[3] Their works are known through

---

Boys in Tudor England', *History of Education Quarterly*, 25(1–2) (1985): 57–70, and Norma McMullen, 'The Education of English Gentlewomen 1540-1640', *History of Education: Journal of the History of Education Society*, 6(2) (1977): 87–101. For a discussion of the traditional education of noble and wealthy gentry women, see Sharon D. Michalove, 'Equal in Opportunity?: The Education of Aristocratic Women 1500–1540', in Barbara J. Whitehead, ed., *Women's Education in Early Modern Europe: A History, 1500–1800* (London: Routledge, 1999), pp. 47–74.

[3]   For an interesting example, see Brenda M. Hosington, 'Translation in the Service of Politics and Religion: A Family Tradition for Thomas More, Margaret Roper, and Mary Clarke Basset', in Jeanine De Landtsheer and Henk Nellen, eds, *Between Scylla and Charybdis: Learned*

manuscripts,[4] in most cases given to their father as new year's gifts, which were carefully saved in his great library – a sign of how much they meant to him.[5] In short, in the manuscripts by Mary and other members of the Arundel family we have a particularly telling example of 'household writing', which says a great deal about interests and preoccupations that they shared with one another and the earl.[6] They provide important evidence of Sussex's literary past, as well as demonstrating the role of humanist education for women across the religious divide of early modern England.

Henry Fitzalan, the Twelfth Earl of Arundel

Henry Fitzalan (1512–80) has been aptly characterised as a magnate.[7] The earldom of Arundel was an ancient one, and the twelfth earl was highly conscious of his noble status and anxious to promote it. One of the wealthiest men in the country, he early figured in the political life of sixteenth-century England, distinguishing himself as an administrator at Calais. He held a variety of offices associated with the courts of Henry VIII and his successors, including that of

---

Letter Writers Navigating the Reefs of Religious and Political Controversy in Early Modern Europe (Leiden: Brill, 2011), pp. 93–108.

⁴ I am particularly grateful to the British Library for permission to cite from manuscripts in its holdings and for photographs of Mary Arundel's signature before and after she was married.

⁵ See Natalie Zemon Davis, 'Beyond the Market: Books as Gifts in Sixteenth-Century France', *Transactions of the Royal Historical Society*, fifth series, 33 (1983): 69–88. Though she is interested in the *book* as a 'bearer of benefits and duties' (p. 69), her discussion is especially applicable to the manuscripts that the Arundel family wrote.

⁶ Household writing has been increasingly studied in the last several years. See, for example, Marion Wynne-Davies, *Women Writers and Familial Discourse in the English Renaissance: Relative Values* (Houndsmills: Palgrave Macmillan, 2007); Roger Ellis, 'Translation for and by the Young in 16th-Century England: Erasmus and the Arundel Children', in Giovanni Iamartino et al., eds, *Thou sittest at another boke … : English Studies in Honour of Domenico Pezzini* (Milan: Polimetrica, 2008), pp. 53–74; Sarah Gwyneth Ross, *The Birth of Feminism: Women as Intellect in Renaissance Italy and England* (Cambridge, MA: Harvard University Press, 2009); Caroline Bicks and Jennifer Summit, eds, *The History of British Women's Writing, 1500–1610*, The History of British Women's Writing, vol. 2 (Houndmills: Palgrave Macmillan, 2010), and Hosington, 'Translation in the Service of Politics and Religion'.

⁷ In addition to consulting the *Dictionary of National Biography* (1921–22), vol. 7, pp. 88–93, and the *DNB* (2004), vol. 19, pp. 758–65, I have drawn upon 'Life of the Last Fitz-Alan, Earl of Arundel', John G. Nichols, ed., *The Gentlemen's Magazine*, first series, 103(2) (December, 1833): 11–18, 118–24, 209–15 and 490–500, and Wynne-Davies, *Women Writers and Familial Discourse*, pp. 63–88.

Lord Chamberlain, later renamed Lord Steward. According to his anonymous biographer, as a very young man he resisted his father's wish to attach him to the service of Cardinal Wolsey, whom he knew was 'of a very lowe and base birth', instead entering the service of Henry VIII, his godfather.[8] It was a wise decision, given Wolsey's subsequent fall from grace, and Henry Fitzalan remained in the service of the king and of his successors – Edward, Mary, and Elizabeth – although in 1553 he briefly supported (or appeared to support) Lady Jane Grey, a relative by his marriage to his first wife. Lady Jane was Protestant, while Mary was Catholic, and his decision has been seen in part as a reflection of his faith. But his insistence upon Mary's legal right of succession, his wish to avoid civil war, and his enmity for the Duke of Northumberland must also have played a large part in his decision.[9] He was obviously socially and politically ambitious; in later years, he had hopes of marrying Queen Elizabeth, hopes that were not reciprocated, and he was implicated in negotiations involving Mary Queen of Scots. In fact, he was imprisoned in the Tower of London in 1551–52 and he experienced house arrest on several occasions. But he was also cautious and/ or shrewd and fortunate enough to survive one of the most turbulent times in English history.[10]

Arundel's survival is evidence of the circumspect nature of many of the Catholic and crypto-Catholic Sussex families during the period. Arundel lost the Chamberlainship and his membership of the Privy Council in 1550 as part of the ongoing power struggle at the court of Edward VI. Arundel's pardon was dependent upon his retirement to Sussex, ostensibly to ensure no further outbreaks of disorder as had been witnessed in the Enclosure disturbances of 1549. As with the removal of Northumberland to Petworth after 1569, Sussex again appears to be a site of internal exile. However, Arundel had acquitted himself well in Sussex when dealing with the Enclosure disturbances; rather than employing violence, he ensured the provision of food. As with other members of the Sussex gentry and nobility, Arundel's political decline can be linked with the increasingly partisan and 'Protestant' nature of central government and with the actions of some of his county neighbours. Arundel was removed from office following the Northern Uprising and Ridolfi named him as a figure prepared to take part in a Catholic uprising. Arundel did return to the Privy Council

---

[8]   'Life', Nichols, p. 12.

[9]   The speech (probably an expansion of the one actually delivered) is included in 'Life', Nichols, pp. 119–20. For an analysis of it, see Wynne-Davies, *Women Writers and Familial Discourse*, pp. 68–70.

[10]   See, in particular, Julian Lock's assessment of Arundel's political career and his character in *DNB* (2004).

in 1574 and remained a member until his death in 1580. His final period in office saw him involved in clashes with local Sussex rivals, notably Sir Thomas Palmer of Angmering – this was a repetition of early rivalries with the Gages. He was also witness to the debacle surrounding Bishop Curteys's attempts to enforce conformity on Sussex's major Catholic families in 1577. Curteys was rebuked by the Privy Council. Arundel's role in this censure, if any, is unclear.

Arundel's cultural and intellectual interests were shaped in large part by what he and his anonymous biographer thought of as the proper display of 'magnificence', a traditional aristocratic virtue, which could also be thought of as conspicuous consumption.[11] During the coronation of Edward VI, he supplied 450 of his own servants for festivities at Westminster hall,[12] and he subsequently enlarged and decorated Nonsuch, a splendid palace built for Henry VIII that remained unfinished when he acquired it in 1556.[13] But though Henry Fitzalan was a member of the old feudal aristocracy, he also adopted new trends, and there are grounds for thinking of him as a humanist.[14] His anonymous biographer describes him as 'not unlearned', and notes that he 'was naturally given unto breefenes in utteringe of his mynde', while 'his wordes, being shorte and fewe, carried matter in them, and weare allwaies fit and pythye' – which helps to explain his attraction to the sententious.[15] He knew Latin and French (though he chose not to speak French), and he probably knew some Italian as well. He was interested in music, history and antiquarian lore, and he owned one of the best libraries in sixteenth-century England, which he acquired in or around 1553.[16] Originally belonging to Archbishop Cranmer, the library was enlarged by the earl and further enlarged by his son-in-law, John, Lord Lumley, a bibliophile and antiquarian, who shared Arundel's interests in promoting the family and its lineage through books, manuscripts, statuary, paintings, buildings and lavish entertainments. The earl served as high steward for the University of Oxford, and, briefly, as chancellor.

---

[11] 'Life', Nichols, p. 122; *DNB* (2004), p. 764.

[12] 'Life', Nichols, pp. 13–14.

[13] He and Lord Lumley also made significant additions to the gardens. See Wynne-Davies, *Women Writers and Familial Discourse*, pp. 72–7; Martin Biddle, 'The Gardens of Nonsuch: Sources and Dating', *Garden History* 271 (1999): 145–83, and Martin Biddle, *Nonsuch Palace: The Material Culture of a Noble Restoration Household* (Oxford: Oxford Books, 2005).

[14] For an excellent discussion of humanism, see Paul Oskar Kristeller, *Renaissance Thought: The Classic, Scholastic, and Humanist Strains* (New York: Harper Torchbooks, 1961), pp. 3–23.

[15] 'Life', Nichols, p. 212.

[16] *The Lumley Library: The Catalogue of 1609*, Sears Jayne and Francis R. Johnson, eds (London: The Trustees of the British Museum, 1956).

He was also a generous patron of the arts, supporting Thomas Tallis, the musician, and Petruccio Ubaldini, a Florentine calligrapher, illuminator and writer. In British Library MS Royal 2B ix, an illuminated manuscript that he presented to Arundel in 1565, Ubaldini called the earl his 'Maecenas'.[17] This is a collection of psalms and canticles, organised for use, which includes a heraldic illustration of the earl's coat of arms, featuring a lion rampant.[18] Even more intriguing, albeit less well-known, is British Library MS Royal 14A i, with specimens of calligraphy and illumination, also written by Ubaldini, which the British Library dates between 1550 and 1553. It is shaped like an autograph album, with many different elaborate frames and borders enclosing extracts in Italian, and Ubaldini could well have intended it as a way to display samples of his art for Henry Fitzalan and his son. At the top of fol. 10v, it is dedicated to the earl's son, Henry Maltravers (or Mautravers), whose name and initials are repeated elsewhere in the manuscript. Ubaldini highlights the name 'Henrico Arvndellio' at the top of fol. 33 and 'Henrico Mautravers' at the bottom, linking the father with his son, and he further flatters the family by several times weaving Maltraver's name or initials into the borders of a collection that names some of the notable rulers of Europe, including Henry II, Charles V and Cosimo Medici.[19] Ubaldini, obviously hoping for patronage, must have designed it to appeal to the two Arundels and the father's ambitions for his only son, ambitions that were dashed by Maltraver's death just a few years later.

The best evidence of the earl's humanist interests – interests that are inseparable from his aspirations for his children and their acquisition of social and cultural capital – is the education, grounded in Erasmian principles and focused on the classics, which his children, both male and female, and other members of the family enjoyed.[20] As far as I can tell, his three children received similar tutoring, although the anonymous biographer speaks only about his son's education, which excelled 'in all manner of good learning and languages'.[21] The same is true of the daughters, who continued their education after they

---

[17]   Fol. 105v. Hereafter, in my notes, British Library will be abbreviated as BL.

[18]   Ibid., fol. 1v.

[19]   See BL MS Royal 14A i, fols 17, 22, 30, 43, 43v (twice), 44, and 45v, besides 10v and 33.

[20]   See J.K. Sowards, 'Erasmus and the Education of Women', *Sixteenth-Century Journal*, 13 (1982): 77–89, and Ellis, 'Translation for and by the Young', which treats the Erasmian presence in the writings of Jane, Lady Lumley, and John, Lord Lumley.

[21]   'Life', Nichols, p. 214. The two daughters may well have received more training in handwriting. The son would have received his initial tutoring (in English), at home, although his later education was elsewhere.

were married, following the practice of the More and Roper families and the advice that another humanist, Thomas Elyot, put into the mouth of Queen Zenobia, a classical exemplar of the learned woman, in his *Defence of Good Women* (1545).[22]

The Younger Family Members, their Writings and their Interest in Sententiae

At times during the 1540s and 1550s, the family circle would have included at least three, perhaps four or five young people, besides the tutor or tutors.[23] The earl's oldest child was a daughter, Jane (1537–78), who married her brother's friend, John, Lord Lumley (c. 1533–1609), in 1550; the couple spent much of their time with her father, and Lumley became the earl's executor. Arundel's only son, Henry (1538–56), attended Queen's College, Cambridge in 1549 and died young, after a promising beginning. A stepson, John Radcliffe, afterwards Sir John Radcliffe of Cleeve (the stepson of Arundel's second wife, Mary Radcliffe, by her first marriage), probably joined the family following his mother's marriage to the earl in 1545.[24] Mary, Arundel's younger daughter, was born in 1539/40 and died in 1557. Her marriage to Thomas Howard, fourth Duke of Norfolk (1538–72), was intended to unite two of England's greatest families, and it was the 'great social event of the spring of 1555'.[25] Her only child, Philip Howard, was born on 28 June 1557, at Arundel House, in London, and was christened four days later at Whitehall, with Philip of Spain and the Earl of Arundel as his godfathers. Less than two months later, Mary Howard died, age 16, and was buried with great ceremony; her sister, Jane, was the chief mourner, and there were 144 torches in the procession, along with many banners and banner rolls.[26]

Thanks to the manuscripts that are now part of the Royal collection in the British Library, we can identify a variety of writings that this group produced, most given to the earl as New Year's Day gifts. Jane, later Lady Lumley, is the best known of this group, on account of her translation (more accurately, a version) of Euripides' *Iphigenia at Aulus* from Greek (or Greek and Latin) into English, which was probably composed in 1557 and staged at the banqueting

---

[22]   Thomas Elyot, *The Defence of Good Women*, in *The Feminist Controversy of the Renaissance*, intro. Diane Bornstein (Delmar, NY: Scholars' Facsimiles & Reprints, 1980).

[23]   For materials consulted, see note 5, above and relevant entries in the *DNB* (2004).

[24]   For dating of the earl's second marriage, see *DNB* (2004), p. 759.

[25]   Neville Williams, *Thomas Howard: Fourth Duke of Norfolk* (London: Barrie and Rockliff, 1964), p. 32.

[26]   Ibid., p. 34.

house at Nonsuch sometime afterwards.[27] It was first published in 1909 for the Malone Society, edited in a Penguin edition in 1998, and successfully staged in 1997 at Clifton Hall Studio, Sunderland.[28] Jane earlier translated six of the orations of Isocrates into Latin: 'Archidamus', 'Ad Demonicum', 'Ad Nicoclem', 'Nicocles', 'Evagoras' and 'De Pace', although her translation of 'Ad Demonicum' is incomplete.[29] The Earl of Arundel's son gave his father an analysis of Cicero's 'De Senectute'; John Radcliffe translated the prayers and meditations composed by Queen Katherine Parr (first printed in 1545) into Latin, probably some time after 1548, as well as a chapter from Thomas Elyot's *Image of Governance*. John Lumley gave Arundel an English version of Erasmus' *Education of a Christian Prince* in 1550, referring to it as 'the golden boke' and signing it, 'Your Lordeshippes obedient sone'.[30]

With the exception of Radcliffe's translation of Katherine Parr's prayers, none of these works is primarily devotional. Their translations, better thought of as adaptations, also display a marked preference for sententiousness. Responding to Erasmus' own description of his *Institutio* as a collection of aphorisms, Lumley organised his abstract into a series of wise counsels addressed to the prince or the good prince.[31] And Jane Lumley emphasised Isocrates' *sententiae* as evidence of his philosophical nature in her letter dedicating her translation of

---

[27]   BL MS Royal 15A ix. See Wynne-Davies, *Women Writers and Familial Discourse*, ch. 4, as updated in Marion Wynne-Davies, 'The Theater', in Bicks and Summit, eds, *History of British Women's Writing*, pp. 175–95, and the introductory chronology, p. xxi, which dates Jane's translation c. 1557, a few years later than usually assumed. See, too, Ellis, 'Translation for and by the Young', and Stephanie Hodgson-Wright, 'Jane Lumley's *Iphigenia at Aulis*', in Susan P. Cerasano and Marion Wynne-Davies, eds, *Readings in Renaissance Women's Drama: Criticism, History, and Performance, 1594–1998* (London: Routledge, 1998), pp. 129–41.

[28]   See *The Tragedie of Iphigeneia: In a Version by Jane, Lady Lumley*, in *Three Tragedies by Renaissance Women*, Diane Purkiss, ed. (London: Penguin Books, 1998), pp. 1–35, together with 'Notes', pp. 167–71, and Purkiss's introduction, pp. xi–xlvi, *passim*; Hodgson-Wright, 'Jane Lumley's *Iphigenia at Aulis*', and Wynne-Davies, *Women Writers and Familial Discourse*, ch. 4.

[29]   See BL MSS Royal 15A i, 15A ii, and 15A ix.

[30]   For Henry Maltravers's analysis of Cicero, which is written as a report, see BL MS Royal 7A xii art. 16, fols 184–91v, addressed to his father, in Latin. For Radcliffe's translation of Parr, see BL MS Royal 7D ix, which includes a short dedicatory letter, fol 1–1v. John Lumley's version of Erasmus' work is BL MS Royal 17A xlix; for the inscription, see fol. 28.

[31]   On the aphoristic quality of the *Institutio*, which is full of maxims and similitudes, see the introduction to the work in Erasmus, *Literary and Educational Writings 5: Panegyricus, Moria, Julius Exclusus, Institutio Principis Christiani, Querela Pacis*, A.H.T. Levi, ed., Neil M. Cheshire and Michael J. Heath, trans. and annot., *Collected Works of Erasmus*, vol. 27 (Toronto: University of Toronto Press, 1986), p. 201. See, too, Ellis, 'Translation for and by the Young', pp. 55–8 and 63–5.

Isocrates' 'Evagoras' to her father.[32] Similarly, she cut out or radically shortened the choruses in her version of *Iphigenia*, sometimes substituting a sententia and highlighting the conflict between duty to family and duty to country, which was of immediate political relevance to the Arundels – recalling a similar choice the earl faced in the summer of 1553, when he supported Princess Mary's claims to the throne, instead of those made for Lady Jane Grey.[33] The family's attraction to sententiae of various sorts is further confirmed by two vellum rolls, over five feet long, of 'divers virtuous and pitthie sentences' that were prepared for the Earl of Arundel and Lady Lumley. Written calligraphically in English and meant to be displayed on a wall, the earl's roll focuses on the accumulation and godly use of temporal goods, Lady Jane's on pride and its great dangers.[34] And, in or around 1576, Sir Nicholas Bacon had an illuminated manuscript, based on the classical sententiae in the long gallery that he had recently added to his estate at Gorhambury, prepared for Lady Lumley, 'at her desire'.[35]

Unlike Jane's play, Mary's writings remain in manuscript at the British Library. They are all in some sense sententious, and often in the form of sententiae, a form prized by the humanists. Rosalie Colie characterises the sententia as 'a sub-literary small form intended to transmit culture and to communicate important values ... and workable into any kind of literature an author might choose'.[36] Sometimes referred to as aphorisms, commonplaces, maxims, adages, or sentences, sententiae, then, are wise and typically brief sayings, normally highly moral, that claim authority, are derived from the classics or wisdom literature, and often are syntactically tight or gnomic. Nichols described Mary's manuscripts in his nineteenth-century edition of Arundel's early biography, but only recently have they otherwise attracted any attention.[37] This is not too

---

[32] BL MS Royal 15A ii, fols 1v–2.

[33] See the following discussions: Ellis, 'Translations for and by the Young', pp. 63, 67–72; Hodgson-Wright, *Jane Lumley's Iphigenia at Aulis*, pp. 132–8; *Three Tragedies by Renaissance Women*, Purkiss, pp. 172–3, and Wynne-Davies, *Women Writers and Familial Discourse*.

[34] BL MS Royal 14B ii and BL MS Royal 14B iii. The roll for Jane Lumley is more richly decorated.

[35] BL MS Royal 17A xxiii, fol. 3. See *Sir Nicholas Bacon's Great House Sententiae*, Elizabeth McCutcheon, ed. and trans. (Amherst, MA: English Literary Renaissance, 1977); like the Arundels and the Lumleys, Bacon embraced the sententious.

[36] Rosalie L. Colie, *The Resources of Kind: Genre-Theory in the Renaissance*, Barbara K. Lewalski, ed. (Berkeley: University of California Press, 1973), p. 33.

[37] 'Life', Nichols, p. 497. Recent studies of Mary Arundel's sententiae, all brief, include Ellis, 'Translations for and by the Young', pp. 60–61 and 67, which mis-states the number of chapters Mary translated from Elyot's work, however; Ross, *The Birth of Feminism*, pp. 85–6; Wynne-Davies, *Women Writers and Familial Discourse*, pp. 66–7, and Brenda M. Hosington, '"Minerva

surprising. With some notable exceptions, scholars and critics have tended to dismiss sententiae as platitudinous and hypocritical or worse. So H.A. Mason insisted that 'It is pathetic to see the Humanists in all walks of life supposing that the mere writing up on the wall of a wise saying will make a difference to those who read the writing on the wall.'[38]

But sententiae were highly valued as a system of thought in early modern Europe and they were an essential part of the culture.[39] They were collected and published in huge numbers and embedded in writing of every sort, whether used 'straight' or ironically (think of Shakespeare's Polonius and his old saws). And they were a major element in the educational system,[40] albeit almost exclusively intended for boys and young men, whose education was based on Latin.[41] By contrast, according to Ann Moss's splendid survey, women were usually not 'among the makers of commonplace books', but 'readers and occasional transcribers, at best, of published compilations of morally edifying sentences and examples in translation'.[42] See, for example, Juan Luis Vives, another humanist and educator, who recommended that the young Princess Mary copy out sententious sayings in a notebook for memorisation.[43]

and the Muses": Women Writers of Latin in Renaissance England', *Journal of Neo-Latin Studies*, 63 (2009): 1–43, at pp. 38–9. I want to thank Brenda Hosington for calling my attention to these sententiae, about which I spoke at a panel she organised for the fifteenth International Congress of the International Association for Neo-Latin Studies, held in Münster in August 2012.

[38] H.A. Mason, *Humanism and Poetry in the Early Tudor Period* (London: Routledge and Paul, 1959), p. 111.

[39] Representative studies include Jacob Zeitlin, 'Commonplaces in Elizabethan Life and Letters', *Journal of English and Germanic Philology*, 19 (1920): 47–65; William G. Crane, *Wit and Rhetoric in the Renaissance* (New York: Columbia University Press, 1937); Sister Joan Marie Lechner, OSU, *Renaissance Concepts of the Commonplaces* (New York: Pageant Press, 1962); Colie, *Resources of Kind*, pp. 32–75; Mary Thomas Crane, *Framing Authority: Sayings, Self, and Society in Sixteenth-Century England* (Princeton, NJ: Princeton University Press, 1993); Ann Moss, *Printed Commonplace-Books and the Structuring of Renaissance Thought* (Oxford: Oxford University Press, 1996); and Earle Havens, *Commonplace Books: A History of Manuscripts and Printed Books from Antiquity to the Twentieth Century* (New Haven, CT: Yale University Press, 2001).

[40] See the very interesting essay by Peter Mack, 'Rhetoric, Ethics and Reading in the Renaissance', *Renaissance Studies*, 19(1) (2005): 1–21, on the way that ethics and rhetoric were linked and the role that commonplaces and sententiae and maxims played in Renaissance schooling.

[41] See Walter J. Ong, SJ, 'Latin Language Study as a Renaissance Puberty Rite', *Studies in Philology*, 56 (1959): 103–24.

[42] Moss, *Printed Common-Place Books*, p. vii. See, too, Crane, *Framing Authority*, p. 206, n. 26.

[43] Pointed out by Charles Fantazzi while discussing a brief manual Vives wrote specifically for her education in his introduction to Juan Luis Vives, *The Education of a Christian Woman:*

It is remarkable, then, that so much of Mary's education was grounded in sententiae and commonplace material used in diverse ways. Spread over a period of at least five or six years, her manuscripts let us follow the progress she made in Latin and Greek as she translated, first from English, and later from Greek, one sort or another of sententious material into Latin. Her education doubtlessly was influenced by the recommendations of humanists like Erasmus, More and Elyot, whose books were in her father's library; by her tutors; by the very lively preoccupation of the Arundels and Lumleys in sententiae, and by what she thought would interest her father. Mary calls her writings 'exercises' and describes them as rude and unlearned, aware both of the modesty topos and her status as a young student. They *are* apprentice work; she was the youngest member in this family circle and died at an early age. But this makes them particularly valuable in so far as they show how a mid-sixteenth-century girl and very young woman, admittedly a socially privileged one, responded to her eminently humanist schooling and the preoccupations of her family. Moreover, she 'owned' this material as she matured and mastered the style and form of the sententia, choosing those that reflected her own lively intelligence and psychological acumen as well as the political issues and personal events affecting her and her family for commonplace books of her making.

There are four manuscripts – British Library Royal MSS 12A i–iv – all in her own hand, an elegant Italic script in which each letter is written separately, whereas letters are often connected in her sister's script. Indeed, Mary's script is so legible and so elegant that it is possible that Ubaldini taught handwriting to her (and her sister).[44] Most sources place him in Italy during the period that the earl's 'school' was flourishing.[45] But one scholar has argued that he was in Scotland and England between 1549 and the summer of 1553, when he returned to Italy.[46]

A Sixteenth-Century Manual, Fantazzi, ed. and trans. (Chicago, IL: The University of Chicago Press, 2000), p. 13.

[44] Ross, *The Birth of Feminism*, stresses what she calls 'the Italian character of the Fitzalan household academy', p. 86. The family certainly had a taste for Italian art, but the children's education seems much more akin to Erasmian ideas. Ross also posits that Ubaldini was a tutor for an extended period (1550–62), which is unlikely, as he seems to have been peripatetic and spent much of that time in Italy. However, I agree that Ubaldini could well have been the writing instructor for both Jane and Mary, p. 86.

[45] See Giuliano Pellegrini, *Un fiorentino alla corte d'Inghilterra nel Cinquecento: Petruccio Ubaldini*, Studi di Filogia Moderna, new series, 7 (Torino: Bottega d'Erasmo, 1967), pp. 15–47, followed in *DNB* (2004). However, Pellegrini does suggest that Ubaldini may have returned to London around 1552.

[46] See Francesca Bugliani, 'Petruccio Ubaldini's *Accounts of England*', *Renaissance Studies*, 8(2) (1994): 175–97.

Moreover, at least two manuscripts in the British Library from the early 1550s – one made for Sir Nicholas Bacon and one for the Earl of Arundel and his son, British Library Royal MS 14A i, discussed above – place him in England then.[47]

Mary signed each of her manuscripts at the end of her dedicatory letter and her translation, but she did not date them, and the order in which they are presently catalogued is misleading. She wrote Royal 12A iii and iv before she was married and Royal 12A i and ii afterwards, as proven by her signature and the increased maturity of her work and her handwriting. The material in each manuscript is sententious, but otherwise different, and each one is accompanied by a dedicatory letter to her father, presenting her manuscript to him as a New Year's Day gift. Some of her expressions are formulaic and resemble the language in her sister's dedicatory letters to their father (also undated).[48] She is also extremely deferential in her salutations, addressing her father as 'your lordship'. I cannot tell to what degree Mary was helped by a tutor in writing her letters, but they show that she was acquiring expertise in *copia* (fullness and fluency), specifically, and rhetoric, more generally, as she learned how to write a personal letter in Latin and to develop her ideas about the texts she had translated.

British Library MS Royal 12A iii, by Mary Arundel

Mary probably finished BL MS Royal 12A iii, the earliest of her four manuscripts, no later than the end of 1552 for the following new year, or, which I think more likely, the end of 1553, presenting it to her father at the beginning of 1554, when she would still have been thirteen.[49] My dating allows time for her initial schooling in English, her subsequent schooling in Latin, and her work on the

---

[47]   See BL MS. Royal 14A xvi, a collection of sententiae or aphorisms from the Bible, written calligraphically, dedicated to Sir Nicholas Bacon and dated 20 July 1550, mentioned in Bugliani, 'Petruccio Ubaldini's *Accounts*', p. 177. See, too, Pellegrini, *Un fiorentino*, p. 44.

[48]   See BL MSS Royal 15A ii and 15A ix.

[49]   My dates for this manuscript and the following one differ from Wynne-Davies, *Women Writers and Familial Discourse*, pp. 66–7. She argues that Mary gave her collection of similitudes (Royal 12A iii) to her father early in 1552, while her father was imprisoned in the Tower of London, and so dates it between 1551 and 1552. But this means that Mary would have had to start her study of Latin by 1550 or even earlier, which is possible but seems unlikely, given her birth in 1539/40. Moreover, all four of her works appear to have been written in successive years, as New Year's gifts, and the last two, written after her marriage, can be dated 1556 and 1557. And while Mary did use for BL MS Royal 12A ii (the later of the two manuscripts she gave her father after her marriage) the 'same pot and flower watermarked paper' that her siblings had used earlier (Wynne-Davies, p. 66), this does not in itself date her manuscripts. Compare 'Life', Nichols, in

manuscript itself, which would have included first reading and then assembling all the material, translating it, and making a presentation copy from a draft. She begins her dedicatory letter by singling out the honour and veneration that her father gave to books of moral philosophy, and adds that she has turned 'egregia dicta grauissimorum prudentissimorumque philosophorum' (outstanding sayings of the most weighty and most prudent philosophers) from English into Latin, hoping that nothing could delight her father more or be more suitable for her age.[50] She also thanks him for his paternal love; he has embraced her from the time that she was a baby and has seen to her education in 'bonae litterae' (good letters), using a characteristically humanist formula.[51] And she begs him to accept this little gift of her intellectual ability as a token of all she owes him at the beginning of this new year. These motifs – of gratitude, gift giving, the particular occasion, her devotion to him and the education she is enjoying, and the nature of the work she is translating – are a constant in her subsequent letters, as is her deferential stance, although her discussion of what she is translating will become more detailed and analytical, her style more epigrammatic.

According to her heading, BL MS Royal 12A iii consists of 'Similitudines eximiae ingeniosissimaeque, ex Platonis, Aristotelis, Senicae, et aliorum philosophorum libris collectae' (Exceptional and very clever similitudes collected out of the books of Plato, Aristotle, Seneca, and other philosophers).[52] Only in her letter of dedication does she acknowledge her English source. There are 109 similes (or 111, counting two instances where she has run two together), which draw upon different aspects of nature and human nature. Sometimes ethical, sometimes psychological, sometimes concerned with governance and the relation between ruler and ruled, occasionally concerned with the relationship between self and God, they constitute recipes for conducting one's life in all sorts of situations, and are applicable for young and old; tellingly, a number are intended for rulers and magistrates like her father. She lists them more or less randomly; except for the occasional 'run' of two, there is very little connection from one simile to another, there are no attributions except in the initial heading, and there are no commonplace headings. She presents them very simply, then, and I suppose that her tutor set this exercise for several reasons: its moral content, its connections with her interests and the interests of the family, and as an effective way to teach Latin grammar and vocabulary and develop her

---

which he comments that 'they were prepared to present to her father on four successive new-year's days' (p. 497).

[50]   BL MS Royal 12A iii, fol. 1v.

[51]   Ibid., fol. 1.

[52]   Ibid., fol. 2. Abbreviations expanded.

skills in translation. Their images, which appeal to occupations such as farming, gardening, sailing and medicine, and objects such as fire, shadows, the sun, a vase and the eye, make otherwise abstract observations livelier and more memorable. Their constructions, which are formulaic, also facilitate translation; there are an assortment of 'just/as ... so' constructions: 'quemadmodum ... sic', 'vt ... sic', 'Veluti ... sic'. At the same time, there is a sense of abundance, the makings of *copia*, a prized Erasmian virtue. In fact, Erasmus was largely responsible for the period's fascination with similitudes or parallels like these, thanks to his *Parabolae*, a mammoth collection, which was first published in 1516 and was frequently reprinted and copied thereafter.

Here are a few examples from Mary's collection. First, a similitude that draws on the nature of metals and earlier appeared in Erasmus's collection and long before that in Plutarch's *Moralia*: 'Vt ferrum et aes usu splendescunt: Sic ingenium exercitatione paratius efficitur' (As iron and copper are bright by use, so the intellect is made more ready by exercise).[53] Another humanist commonplace, also reminiscent of Plutarch and Erasmus, is directed to the ruler: 'Vt pastor se habet inter oues suas: Sic rex debet gerere seipsum erga subditos' (As a shepherd carries himself among his sheep, so a king ought to carry himself among his subjects).[54] The bee analogy, itself a self-reflexive and much-loved commentary on the commonplace method, is a third similitude from Mary's collection: 'Quemadmodum apes colligunt ex floribus dulcissima: sic homines ex uarijs librorum uoluminibus debent comparare optima' (Just as bees collect the sweetest [nectar] out of flowers, so human beings ought to gather the best out of diverse volumes of books).[55] It was with this similitude in mind that Erasmus described the three daughters of Thomas More in a letter to their brother, imagining them 'flitting like honey-bees through every sort of text in the two learned tongues – here jotting down a good phrase to reuse, there gathering some outstanding maxim on which to model their way of life ... '.[56] Finally, here is an example of what is actually

---

[53]   BL MS Royal 12A iii, fol. 3v. Compare Erasmus, *Parallels*, in *Literary and Educational Writings 1: Antibarbari / Parabolae*, Craig R. Thompson, ed., R.A.B. Mynors, trans. and annot., *Collected Works of Erasmus*, vol. 23 (Toronto: University of Toronto Press, 1978): 'Iron or bronze gleams from hard use, and powers of mind are polished by the conduct of business', p. 141 and n. 27, p. 140, on inspiration from Plutarch.

[54]   BL MS Royal 12A iii, fols 5v–6. Compare Erasmus, *Parallels*, p. 149, for the parallel between the sheepdog who looks after the sheep and the king who should look after his people.

[55]   BL MS Royal 12A iii, fol. 8v.

[56]   Erasmus, *The Correspondence of Erasmus: Letters 1356 to 1534: 1523 to 1524*, R.A.B. Mynors and Alexander Dalzell, trans., James M. Estes, annot., *Collected Works of Erasmus*, vol. 10 (Toronto: University of Toronto Press, 1992), Letter 1402, to John More, p. 130.

an epigrammatic *sententia* in her collection, as it relies on wit and antithesis rather than imagery: 'Vt liberalitas ex inimicis amicos: sic superbia inimicos ex amicis efficit' (As liberality makes friends out of enemies, so pride makes enemies out of friends) [57] Like the proverbial bees, then, Mary selected and translated what she (and her tutor) considered some of the more remarkable or instructive similes from a variety of Greek and Latin authors, already conveniently at hand in a compendious English collection, not as yet identified.[58]

British Library MS Royal 12A iv, by Mary Arundel

Mary Arundel faced a still sententious, but otherwise quite different task in BL MS Royal 12A iv, an exercise which she prepared at least a year after Royal 12A iii and probably gave to her father early in 1555, prior to her marriage later that year. Instead of turning a miscellaneous collection of similes from English into Latin, she translated the first six chapters of an English work by Thomas Elyot, first published in 1541. His descriptive title-page, with its mention of '*Actes and Sentences notable*', gives some clues as to why this work was chosen, whether by her or her tutor: *The Image of Governance Compiled of the Actes and Sentences notable, of the moste noble Emperour Alexander Seuerus, late translated out of Greke into Englyshe, by syr Thomas Eliot knight, in the favour of Nobylitie*.[59] Elyot, best known for his educational-political work, the *Governour*, had published *The Bankette of Sapience*, a collection of *sententiae* arranged alphabetically and dedicated to Henry VIII, in 1534, augmenting it in 1539; the Arundel family shared many of his intellectual and political interests.[60] His biography of Alexander Severus, which purports to be based upon a work written in Greek by the emperor's secretary, Eucolpius, is an extensive, ethical treatment of Severus's life and reign that emphasises his excellent education and what appears to be his wise reign, in sharp contrast to that of his predecessor, Heliogabalus, a tyrant.[61]

---

[57] BL MS Royal 12A iii, fol. 8v.

[58] Because of the constant printing and reprinting of such collections, and the way they borrow from one another, it is usually a fruitless chase to try to find an exact source, much less the text or edition used.

[59] This is the last treatise included in Sir Thomas Elyot, *Four Political Treatises: Facsimile Reproductions*, Lillian Gottesman (intro.) (Gainesville, FL: The Scholars' Facsimiles & Reprints, 1967), pp. 203–426.

[60] *The Bankette of Sapience* is included in Elyot, *Four Political Treatises*, pp. 101–202.

[61] See Uwe Baumann, 'Sir Thomas Elyot's *The Image of Governance*: A Humanist's *Speculum Principis* and a Literary Puzzle', in Dieter Stein and Rosanna Sornicola, eds, *The Virtues*

It usually has been read as an idealised picture of the good prince, although at least one critic has detected an intermittent irony on Elyot's part that invites reflection upon discrepancies between Severus's noble speeches and actions that seem like the cruel deeds of a tyrant rather than the just actions of a good king.[62] Instead of reading, collecting and translating fragmentary bits of wisdom, then, Mary was now working with an extended narrative history that embodied sententious material and showed ethical and political matters in action, always a serious humanist concern and one that Elyot's title highlights. In her letter dedicating her translation to her father, she signals his interest in politics and history and comments that she thought Elyot's work was most suitable for his position and authority, implicitly comparing him to Severus, who, she explained, taking Elyot at his word, was an ideal ruler: 'Nam ille ipse quamdiu uixit, felicissime praefuit, absolutissimumque reliquit exemplar absolutissimae reipublicae' (For he, as long as he lived, most auspiciously was in charge, and left behind the most accomplished model of the most accomplished commonwealth).[63] She worked systematically from Chapter 1 through Chapter 6, though she treats the fourth and fifth chapters as one, omitting the title for Elyot's fifth chapter. Her version is close, though not word for word, and less wordy than Elyot's English, sometimes at the cost of any potential irony. For example, she shortened Elyot's title for Chapter 2, 'The education of Alexander, and howe he profyted in vertue and doctryne', which obliquely invites the question (how did he profit, if he did?), to 'De Alexandri educatione, atque illius uirtutibus'.[64] She also omitted some of the more horrific crimes committed by Heliogabalus, but it is impossible to know if her tutor had altered the text that she was working with at that point on moral grounds.

There is one puzzling aspect to her translation, which ends at the end of Chapter 6. This seems intentional on her part; she signs her maiden name, 'Maria Arundell', underneath.[65] But as it stands, it is incomplete. Chapter 6 consists of a letter that a revered senator, Gordian, wrote to Alexander Severus, urging him to be less approachable and maintain a greater distance from his subjects, so that he might seem more majestic and instil more fear. Severus answers this letter in the

of Language: History in Language, Linguistics and Texts: Papers in Memory of Thomas Frank, Amsterdam Studies in the Theory and History of Linguistic Science, series 3 (Amsterdam: John Benjamin, 1998), pp. 177–99, and Greg Walker, *Writing under Tyranny: English Literature and the Henrician Reformation* (Oxford: Oxford University Press, 2005), pp. 240–75.

62   Ibid., pp. 264–68.
63   BL MS Royal 12A iv, fol. 1v, abbreviations expanded.
64   Elyot, *Image of Governance*, p. 217; Royal MS 12A iv, fol. 4, abbreviation expanded.
65   Royal MS 12A iv, fol. 19v.

next chapter, thanking him for his counsel but defending his approachability, pointing out that Tiberius ruled quietly while he displayed his humanity but was 'of all men abandoned' and slain 'lyke an horrible monstre' when he 'compelled the senate and people to worshyp hym'.[66] Taken together, these two letters raise a crucial issue for Renaissance politics in general and Tudor politics in particular: is it better for the ruler to be feared or loved? They also raise an important question for an interpretation of Severus, who failed to follow his own good advice and ultimately was murdered by his soldiers on account of his severity. Of more immediate relevance to readers like the Earl of Arundel, they raise important questions about the nature of the relationship between ruler and adviser or counsellor and the value of approachability and moderation. I wonder if Mary stopped at the end of Chapter 6 because she was distracted by negotiations and/or preparations that were then underway for her marriage to the fourth Duke of Norfolk. Clearly someone sensed the need for this second letter, because Mary's stepbrother, John Radcliffe, who had already given a translation to the earl, stepped in, translating Severus's reply in Chapter 7 in an italic hand that is clear but bolder and less elegant than Mary's.[67]

British Library MSS Royal 12A i and ii, by Mary, Duchess of Norfolk

BL MSS Royal 12A i and ii, which Mary composed after her marriage in 1555, mark a real advance in her education. They are both compilations of *sententiae* arranged under commonplace headings, and translated, not from English, but out of Greek into Latin. The only authors she cites, some of them quite rare, are Greek; in citing an epigram attributed to Palladas, she even writes two letters and two words in Greek to distinguish one word from the other.[68] Almost certainly she turned to an anthology of Greek materials gathered by Stobaeus, a fifth-century Greek anthologist, for BL MS Royal 12A i, and probably used it for BL MS Royal 12A ii, as well; an edition of 1543 was part of her father's library.[69] But she must have used other collections as well. For instance, Palladas's epigrams, which she used in BL MS Royal 12A ii, are in the *Greek Anthology*, but they are

---

[66]   Elyot, *Image of Governance*, p. 243.

[67]   BL MS Royal 12A iv, fols 20–26.

[68]   BL MS Royal 12A ii, fol. 14.

[69]   Ellis, 'Translations for and by the Young', pp. 60, 62; for Stobaeus and his importance, see P.G. Stanwood, 'Stobaeus and Classical Borrowing in the Renaissance, with Special Reference to Richard Hooker and Jeremy Taylor', *Neophilologus*, 59(1) (1975): 141–6, and Havens, *Commonplace Books*, pp. 35–6.

not in Stobaeus.[70] In her dedicatory letter to 12A i, which she likely completed in time for New Year's gift giving at the beginning of 1556, she explains that she thought that the best gift she could give her father from her literary exercises was her translation of short Greek sentences, which she praises for the elegance of their language and the inexhaustible fruitfulness of their ideas. She goes on to explain that 'Ex his enim intelligi potest, quid in hac uita faciendum, quidque fugiendum est' (And from these can be understood what ought to be done in this life and what ought to be avoided).[71]

She dramatises her search for a suitable gift, and many of the sententiae she translates are also dramatic and/or epigrammatic. She also seems to have translated them independently of the Latin versions of the Greek in the bilingual edition of Stobaeus, although she might have found them helpful.[72] Of the thirty Greek authors that she identifies in BL MS Royal 12A i, Euripides leads the list, with eleven selections, followed by Theognis, a poet given to smart epigrams, and Menander, a writer of the new comedy, whose works were then known only through his sententiae. Her choice of topics (eight altogether) and sententiae is also striking; Injustice (under which she also treats Avarice) accounts for one-third of the sententiae she identifies in BL MS Royal 12A i. Her association of the two vices, the latter a result of the former, probably is due to her use of Stobaeus, who joins Injustice with Avarice in his index of categories.[73] A distant second is Modesty, followed by Intemperance and a double topic, Prodigality and Luxury, while the remaining categories (Impudence, Patience, Truth and Secrecy) are about equally treated. So she seems generally less concerned now with governance or rule in a political arena than with ethical and psychological issues that are particularly relevant for a young woman of great wealth and social status. In this connection, Mary includes a sententia, attributed to Pythagoras, which is very like the problem of love versus fear that was at the heart of Chapters 6 and 7 of Elyot's biography of Severus: 'Opta potius a familiaribus tuis reuereri, quam metui: nam reuerentiae honor sed timori odium adiunctum est' (Choose rather to be revered by your household than to be feared, for honour is next to reverence but hatred is connected to

---

[70]   I consulted *Ioannis Stobei Sententiae ex Thesauris Graecorum Delectae*, Conrad Gesner, ed. (Tiguri, 1543), in the British Library, a bilingual (Greek and Latin) edition. For an illustration of a page from a later edition of Gesner's compilation (Basel, 1549), see Havens, *Commonplace Books*, p. 36.

[71]   BL MS Royal 12A i, fol. 1v, abbreviation expanded.

[72]   My comments are based on a check of a number of Mary's sententiae with the Latin versions in Gesner's *Stobaei Sententiae ex Thesauris Graecorum* (1543).

[73]   Ibid., 'Index'. 'De iniustitia & auaritia' is seventh out of 123 categories.

fear).[74] In this case, though, the context is not the kingdom, but the family and the household, which would have been thought of as a kingdom in microcosm, and 'were, to an extent inconceivable today, the central institution of society'.[75]

BL MS Royal 12A ii is by far the most sophisticated and mature of Mary's compilations, the most aculeate, and in some ways the most personal. She must have been working on it throughout 1556, so as to present it to her father at the beginning of 1557. Both her dedicatory letter and her selection of *sententiae* show that she has absorbed the form and style as well as the substance of the *sententia*. While continuing to dramatise her situation, even referring to her reading with the advice of her tutor, she emphasises that she has picked out certain Greek *sententiae* that especially pleased her. Her choices now reflect a taste for the aculeate and epigrammatic. She has ranged more widely among Greek writers than in her previous collection and includes numerous lines from Palladas, now her favourite author after Theognis. Her own writing likewise has become tighter and more fully developed. In her dedicatory letter, which is the longest of the four she wrote to her father, she builds her case for giving her father a collection of *sententiae* rather than more usual New Year's gifts such as gems, gold, clothes, or horses as signs of love. And she emphasises their high value by alluding to three authorities – Cicero, Socrates and one unnamed – who call the knowledge of things the medicine of our soul, the staff of life, and the ruler of heaven and earth. She adds that this sort of knowledge 'iuuenes moderatos facit, senes consolatur, pauperes locupletat, diuitesque exornat' (makes young persons restrained, consoles the elderly, enriches the poor, and embellishes the wealthy).[76] Likewise, her entries under a particular heading (there are seven all together) frequently turn into essays, as she builds from one *sententia* to another.

Even more striking is the way she organises many of her *sententiae* by antithesis. For example, she begins her first category, about the nature of human life, with a series of negative remarks, themselves structured antithetically: in public life, one finds lawsuits; in private, trouble; in the fields, labour; at sea, danger, and so on. Then she lists a parallel series of positive claims: in public life, there will be honour; in your own home, great peace; in the countryside, wonderful pleasure of nature; at sea, wealth. So she develops each side of a question: is it better not to have been born or does every state of life have its

---

[74]   BL MS Royal 12A i, fol. 3–3v.

[75]   See David Starkey, 'The Age of the Household: Politics, Society and the Arts *c*. 1350–*c*. 1550', Chapter 5 in Stephen Metcalf, ed., *The Later Middle Ages* (London: Methuen, 1981), quoted on p. 225. Starkey is particularly well-informed on what he calls the 'great family', a category that would include the Arundels, the Lumleys and the Howards.

[76]   BL MS Royal 12A ii, fol. 1v.

good points?[77] Implicit here and throughout her collection is her awareness of how ironic, how fragile and how unstable, if not dangerous, life is. And she repeatedly selects sententiae that are sceptical, occasionally cynical, and often cautionary, as when she writes, 'Multi mensae tuae sunt amici, at in re seria paucissimi' (Many are friends of your table, but in a serious matter, very few).[78] This probably reflects a stage in her development, a *mentalité* that is not unusual in a period of such rapid and often violent change, and her own experiences of rapid changes of fortune and of loss. We only need to consider the changes in the fortunes of her father, who was imprisoned in the Tower of London for over a year, and, less than a year later, became a close friend (to use the customary Tudor term) of Queen Mary and, subsequently, of her husband, Philip of Spain. Think, too, of the execution of her first cousin, Lady Jane Grey, in 1554, and of recent deaths in her family: her brother had died, unexpectedly, in 1556, and it seems likely that some or perhaps all three of her sister's children, who died in infancy, died during the 1550s.

Mary's selection in BL MS Royal 12A ii also gives us a sharper sense of her character, personality and interests. Here she focuses on issues that must have been particularly meaningful to her. Following her extensive discussion of human life, she dwells on troubling questions about riches and poverty; just what is enough; the nature of human beings, intellects and customs; crafty human beings and flatterers; envy and anxiety; and friends, foreigners, flatterers and ungrateful persons. A nineteenth-century family biographer has described her as 'being of so sweet and amiable Disposition, so prudent, pious, vertuous and religious, that all who knew her could not but love and esteem her much ... ', and her portrait shows a very elegantly dressed young woman in a rich dress with a red cape trimmed with ermine, holding a book of hours.[79] But her sententiae show a lively mind and a keen interest in the nature of human behaviour and life, and of the many difficulties one may encounter. Wariness, caution and an embrace of the 'middle way' seem to be attitudes that she feels she can trust. Moreover, she has developed an acute sense of irony, shown by her juxtaposition of sententiae that take an almost cynical or pessimistic attitude towards life with sententiae that acknowledge its value. So she is aware of both sides of a question,

[77]   Ibid., fols 3v–4.
[78]   Ibid., fol. 15v.
[79]   *The Lives of Philip Howard, Earl of Arundel, and of Anne Dacres, His Wife*, Duke of Norfolk, E.M., ed. (London: Hurst and Blackett, 1857), p. 4. Williams, *Thomas Howard*, reproduces her portrait in black and white, facing p. 114. For a picture in colour, see John Martin Robinson, *Arundel Castle*, compiled by Roland W. Puttock (Arundel Castle, West Sussex: Arundel Castle Trustees Ltd.[1989]), p. 12.

testing the sententiae and the ideas they represent, rather than simply taking them at face value.

In her last dedicatory letter, Mary wrote, 'De reliquo, precor deum Optimum Maximum, ut Dominationem Tuam nobis, republicaequae nostrae diu seruet saluam atque incolumem' (For the rest, I pray to the best and greatest God that he long keep your Lordship safe and unharmed for us and for our commonwealth).[80] Some part of her prayer was granted: the twelfth Earl of Arundel did not die until 1580, outliving both his first wife and his second, as well as all three of his children; his son-in law, Thomas Howard, who was beheaded in 1572; and all but one of his grandchildren, Philip, the son of Mary and Thomas Howard. Philip, who was raised by the Norfolks rather than the Arundels, lived to become the 13th Earl of Arundel through his mother. Later imprisoned in the Tower of London on account of his Catholic faith, he was canonised in 1970.[81] Out of his immediate family, then, Henry Fitzalan left only two survivors: Jane's husband, John, Lord Lumley, and Mary's son, Philip.

But I want to return to Philip's mother, Mary Fitzalan, first an Arundel, then a Norfolk, as the daughter of one highly placed nobleman and the wife of another. When she died in the summer of 1557, she was not only a new mother but very close to what would have been the next stage of her schooling, had she lived longer. This would have meant reading a complete work in Greek, translating it into Latin, and preparing an argument or abstract of it, following the practice of her older sister. And there would have been one more major step, similar to John and Jane Lumley translating or adapting an entire work from Greek or Latin into English. Even so, her four manuscripts, each in its own way sententious, are a valuable record of how one very young woman was educated at home and acquired the culture and the humanist values that were embraced by the sophisticated world of the mid-century Tudor court, in general, and her family, in particular. More striking still, she shaped her own identity as she matured and made the sententiae her own by selecting, translating and arranging them in increasingly thoughtful and distinctive ways.

---

[80]   BL MS Royal 12A ii, fol. 2v, abbreviations expanded. Compare a similar ending at the end of John Radcliffe's letter preceding his translation of Parr's devotional writings – BL MS Royal 7D ix, fols 1v–2 – which omits any mention of the commonwealth, and Jane, Lady Lumley's letter to her father in BL MS Royal 15A ix, fol 4v. However, Jane refers to her father there as 'te', whereas Mary uses an honorific and abbreviates 'Optimum Maximum'. Note the classicising of God.

[81]   Philip Caraman SJ, *Notes on St. Philip Howard* (London: Lincoln Inn Press Ltd. for the Catholic Truth Society, 1985). Like his mother, his aunt and his grandfather, the poet Earl of Surrey, Philip was a writer: see Steven W. May, *The Elizabethan Courtier Poets: The Poems and the Contexts* (Asheville, NC: Pegasus Press, 1999), pp. 347–55.

Chapter 7

'The Government of this Church by Catholic Bishops hath always been a Strength and Defence unto the Kingdom':[1] Episcopacy and the Catholic Community in Early Seventeenth-century Sussex and Beyond

Michael Questier

Most historians now accept that Catholicism is a major topic in the historiography of post-Reformation England and Britain. While not everyone agrees how to define exactly what a Catholic was during that period, there is a broad consensus that there were quite a lot of Catholics and that the Reformation in the British Isles was not necessarily the smooth consensual process that some historians of the topic used to assume.[2]

---

[1]   Matthew Kellison, *A Treatise of the Hierarchie and Divers Orders of the Church against the Anarchie of Calvin ...* (Douai, 1629), p. 395.

[2]   There is still a residual assumption among historians of the post-Reformation period that it is anti-popery which characterised the national English response to much of Europe and western Christendom although, in recent years, the assumptions in the work of historians as diverse as Christopher Hill, Robin Clifton and David Underdown about the centrality of anti-popery in English and British culture have been called into question, not just in Kevin Sharpe's magisterial (if controversial) version of the personal rule of Charles I, but also by, for example, Anthony Milton's reading of the place of Catholicism within the national Church in the period before the Civil War. See C. Hill, *Antichrist in Seventeenth-Century England* (London: Verso, 1990); R. Clifton, 'The Popular Fear of Catholics during the English Revolution', *Past and Present*, 52 (1971): 23–55; idem, 'Fear of Popery', in *The Origins of the English Civil War*, C. Russell, ed. (London: Clarendon, 1973), pp. 144–67; D. Underdown, *A Freeborn People* (Oxford: Clarendon, 1996), pp. 13, 17–18; K. Sharpe, *The Personal Rule of Charles I* (London: Yale University Press, 1992); A. Milton, *Catholic and Reformed* (Cambridge: Cambridge

But would it be true to say that Catholics in post-Reformation England have an intellectual history? That topic – English Catholicism – has very often been dumped in the box marked 'local studies' and has been taken to be largely free of real ideological and political baggage, despite a number of contemporary Catholics' vehement opposition to the imposition of a Protestant settlement in Church and State. There were of course several major Catholic philosophers, theologians and political theorists from the British Isles during the later sixteenth and the early seventeenth centuries, notably Thomas White but, put alongside the likes of Hobbes and Locke, such people usually fail to register.[3] The dominant image of the post-Reformation Catholic, in the provinces at any rate, is that of the recusant or occasional-conformist gentleman who had opted out of almost everything – not just attendance at his local parish church, but also the tasks in government of the locality which were traditionally carried out by those of higher social status. So limited are the historical sources which tell us what individual Catholics actually thought about things that it has often seemed easier to accept John Bossy's dictum that post-Reformation Catholicism became an essentially sectarian manoeuvre, and to assume that separatist Catholics, by their own choice, had nothing much to say about major ideological issues.[4]

Yet is this where we should leave the topic? The Catholic question positively erupted into mid- and late Elizabethan politics. One of the ironies of Bossy's work was that his original doctoral dissertation was rooted in a narrative of English Catholics' participation in the radical politics of the French Holy League and the intellectually transformative impact that this had on English politics. When, however, in the mid-1970s he came to publish a 'big book' on the subject of post-Reformation Catholicism, almost all of that material was missing. Instead, Bossy presented a sociological reading of Catholic dissent which was, if not exactly anti-intellectual, then certainly without a

University Press, 1995); A. Milton, 'A Qualified Intolerance: the Limits and Ambiguities of Early Stuart Anti-Catholicism', in *Catholicism and Anti-Catholicism in Early Modern English Texts*, A. Marotti, ed. (London: Macmillan, 1999), pp. 85–115.

[3] We know, however, from the work of the bibliographers Antony Allison and David Rogers that there was a stream of published works which came mainly from foreign presses in English and in other languages and that these, especially the English ones, were imported and distributed around what Professor Bossy chose to call the 'Catholic community'; see A.F. Allison and D.M. Rogers, *The Contemporary Printed Literature of the English Counter-Reformation between 1558 and 1640*, 2 vols (Aldershot: Scolar Press, 1989–94).

[4] See J. Bossy, *The English Catholic Community 1570–1850* (London: Darton, Longman and Todd, 1975).

great deal of the underpinning which had been so striking in his staggeringly brilliant PhD.[5]

So how might one trace intellectual currents outside the world of printed literature and the occasional high-profile confrontation between leading Catholic clergy and royal government? How can one find out about this sort of thing, for example, in an average English county? One imagines that big political issues of the day were discussed in the houses of the gentry, and indeed elsewhere, but in general, the thoughts of these people were not written down, certainly not by Catholics themselves. If one does know what leading Catholic gentry thought about major political questions it is usually through fortuitous survival, for instance, the accidental discovery of Sir Thomas Tresham's papers (now in the British Library), which had been concealed after the Gunpowder Plot and were unearthed in the early nineteenth century.[6] One knows from the odd snippets of information (often supplied by government informers) that arguments about this and that topic did take place in such-and-such a Catholic's house. But this becomes an increasingly rare occurrence in the seventeenth century and it is usually impossible to check whether the things that are supposed to have been said by so-and-so are in any sense accurate.

Another methodological difficulty, as far as this chapter is concerned, is that there is no archival law which says that the discussion of philosophical or other matters must be pegged to or confined within a particular county, or indeed any territorial unit. What I want to trace here, however, is the way in which one specific intellectual controversy (in fact, an ecclesiological one) took shape. And I propose to do this with reference to the immediate context in which it was talked about and debated – primarily, though not exclusively, in one geographical region, in this case the English south coast and, in particular, the county of Sussex. For what it is worth, in Sussex there is a reasonably easy-to-trace network of Catholic gentry and peers who, by the early seventeenth century, were ready enough to articulate particular versions of the way their community should be regulated although, about such people, so-called 'mainstream' accounts of the later English Reformation have had remarkably little to say.

The topic which I propose to address here is one which I have glanced at before, following as best I could in the footsteps of my old friend Mr Antony Allison, a peerless scholar and bibliographer who, as much as anyone, tracked

---

[5]   To be fair, a good deal of Professor Bossy's PhD (J. Bossy, 'Elizabethan Catholicism: The Link with France' (PhD, Cambridge, 1961), had already been published in article form in academic journals.

[6]   British Library, Additional MS 39828–38; S.C. Lomas, ed., *Report on Manuscripts in Various Collections*, vol. III (London: Historical Manuscripts Commission, 1904), pp. 1–154.

down and opened up the intellectual world of post-Reformation English Catholicism. One of his many projects was to find, transcribe, translate and analyse the documents generated by the disputes about the appointment of a titular bishop in England in the later 1620s. This was the so-called 'approbation' controversy caused by the extremely divisive programme of Richard Smith who was consecrated as Bishop of Chalcedon in 1624 and then returned to England in 1625, that is, almost exactly at the point that Henrietta Maria crossed the Channel to wed Charles I.[7]

Very briefly, the elevation and sending to England of Bishop Smith, and indeed of his equally divisive though short-lived predecessor William Bishop, were part of Rome's reaction to the Stuart court's foreign policy of the early and mid-1620s. It seems clear enough that Rome, as it responded to the calls of an influential section of the English Catholic community to provide it with direct episcopal government, was also anticipating what the papal curia took to be the imminent good effects of the Stuart monarchy's decision to bind itself, through a dynastic marriage alliance, to one of the major European Catholic royal houses. William Bishop had sweeping ambitions to reform and to regulate the Catholic community but survived only one year in office, and thus left the field to his successor, Smith.[8]

The debates among English Catholics about whether the papacy ought to appoint bishops to govern them directly were, of course, not in themselves particularly novel. That kind of dispute was one of the problems which tended to crop up in any territory which was not (or parts of which were not) formally in communion with Rome, but which contained sizeable numbers of Catholics.[9] One additional difficulty here was that, among the English, those who had now secured the appointment of a bishop were the precisely the ones who, for the past twenty years and more, had caused considerable controversy by claiming that the troubles of the Catholic fraction of the English Church were essentially of its own making; that the State had every reason to distrust the political impulses of

---

[7]   See A.F. Allison, 'Richard Smith, Richelieu and the French Marriage. The political context of Smith's appointment as bishop for England in 1624', *Recusant History*, 7 (1964): 148–211; idem, 'A Question of Jurisdiction: Richard Smith, Bishop of Chalcedon and the Catholic Laity, 1625–1631', *Recusant History*, 16 (1982): 111–45; see also M. Questier, *Catholicism and Community in Early Modern England: Politics, Aristocratic Patronage and Religion, c. 1550–1640* (Cambridge: Cambridge University Press, 2006), chapters 12, 13.

[8]   Questier, *Catholicism and Community*, pp. 400–408.

[9]   For the regions in Flanders where Rome appointed titular bishops, see M. Questier, ed., *Stuart Dynastic Policy and Religious Politics, 1621–1625* (Camden Society, fifth series, 34: London, 2009), pp. 161, 197–8, 315–16, 341, 360, 362.

(some) Catholics, and even to use a raft of penal statutes against them; that some English Catholic clergymen, particularly within the Society of Jesus, had been guilty of sedition exactly as the spokesmen of successive regimes (both Tudor and Stuart) had claimed. The line taken by the champions of episcopacy was that the appointment of bishops would be a way of reconciling English Catholics with the State because episcopal regulation would itself guarantee that English Catholics would be both good Catholics and good subjects; if Catholicism had at any point become tainted by notions of radical politics, then the restoration of the normal modes of ecclesiastical governance, at least as found in Churches in communion with Rome, would serve to cleanse the practice of Catholicism of those associations. Put simply, a good bishop would be able to police the community over which he had authority and purge it of political radicalism and disobedience. Out of this could come the kind of tolerance, and perhaps one day a formal toleration, which would square the circle and mark the end of the needless hostility of the crown towards those who had always claimed that their religion was a matter of conscience and not one of 'politics' at all.

The sometimes rather complex arguments in the 1620s over this issue reprised the twists and turns of much of the so-called (and better-known) archpriest dispute of 1598–1602.[10] This new stage of intra-Catholic in-fighting went viral, as it were, because Richard Smith claimed that he had full ordinary jurisdiction, that is, the same as was possessed by any diocesan bishop, and that this allowed him to demand that all the clergy working within the country should sue to him for 'approbation', in other words, for his approval of their faculties as priests, notably to hear the confessions of their penitents, and particularly those who were their patrons and benefactors.[11] What was at one level (merely) their basic function as clergymen, the same as priests the world over, now became the topic at the centre of a struggle to define the nature of Catholicism among the English.

To rehearse the ins and outs of this debate would take some considerable time, and much more space than is available in a short chapter.[12] It was, in its formal and theoretical articulations, often stunningly tedious. For the purposes of a piece about the intellectual history of Sussex, the approbation business is, however, extraordinarily apposite. As the controversy spilled out all through the provinces as well as in the metropolis and around the court, we have, here and there, a slew of reports about how different Catholics understood the question, and whether

---

[10]   See, for example, J.H. Pollen, *The Institution of the Archpriest Blackwell* (London: Longman, 1916).

[11]   Questier, *Catholicism and Community*, chapter 13.

[12]   See, however, M. Questier, 'The Politics of Episcopacy in the Caroline Catholic Community: the Approbation Controversy in Context' (forthcoming).

they thought that Smith and his friends were right to be doing as they did, and whether Rome had given him the authority that he claimed. We know what a big deal this was because there are so many surviving manuscripts of the arguments adduced in support of, or in opposition to, Bishop Smith. These debates during the later 1620s, we know, occurred in several English counties but particularly along the Sussex coast where there were many Catholic houses, and especially the principal residence of the second Viscount Montague, that is, Cowdray Park. Montague was one of Smith's principal lay patrons and, though he had broken with him during the 1610s, now turned decisively to support him as the approbation controversy unfolded. (One of the major theoretical contributions to the debate came from Montague himself, presumably the product of long discussions with his chaplains and other Catholics.[13]) The dispute reverberated around these houses which themselves supplied a kind of institutional structure among English Catholics in their own country (at least in so far as those houses sustained a resident clergy) and, in the absence of an official Church establishment, were in some sense *the* Church in England.

The sharp differences of opinion among these Catholics led to, in effect, the popularising and public discussion of a subject which, under other circumstances, would generally be the preserve of some of the nerdiest of contemporary theologians and ecclesiologists. For the rest of this chapter, I want to talk about the extent of this debate within the confines of the county of Sussex. It was, as I have suggested, likely to be pretty intense because of the support there for the new bishop. The clergyman George Birkhead (d. 1614), who had in 1608–09 launched an appeal to the papacy for reform of the English Catholic community, had also been one of Montague's senior chaplains and had appointed Richard Smith as his agent in Rome. Smith's predecessor as Bishop of Chalcedon, William Bishop, had not been a Cowdray chaplain, but he had been ostentatiously welcomed by Montague when he (Bishop) returned to the country in 1623 following his consecration in Paris in the same year. The long-serving secular clergy agent in Rome in the 1610s and into the early 1620s was a man called Thomas More, another Cowdray priest, who formerly, like Smith, had served as a chaplain to the wife of the first Viscount Montague, the formidable Magdalen Dacre, who had established her own visibly Catholic outpost in East Sussex at Battle Abbey. Elsewhere in rural Sussex we find prolific

---

13   Anthony Maria Browne, Viscount Montague, 'An Apologeticall Answere of the Vicount Montague unto sundrie important aspersions in the seven Reasons, and some other partes of a Letter of a namelesse author cov[e]red under the Letters A.B.' (Gillow Library MS, Downside Abbey MS 28000, thankfully available on microfilm at the West Sussex Record Office).

newsletter writers such as Benjamin Norton who was also a critic of the Jesuit clergy and was appointed as an official of the new bishop.[14]

Within the aristocratic and gentry network in Sussex, we can look for echoes of the often intense bitching and unpleasantness over the series of linked and otherwise rather theoretical issues concerned with Church government which came out into the open during the approbation business. So let us see which voices we can recover from the swirl of speculation and uncertainty in early Caroline Sussex over the question of the new bishop and his powers. We can pick up, here and there, the real antagonism which these things caused and which demonstrates that, on the ground, this question, though based on a set of contested theories about the nature of Church government, was far from purely theoretical.

The basic position was this. The Council of Trent (session 23, c. 15) had given diocesan bishops the power to require regular clergy to obtain their approval, or approbation, for hearing the confessions of the laity. (Such approbation could be required from all priests in a bishop's diocese who did not hold a parochial benefice, both regulars and seculars.) Richard Smith claimed that it was a purely formal process. It would not expunge any of the regulars' faculties. The only reason he had for demanding it was that he needed to satisfy his own conscience that all Catholics' confessions were in fact valid.[15] Following the Tridentine decree and a host of other authorities, Smith therefore pronounced that all the clergy in the realm, including the regulars, required episcopal (that is, his) approbation if they were to hear the confessions of their penitents.[16]

Unsurprisingly, his Catholic opponents saw it differently. To them, his insistence on approbation bore all the hallmarks of a quasi-Whitgiftian subscription campaign against puritan nonconformity. Probably with justification, they feared that once they acknowledged his authority he would start to expel them from what they regarded as, in effect, their benefices – that is, the gentry and aristocratic residences which they occupied – and that he would attempt to create a monopoly of ecclesiastical patronage and authority within the realm largely at their expense.

By a decree of 26 May/5 June 1627, the congregation for the Propagation of the Faith (Propaganda), in response to complaints that Smith was simply not available to deal with and approve missionary faculties, advised him to examine

---

[14]   Questier, *Catholicism and Community*, passim.

[15]   P. Hughes, *Rome and the Counter-Reformation in England* (London: Burns and Oates, 1942), pp. 347–9.

[16]   Archives of the Archdiocese of Westminster [hereafter AAW], B 48, no. 25 ('Certaine Observations ... ', a work, unfoliated, written by Richard Smith); Allison, 'A Question of Jurisdiction', pp. 118–19.

('recognoscere') the faculties of priests in England, and ordered him to delegate his authority in this respect.[17] Smith's supporters were determined to exploit this opportunity for all it was worth. According to the Benedictines, this 'decree', which did not specifically mention regulars at all, 'ys shewed up and downe in papers by the priestes to justify the bishop of Chalcedon his act of calling regulars to his approbation'. Everyone knew, they said, that what Smith really wanted was to 'examyne our sufficiency', which was a rather different matter from simply proving faculties. They claimed that the decree was no proof that Smith had ordinary jurisdiction.[18]

The regulars were certain, therefore, that Smith and his officials would try, as indeed they now did, to prohibit the religious from performing their sacramental function of hearing confessions if they refused to seek approbation. They were equally sure that the real agenda was to prise the noncompliant out of the community altogether. If Smith's authority were to be widely accepted, a chaplain without his approbation would be no chaplain at all. Such a priest's credit would be ruined. He would be unemployable. On 27 December 1627, a Benedictine called William Johnson wrote a letter to the Midhurst-based Benjamin Norton addressing it 'to my verie lovinge freinde hertofore Mr Norton'. Johnson was grieved and enraged that Norton, in his official capacity as one of Smith's officials, had proceeded formally against him: 'Sir, the troble you have brought me into, and the injurie I receive from you, are the motives of my sendinge thease fewe lines of complainte at this time unto you.' Johnson said that his only function in England was 'with a quiet minde to serve my God and Saviour in the best manner I coulde'. But 'in my followinge of this course, and in adheringe to my order, you much disquiet me, makinge me nowe to become irreligiouse and of a regular, irregular, by deprivinge me of absolutione both active and passive, as if I could neyther absolve nor be absolved.'

Here we have all the rage of the period's generally conforming or 'moderate' man caught out and embarrassed in the sight of the world and his flock by the (many would say) misplaced zeal of an over-enthusiastic agent and enforcer of an unreasonably thorough conformity and obedience to ecclesiastical authority. Johnson was 'shure I goe uppon a firme and sounde grounde, allowed by all the universities in Christendome; neyther have I donne anie thinge to deserve this at your handes.' Johnson averred that the matter had not yet been settled at Rome, and in the meantime Norton ought 'not to give sentence agaynst me as you have done, and that also most unjustlie to the scandalle of the countrie, and to the

---

17	AAW, A XX, no. 86, p. 305; Hughes, *Rome*, pp. 341–4; The National Archives, SP 16/64/66, fo. 119r; Questier, *Catholicism and Community*, p. 445.

18	AAW, A XX, no. 100, p. 341.

great perplexitie of my gostlie children which you knowe are manie: wherby you have likewise driven me into an inextricable labarinth'.[19]

What clearly aggrieved Johnson was the sense that someone whom he reckoned to have been a friend, or at least someone he could have cooperated with in the loose and uncertain structure comprising the Catholic fraction of the county community, had sold out to a set of external forces, forces which were at odds with the natural balance of interests inside the region, interests which had served to maintain the Catholic faith there in the period after the Reformation in the face, sometimes, of the regime's enforcement agencies.

Those who wanted to see the new bishop's authority spread through the community saw the matter differently. They thought that their slate of reforming measures would enhance the practice of Catholicism as a true expression of the Christian faith. These people thought that lurking within the unregulated and shapeless mass of the Catholic community was a reprehensible disdain for what, after all, was the usual and apostolically warranted mode of government of the true Church. These red-tape merchants (as their opponents undoubtedly saw them) did have a relatively coherent mission statement. As with so many institutional administrators, they believed, or could claim, that their style of governance, indeed in their case their actual presence in the Church, was essential to the well-being of that Church. One advice paper sent to Rome in July 1627 advised the secular clergy's agent there that

> ... the necessity of having this authority here well established and continued is apparent to any indifferent judge, both for the comfort of the good, and for the correction of the bad. For, without this authority, the wisest men that understand the case of England truly are of opinion that this great work of the conversion of our country will advance nothing at all, and never be achived, and that the abuses and inward impediments which have hitherto chiefly hindered the same will rather grow and encrease daily, as by experience we see they doe.

The lack of direct episcopal government in England was the cause of 'intolerable abuses'. Some priests, it was said,

> ... have come into England, and have practised their priestly function without a lawfull mission. Others have practised beyond the extent of their faculties. There are divers particular religious men here that do acknowledge no superiour in England. Some have committed notorious and daungerous indiscretions. Some live scandalously, and the like.[20]

---

[19]   AAW, A XXI, no. 13, p. 51. For Johnson, see D. Lunn, *The English Benedictines, 1540–1688* (London: Burns and Oates, 1980), p. 149; see also idem, 'Benedictine Opposition to Bishop Richard Smith (1625–1629)', *Recusant History*, 11 (1971–72), pp. 1–20.

[20]   AAW, A XX, no. 102, p. 354.

From several sources, we get a sense of the knockabout style of the resulting conflict from the general and much-reported dissing of Smith and his associates, just as he and his friends told increasingly rude stories about Jesuits and Benedictines, and recorded every sleight and rudery about themselves to use as evidence of the regulars' lack of respect for all, but especially episcopal, authority. This lack of respect could, said Smith's men, be found even in the schools which the Society ran on the Continent. Thus, in May 1626, Benjamin Norton recounted how 'latelye I delte with the cheefe of the Societie in these shires to have a fault reformed and amended, which is this. In theire scooles at St Omers theye have emperors, senators, equites, decuriones, and the verryest asse of everye classe is putt after all thease and cauled a bishop.' After years and years of clerical bitching over whether episcopal authority was necessary among the English nation, one can hardly believe that Norton was very surprised at being told that the administrators of Jesuit schools thought it a capital joke to burden their idiot pupils with the title of 'bishop'. However, Norton protested: 'I accoumpt this a preposterouse order and I might geve it a woorse name.' The unnamed Jesuit, with whom Norton was speaking, 'denyed thatt theire was any suche thinge in the Englishe scooles 3 yeares since'. Norton said, 'I did not altogether beleeve him: yett I answered after this manner: "Soe muche the woorse quoth I that you shoulde beegin to caule your verriest foole a bishop just abought the tyme thatt wee beegan to have a bishop."'[21]

Of course, the prospect of having to deal with someone quite as prissy and humourless as Norton would undoubtedly be enough to drive many people up the wall. In the secular clergy's agent's papers in Rome, there is an officially attested account of the words of one Thomas Percy concerning Norton. Percy was alleged to have said 'that the law which made religious men uncapable of heritage after profession was a barbarous lawe'. When Percy was 'tould that it was the opinion of Catholike preists that the law was good in Catholique cuntryes and was made here in Catholike tymes', he replied that those clerics that said so were 'knaves, prusevantes [*sic*] and worse, yea though Mr Norton himself shold say soe, hee were a knave and a damned knave.' On being informed that he should 'take heede what he sayd of Mr Norton for hee was vicar generall' and 'hee might punish him', Percy exploded: 'vicar generall, vicar turd, he hath nothing to doe with mee, I ame a religious man, hee hath nothing to doe with mee.'[22]

---

[21]   J.H. Pollen, ed., *Unpublished Documents Relating to the English Martyrs* (London: Catholic Record Society, no. 5, 1908), pp. 396–7.

[22]   AAW, A XX, no. 27, p. 99. Percy's identity is not clear, and his name may well have been an alias. For a copy of this and other similar stories, see AAW, A XXII, no. 69.

This sort of thing was, predictably, not confined to Sussex. It was replicated almost everywhere that Smith and his high-handed friends conspired to alienate people. But why this really mattered in Sussex was because, as we have already observed, Smith had Viscount Montague as a patron. The way in which this ageing peer, whose patronage network was actually quite diverse and incorporated clergymen of several different stripes, saw matters would undoubtedly be very significant. One newsletter sent to Rome in November 1627 incorporated a list of trenchant and allegedly defamatory statements made by the regulars about Smith, and some of them evidently originated in Sussex: 'now, as for speeches and slanders', one Benedictine had said 'the bishop plaied the divell' at Montague's palatial residence of Cowdray.[23]

There would inevitably be consternation among the clergy who were part of this Catholic network but who would not fully accept Smith's declaration of his authority. Famously, there was a bust-up between Montague himself and a Benedictine monk, David Codner, when Montague started to swing away from a kind of *via media* position to one in which he began to offer his support more or less unequivocally to Smith.[24] Another Benedictine, Edward Ashe, Lord Montague's own chaplain, said that an (admittedly provocative) sermon delivered by Smith on Palm Sunday 1627, concerning the nature of true obedience, 'savoured of heresie'. These people's hostility was echoed and amplified by others. Ashe's confrere, 'Mr [Thomas] Hill from the North, writes that there it is reported that the bishop preached heresie.' Benedict Jones, one of the leaders of the Benedictine opposition to Smith, had said that 'in Spaine the bishop would have been putt into the Inquisition for his sermon.' Yet another had remarked that 'he deserved to be sent to the gallies' and a 'fift[h] [said] that he was to be excommunicated.' Others claimed that the bishop 'takes money for making of officers'. It was said also 'that he goes about to thrust religious men out of their residences, and that he hath saied that within two yeeres he would not leave a religious man in England.' Another Benedictine, Robert Sherwood, whose patrons were a branch of the Browne family located at Kiddington in Oxfordshire, 'sayd to the bishops face, and in the presence of his owne superiour, that he would sinke, yea die rather then aske the bishops approbation, though the bishop required it not as a thing due to himselfe, but as a charitie done to his penitents'.[25] The Jesuit Lawrence Anderton (who was

---

23 AAW, A XX, no. 159, p. 602; Questier, *Catholicism and Community*, p. 450, citing Anthony Maria Browne, Viscount Montague, 'An Apologeticall Answere', p. 464.

24 Questier, *Catholicism and Community*, p. 449.

25 AAW, A XX, no. 159, p. 602; Anthony Maria Browne, Viscount Montague, 'An Apologeticall Answere', pp. 511–13; Lunn, 'Benedictine Opposition', pp. 8–9; AAW, A XXII, no. 66, p. 378.

to be found serving as a chaplain to Montague in London in 1627) 'sayd in the presence of a nobleman and a priest that he would not goe over' the threshold 'to aske the bishops approbation'. The Benedictine Peter Wilford 'saied to a lay Catholick, that he was an idle foole and a cockes-combe who would mainetaine that which was expressed in the bishops letter to the lay Catholicks'. The crucial claim made by the new bishop and his supporters was that the bad intentions and disobedient humours of the bishop's enemies were actually leading them to reject the authority of Rome itself. Thus the Jesuit Michael Freeman, 'being urged with the late decree of the Congregation de Propaganda Fide' (that is, of 26 May/5 June 1627 allowing the Bishop of Chalcedon to approve the clerical faculties of the religious), 'replyed that that congregation did many things that could not be justified'. And 'another, speaking of that congregation, sayd it was de destruenda, not de propaganda fide.' Furthermore, 'some Catholicks' who were 'penitents unto regulars' had gone so far as to say that if the pope 'should define this question against the regulars, they would hould him [to be] Antichrist'.[26]

It may be worth a preliminary glance at how far this kind of rhetoric was mere flim-flam. Smith and his supporters knew that they were scoring palpable hits when they floated their claims through an appeal for decorum and order in the Church, and through a critique which was aimed at those whose clerical status meant that they lived outside the conventional modes of ecclesiastical governance. As Thomas McCoog has shown, the Jesuit general Everard Mercurian had, even in the 1570s, been reluctant to inaugurate an English Jesuit mission because he could foresee exactly the kind of difficulties which Jesuits would experience when they arrived in England and tried to live there according to their institute.[27] Privately, the Jesuits continued to air their worries about how well they fulfilled their mission, and how far mission superiors were able to visit their communities and provide spiritual and other direction, although the Jesuit clergy in England were organised into a vice-province in 1619 and a full province in 1623. As McCoog asks, 'would the patron take advantage of his position and demand that the priest involve himself in occupations inappropriate for a religious?' As far back as January 1607 Mercurian's successor, Claudio Acquaviva, had advised that in place of external poverty, where it could not be practised, an interior one should be cultivated instead. The fact that they could not simply apply to their superior for financial supply meant that they would have to be even more

---

[26]   AAW, A XX, no. 159, p. 602.
[27]   T.M. McCoog, *The Society of Jesus in Ireland, Scotland, and England 1541–1588: 'Our Way of Proceeding?'* (Leiden: Brill, 1996); idem, 'The Religious Life of the English Jesuits' (I am very grateful to Dr McCoog for permission to cite this draft essay).

careful about their supposed calling of evangelical poverty. Jesuits should also avoid familiarity with the patron's family in order to fend off threats to chastity.[28]

The freedoms which the Society of Jesus' *Constitutions* allowed it could, undoubtedly, be represented, by some, as tantamount to licence. St Ignatius gave the Society, as McCoog says, 'a flexible, adaptable structure that would enable it at all times' to perform its apostolic labours: in particular, 'the *Constitutions* prescribed neither choral recitation of the office, common religious exercises, regular and obligatory corporal austerity, nor a vow of stability', in other words freeing the Society 'from a monastic conception of religious life'.[29] This was not necessarily an unalloyed blessing. David Lunn suggests that 'the loose, Jesuit-type organisation, which had its heyday among the Benedictines between 1603 and 1619, was less advantageous to all concerned than might be supposed', and 'even after 1619 ... it has to be said that proper discipline, monastic observance and supervision were unsolved problems.'[30] Furthermore, when a local superior, such as Thomas Preston (head of the Cassinese Benedictines in England), wobbled, as he did, on an important political issue such as the 1606 oath of allegiance, or was generally incapable of keeping order, as was the irascible and largely hopeless Leander Jones (the vicar general of the Spanish congregation in England), then there was likely to be trouble.[31] The result, among the Benedictines, was a series of anxieties and discussions, similar to that which McCoog traces among the Jesuits, about how to regularise the often rather irregular aspects of the mission in a country where there were no cloisters.[32]

Without wanting to go into the minutiae of the authority structures which were created in order to address some of these problems, it is clear that there remained real difficulties, and that the episcopalian (if that is the right word) lobby among the secular clergy could make a decent prima facie case for their remarks about the regulars' irregularity.

---

[28]   McCoog, 'Religious Life'. McCoog notes that another general, Mutio Vitelleschi, 'issued a series of ordinances and regulations for the religious life of the missioners in England' in 1626, that is, just before the approbation crisis broke, ibid. In December 1628, he instructed the provincial, Richard Blount, to make sure that each house where a Jesuit served as chaplain was visited by himself or by a deputy at least once a year: ARSJ, Anglia MS 1 (Letters of the Jesuit general, Mutio Vitelleschi, to members of the English province (summaries at ABSJ, XLVII/3 (vol. i: 1605–23), XLVII/4 (vol. ii: 1624–32) and XLVII/5 (vol. iii: 1633–41), vol. ii, fo. 286v. For the domestic problems experienced by clergy in gentry and other households, see Bossy, *The English Catholic Community*, pp. 254–61.

[29]   McCoog, 'Religious Life'.

[30]   Lunn, *The English Benedictines*, p. 148.

[31]   For the complex reconstitution of the English Benedictine Congregation in 1619, producing no end of constitutional difficulties, see Lunn, 'Benedictine Opposition', pp. 4–5.

[32]   See Lunn, *The English Benedictines*, pp. 147–8, 149–50.

Anyway, if we put the religious orders' own agenda for promoting peace, harmony and godliness within their own ranks in the context of the 'evidence' which some of the secular priests collected that the religious lacked all these things, we can see how the approbation controversy, technically a rather dry dispute about the precise legal extent of Richard Smith's powers, could look to some contemporaries like the product of a bold attempt at a wide-ranging reform programme. The lack of episcopal authority over chaplains living in the lay-dominated locale of the gentry or aristocratic household could well appear to be a fit subject for the attentions of a zealous Counter-Reformation bishop such as Smith who said that he worried about these matters.

In this context, it is possible to see the Society's well-known annual letters not just as upbeat reports of the Jesuits' activities, but also as carefully crafted polemical replies to their enemies' accusations. It seems very likely that the Society's account of itself in England at this time (that is, in the annual letters), a kind of moral self-fashioning exercise, must have come partly in response to what people were saying about the Society.[33] At the Jesuits' residence at Clerkenwell in March 1628, government searchers seized, among other papers, the list of points to be included in compiling the Society's annual letter for England. This list included not just numbers of baptisms and 'generall confessions', but also how many people had been reconciled and converted (especially 'straung and notable conversions'), 'how many have bene recalled or kept from taking the oath [of allegiance] or falling otherwise', 'how many have bene directed to the seminaryes, or religious howses, men or women', 'how many prisoners, or what persecution hath befallen us or our friends', and 'what reliefe prisoners or pore Catholikes have had by our meanes', 'what good example or edification hath bene given by us or our freindes in life or death', and 'what opinion the Society hath in those ... parts'.[34] The results of such surveys would inevitably be taken, by a significant section of the Catholic community, as direct challenges to the claims of the episcopal lobby which often implied that the religious, and the Jesuits in particular, did none of these things properly, if at all, because they were not under episcopal authority and discipline.

---

[33]   As McCoog shows, reports of the Society in England forwarded to Rome by such Jesuits as the provincial, Henry More, in 1636 specifically list complaints against the Society. More listed allegations of 'excessive involvement in the financial affairs of laymen' as well as the 'persistent use of tobacco', ibid.; ARSJ, Anglia MS 1/ii, fo. 441r. For an earlier Jesuit directive against the use of tobacco, see CSPD 1628–9, p. 54. For the annual letters, see T. McCoog, 'The Society of Jesus in England, 1623–1688: an Institutional Study' (Ph D, Warwick, 1984), appendix 2.

[34]   H. Foley, ed., *Records of the English Province of the Society of Jesus*, 8 vols (London: Burns and Oates, 1875–83), I, pp. 127–8.

The critics of the regular clergy wanted to probe the scandals in Catholic patron-chaplain relationships where the religious seemed to be at fault. Among the Jesuit vices which Smith noted, during the approbation controversy, as evidence of their dissolute life was their willingness to engage in the running of 'temporal states'. One Jesuit, recounted Smith, who was 'desirous to have the managing' of an unnamed 'gentlemans [e]state in Sussex, told him that if he wold permit him so to doe, where now he ate beef and mutton, he shold eate turkeys and capons. But the gentleman was too wise to be taken with so fond a baite.'[35]

The Society's English vice-provincial congregation of 1622 issued instructions which advised Jesuit missioners to extract themselves from any kind of involvement in 'marital and domestic arguments'.[36] Supposed or alleged involvement in such disputes was a major source of Catholic accusations that the religious disrupted the life of the community. As McCoog notes, from a memorandum in 1630 which codified the instructions put forward to regulate missioners' lives since the English province of the Society came into being, there were strict warnings against 'involvement both in the management of the house and the inner workings of the marriage'.[37]

The opponents of the regulars frequently alleged that the religious did not balk at such meddling. Among the stories of marital interference which the seculars collected for use in their campaign against the regulars were, for instance, the complaints of one Henry Good. Good attested on 2 October 1627 that he had, of late, run into the monk David Codner (coincidentally just at the point when he was allegedly so rude to Lord Montague) and took the opportunity to ask him 'why he tould my wife' Anne that 'she was a stinckinge peece of fleshe.' Good had been married to his wife for some fifteen years but that did not prevent Codner, who had recently been confessor to both of them, from saying that 'he had a tender nose and that he did often smell an ill savor come from her.' Codner had been told by a priest that 'my wyfe had byn a most leaude loose liver, and that she had lived aparte from me.' Good swore that 'it was most false', and demanded to 'knowe the prists name', but Codner refused to tell him. Good was sure that Codner had 'much wronged her for had she bin soe in the 15 ... yeres I have bin maried to her I should have founde it but what shall I saie when by reason of his function I am reameadiles, but leave all reav[e]ndge to God.' Good mentioned also that Codner

---

35 AAW, A XXI, no. 49, p. 175.
36 McCoog, 'Religious Life'. In November 1632, the Jesuit general warned Lawrence Anderton SJ about the scandal caused by Jesuits getting involved in lawsuits between leading Catholic families in England: ARSJ, Anglia MS 1/ii, fo. 362v.
37 McCoog, 'Religious Life'.

had often called the secular priest George Fisher an 'arrant knave and saies he is the bellowes that blowes up the lord bushopp', that is, Smith, 'with pride'.

For Smith and his friends, this kind of thing was a reminder of how many other sins could be detected in the lives of the religious – their unsoundness on papal ordinances as much as their own sexual licentiousness. Good added as a parting shot that Codner had said the oath of allegiance might be taken by Catholics. Also a French gentleman (one Mr Burgoyne) had told him that Codner did much 'importune' one of his female converts (his landlady in fact, one Mrs Smith who was Good's own sister) that 'she would have had her picture to have bin drawne naked to present to the Venetian imbasidor.' The experience apparently convinced the woman to become a Protestant again.[38] In July 1628, the still furious Good, temporarily forgetting that he had vowed to leave vengeance to the Almighty, produced another blast of accusatory material against Codner, in particular that 'he many times would take phisicke coulorably to goe up in to a certayne garrett in their house where usually one Martha Birde, sister in lawe to this [Mrs] Smyth, did meete him, and there they were dishonest togeither.'[39] Anne Good added that 'occation he [Codner] never had from me while he lived with me', that is, for hostility or offence, 'but only once, seinge' two of Smith's officials, John Jackson and George Fisher 'at my house, he fell fowell with me, sainge it was not safe for him to be wher the bishops spies' were, 'for soe he termed them'.[40]

Of course, one might think, if English Catholicism had moved resolutely into full separation from the national Church, who would actually be bothered with this sort of thing, other than the petty gossip-mongers who spread this stuff about? One answer is that it is possible to make a connection between the difficulties inside the separated Catholic community and some of the ructions caused by, as scholars have traced them out, the avant-garde conformist agenda in the early Stuart, and particularly the Caroline, Church.[41] Now, of course, at some level, what Smith and his friends were doing was simply what episcopal administrators were supposed to do everywhere in Christian Europe; and that was exactly the case that Smith himself made. However, there was a clear enough similarity between, on the one hand, this Smithian Catholic impulse to impose discipline and order and, on the other, the harsher face which was being turned

---

[38]   AAW, A XX, no. 136, p. 499.

[39]   AAW, A XXII, no. 76, p. 405.

[40]   AAW, A XXII, no. 76, p. 407.

[41]   K. Fincham and P. Lake, 'The Ecclesiastical Policies of James I and Charles I', *The Early Stuart Church 1603–1642* , in K. Fincham, ed. (London: Macmillan, 1993), pp. 23–49.

towards what some Caroline churchmen called 'puritanism', as they attempted to deal with what they took to be the danger represented by failure to conform.[42]

The scattering of approbation controversy documents, in a range of archives, shows also how far this question became in part a public one.[43] There was a good deal of back-and-forth petitioning and lobbying. As much as in the archpriest dispute, we have here, in the later 1620s, evidence of a news network in and through which comments and stories were repeated and collated for quite sophisticated political purposes. Many of the principal documents of the controversy, even allegedly private 'letters', were circulated widely. What drove Bishop Smith nearly berserk was that his enemies were taking their case to a much wider public than Smith considered apposite (though, of course, he would proceed to do exactly the same thing in retaliation against them). They were courting, he claimed, a form of popularity. This had long been an accusation in the mouths of the Jesuits' opponents. Smith's enemies had, he said, never even bothered to ensure that their first broadside against him, known as the 'Interrogatories of the Laity', 'should come to the bishops hands'. Instead, they had scattered 'coppies ... amongst the laity without any hands at all to them wherin they shew that neither they had any reall intention to have any such satisfaction of the bishop for els they would have sent the articles to him'.[44] Smith declared further that his enemies 'spred them al England over, in such sorte as they came into the hands of the State, which whether it were their intention or no I leave to God to judge',[45] and they deliberately did it at precisely the time

> ... when the bishop (to his great paines and danger) was visiting, instructing, and bishoping [that is, confirming] the laiety of all sortes, in the remotest parts of England to theyr wonderfull comfort which might have moved the devisers of these articles to deferr them to another time, least they should have interrupted the bishop in so good an imployment and so comfortable and profitable to some, [but they were blinded by their] passion.[46]

---

[42]   See especially K. Fincham, 'Clerical Conformity from Whitgift to Laud', *Conformity and Orthodoxy in the English Church, c. 1560–1660*, P. Lake and M. Questier, eds (London: Boydell, 2000), pp. 125–58.

[43]   For copies of several approbation controversy documents in the Trumbull manuscripts, see BL, Additional MS 72415, fols 72r–109r.

[44]   AAW, A XXI, no. 101, p. 409.

[45]   AAW, A XXI, no. 32, p. 103.

[46]   AAW, B 48, no. 25.

This was obviously not confined to the county of Sussex, though we have, here and there, evidence that prominent Sussex gentry, in addition of course to Montague, became involved. Thus, for instance, on 28 December 1627, a letter addressed by, among others, Edward Gage to Sir John Gage at London went up from Sussex, asking about a recently written and now widely circulating document, dated 25 November 1627, which challenged Smith's authority. It was known, accurately though rather unimaginatively, as the 'letter of the three gentlemen' since it was written by three of Smith's leading lay critics; it claimed to represent, however, the opinion of the entire Catholic laity. Lord Arundell, one of Smith's aristocratic champions, commented that 'I have heard that some copies of the letter were scattered abroad, before the letter it selfe was subscribed.' Well, said Edward Gage, it definitely was not the sense of the majority of Catholic lay men, and no

> ... lay Catholik in this countie to my knowedg did ever knowe or alowe of the sayd letter, but do utterly disdaine from it and much dislik some thinges therin as nott beseeminge good Catholiks, and we much marvel that some few gentlmen [sic] showld thus take uppon them the name of the laytie without their allowance therof: especially in a manner of so gret importance and to theire great prejudice and indignitie.[47]

The principal issue raised in that document, as in several of the petitions which questioned Bishop Smith's strategy and motives at this time, was the not unreasonable fear of some Catholics that Smith's known determination to set up an episcopal tribunal and enforce its judgments would potentially set Catholics at odds with the royal courts.[48] Here, then, the petty personal disputes, of which we have evidence in the advice papers sent to the secular clergy's agent in Rome, could be seen as the sharp end of a much broader contemporary theoretical question, that is, whether Smith's jurisdiction was all that he claimed, and how far he could exercise his authority in the same way as a Church-of-England bishop.

We do not know, of course, exactly how far the technical jurisdictional concerns involved in the approbation controversy were fully comprehended by those who were potentially affected by it. But the fact remained that the way in which the dispute panned out and was contested by a range of interested parties did indeed mimic, or rather conformed to, some of the outlines of public-sphere politics as it has figured in the writing on the period from the pens of, for example, Peter

---

[47]   AAW, A XXI, no. 14, p. 55; AAW, A XX, no. 166, p. 636; see also Questier, *Catholicism and Community*, p. 437.

[48]   Allison, 'Question of Jurisdiction', pp. 119–20.

Lake and Steven Pincus, that is, as opposing groups tried to appeal to different and wider audiences when they were faced with the uncertain responses of higher authority to the case that they made against their opponents.[49]

Because Smith's authority was itself uncertain and open to question, his critics decided to challenge him directly by appealing to Rome, and also to the English Catholic community and finally to the Stuart regime. They were determined not to allow him a monopoly of the rhetoric of order and discipline, a rhetoric which Smith and his friends were undoubtedly determined to appropriate and, in so doing, to make the claim that if the crown were to permit the newly appointed bishop to function as a bishop might do pretty much anywhere else in the Western Christian Church, the commonwealth as a whole would benefit from the setting to rights of the Catholic community which had been beset by so many difficulties.

By looking at the few extant pieces of evidence about individual cases which involved wills and bequests, and disputed marriage contracts, and the like, which were kept on file by the secular clergy officials of Bishop Smith, one can see exactly how the exercise of episcopal authority to sort out marital and other disputes might also have transformative effects on the structure of the Catholic community in England. The opportunity to decide such cases would confer enormous coercive authority over Smith's enemies and the ability to interfere in the crucial relationships between lay gentry patrons and their chaplains.

For example, among the papers of the secular clergy's Roman agent, there is an account of a form of marriage gone through, at some point between October 1621 and mid-1623, and subsequently consummated, by William Roper, 'second sonne to the late deceased and brother to the present Lord Teynham'. This was a marriage which the Ropers had repudiated, apparently on the advice of their Jesuit friends and spiritual counsellors.[50] The Teynham Roper family was primarily located in Kent. Despite its known Catholic inclinations, a peerage had been acquired by the family in the 1610s. (The monuments of the first and second barons in Lynsted Church are very impressive.[51]) However, the wider Roper family extended into Sussex, not least because the Brownes of Cowdray had married into the Eltham and Canterbury branch of the Ropers

---

[49]   P. Lake and S. Pincus, 'Rethinking the Public Sphere in Early Modern England', in *The Politics of the Public Sphere in Early Modern England*, idem, eds (Manchester: Manchester University Press, 2007), pp. 1–30.

[50]   The Teynham branch of the Roper family was strongly inclined towards the Jesuits. It had little contact with the secular clergy, and not much with its Roper cousins at Canterbury and Eltham, who were consistent supporters of the secular clergy at this date.

[51]   <http://www.geograph.org.uk/snippet/7197> accessed 10 April 2014.

who, because of their well-known marital connection with the More family, were of some real significance in Catholic circles.

William Roper's unfortunate bride, Mary, protested that her good name was being besmirched. The Teynham branch of the Roper family was saying that she had 'heynously wronged them'. And now she had been abandoned by the person she still regarded as her husband, who had fled abroad, 'leaving an unfaythfull relation of the case betweene him and me'. She wanted justice, and she evidently knew exactly who might give it to her. For their part, the secular clergy leadership had, in this kind of testimonial, a case which demonstrated most of their claims about the bad effects of the unregulated regulars on the lives of English Catholics. Not only was anguish caused to the unsuspecting likes of the unfortunate Mary Roper, but scandal was given to others by the bad example of known Catholics. More fundamentally, the nature and function of the sacraments were publicly mocked, and all because of the perverse and corrupting spiritual advice of the chaplains who were drawn from the religious orders. Mary Roper's testimony was annotated by the secular priest Edward Bennett and sent off to his brother John in Rome with the message that 'this information is sent you that you may see what want there is of a bushop to determin bussinesses', for 'this matter hath bred and doth still [breed] great scandall.' William Roper was now at either Louvain or Liège, 'at the Jesswetes direction'. The rumour among his deserted wife's friends was that 'the Jesswetes would fayne make hym a Jesswete that they may possess all he hath.'[52] As one sacrament was being perverted and ridiculed, so these Jesuits were exploiting the young man's entry into a religious order for their own material gain.

In 1627, Benjamin Norton was involved in a dispute with the Benedictines about a case of a family where the daughter was intending to marry without her mother's consent. Norton supported the mother, but a Benedictine chaplain of the girl's intended spouse opposed Norton. The situation was made worse because the Benedictine, 'to cowntenance' the girl's frequenting the company of her lover, 'used his authoritie in sending for her to playe with him at cardes; whearewith the mother was much disedified and complayned to me of him, whoe could nott helpe her against such a kinde of man'. (Here the vice of gambling, in which the Benedictine was indulging, was presented as the means by which he persuaded the girl to refuse to obtain parental consent for marriage.) Norton threatened excommunication unless they separated. He used his report of this

---

[52]   AAW, B 25, no. 46. Edward Bennett added, however, that 'he that married them is a Benedictyn and a very good man', ibid.

incident to launch into a general attack on the regulars in his district, and to accuse them of fomenting all kinds of indiscipline and scandal.[53]

Smith raged at the power which chaplains from the religious orders exercised over the marriages of wealthy Catholics. 'As for mariages', wrote Smith, a baronet 'having in a maner fully agreed for a mach betwene his eldest daughter and the sonne of an other principal Catholic, becaus[e] the knight was not addicted to Jesuits, they brake the mach, and procured the gentleman to marie a daughter of a freind of theirs.' Smith commented that 'their hindrance of mariages which they like not is so manifest as a principal gentleman in Lancashire said openly that in that countie no mariages could be made betwene Catholics of account which Jesuits liked not.' He also knew of 'another principal gentleman, of Dorsetshire' who said that 'such Catholics as are not favored of Jesuits must seek there maches amongst Protestantes, becaus[e] among Catholics they shold not speed.' With a quick bit of lateral thinking, Smith recalled that 'it is commonly talked that they had a great hand in breaking the mach with Spayne', in other words, the negotiations up to and during the first part of 1623 when it appeared that Prince Charles (as he then was) might wed the infanta Maria. Smith added that 'a gentleman who was then in Madrid doubteth not to saye that after one of theirs', evidently a reference to the Jesuited priest Sir Tobias Matthew, 'came thither, the mach went more and more backward, and for his good service therin he was presently knighted at his returne'.[54]

But while Smith and his officials could represent their intervention in such cases as a positive good to correct the mistakes and infidelities of certain errant Catholics, it was clear that the inevitable product of settling such cases must be to drive families such as the Teynham Ropers from their reliance on the regulars for spiritual counsel. Thus would the balance of power between various interest groups within the community be substantially and permanently altered.

The point was that the regulation of these webs of relationship was one of the crucial modes of exercise of authority and control over contemporary society. One could see this in the alleged 'scandal' of Lord Baltimore's supposed and then failed marriage to a maidservant in the early 1630s. News of the involvement of Baltimore's chaplains' attempts to get the unfortunate maidservant into a

---

[53]   AAW, A XXI, no. 46, pp. 165–8; Lunn, 'Benedictine Opposition', p. 10. For a case of a religious (George Gaire OSB) dispensing a man and woman wanting to marry within the prohibited degrees of consanguinity, see AAW, A XXII, no. 105, p. 509. For other similar cases, see AAW, A XXII, no. 115, p. 535 and in particular the long-running suit in the 1630s between William Worthington and Penelope Parkins, for which see M. Questier, ed., *Newsletters from the Caroline Court, 1631–1638: Catholicism and the Politics of the Personal Rule* (London: Camden Society, fifth series, 26, 2005) [hereafter Questier, *NCC*], pp. 20, 66–7, 72–4, 75, 76, 110, 123, 163, 179, 188.
[54]   AAW, A XXI, no. 49, pp. 173–4.

convent in order to bury the scandal buzzed around the Catholic network; the peer's tame clergy did this on the basis of a (specious) claim that 'there was a spirituall kindried betwixt him and her which did make the marriage invalide.'[55]

This was a crucial indictment of the regulars. Here it could be alleged that they were opposing the papacy's own reform programme enshrined at Trent, and all on entirely specious and self-serving grounds. The council had laid out a number of rules governing such things as degrees of kinship in order to govern the contracting of marriages. As John Southcot (another of Smith's officials) reiterated, 'I heare that Father John Floid and Father Rudesindo [Barlow] have given their verdict' on Baltimore's case and 'pronounce that it is no marriage, giving only for reason the not reception of the Councell of Trent here which hath taken away that impediment of compaternity derived from the wife to the husband'. Southcot had seen 'Father Floids verdict but I could not gett a coppy of it, for, it seemes, they are loath to lett anything be seen under their hands wherin they oppose the reception of the councell'. By contrast, the secular clergy 'consulted of this case the last week, and resolved that the mariage was good'.[56] The prominent Catholic gentleman and former courtier Sir Nicholas Fortescue was another sinner. 'It is well known' wrote George Leyburn 'how lude ever he haith been'. He was another one who had 'maryed his owne ma[i]de', and he 'keepeth her obscurely in the country'.[57]

When Lady Kirkham was sought in marriage by Francis Plowden jnr (son of the Francis Plowden who was one of Bishop Smith's leading gentry opponents), Plowden subsequently backed out of the marriage contract. He did this on the advice of the Jesuit Richard Blount who said that this was morally licit if Plowden jnr had reserved an intention not to go through with it.[58] This was, it could be alleged, an instance of the Jesuits' well-known (alleged) perversions of the rules relating to casuistry being used to play fast and loose with the marital arrangements of their gentry patrons and penitents, and all in order to indulge their lust.[59]

---

[55] Questier, *NCC*, p. 51.

[56] Ibid., pp. 63–4.

[57] Ibid., pp. 51–2.

[58] Ibid., pp. 127–8, 178. In 1632, Southcot alleged that the Jesuits were not even using a proper form of marriage service. Southcot said that 'my cosen [Richard] White (Mr Blacklows brother) his daughter and young [Robert] Brett' were married by 'one [George] Ward a young Jesuit (as I was tould)' who simply joined 'their hands togeather and [said] ... thus, be married', ibid., p. 128.

[59] For contemporary Jesuit casuistical teaching on these and other issues, see, for example, P.J. Holmes, ed., *Caroline Casuistry: The Cases of Conscience of Fr Thomas Southwell SJ* (Woodbridge: Catholic Record Society, 84, 2012).

Another and equally important question which the bishop's tribunal would inevitably address was the topic of money. Clearly, it was going to be difficult to stop a Jesuited patron leaving cash to the Society if that was what he really wanted to do. But it was feared by some lay patrons that the slightest hint of a dispute about the testator's intentions or his trustees' capacity would allow the bishop to be in there like a not particularly impartial shot to strike down provisions in their wills in favour of the religious orders. It had, after all, been one of the most regularly repeated gripes of the appellants that the Jesuits greedily collared patronage resources and then dispatched funds out of the country for the benefit of their own order and to the detriment of the English Catholic community as a whole.

In c. 1627, Smith complained that a 'knight dying the last yeare in London was refused absolution upon his death bed by a Jesuit, his confessor, becaus[e] he wold not dispose of his goodes according to the Jesuits mynde.' Smith wondered to himself, 'if they delt thus with men' what might they not be expected to do with women; and if they practised their trickery in London, where there were so many other priests, what might they not be expected to get away with 'in the countrie, where in some places scarce an other priest is to be had. Wherfor' it was 'no mervel if they feare the bishop shold have the proving of wills'.[60]

If the new Catholic episcopate were to appropriate this sort of authority and to create a consensus among Catholics that it was entitled to exercise it at the expense of those members of the religious orders who rejected this level and style of episcopal governance then, as we have seen, the implications of this manoeuvre would extend far beyond the merely administrative.

There is also, in all these stories and jibes, a more general and latent rhetoric or thesis about the proper format of the community of the godly, that is, what the Catholic community in England ought to be like. In a truly godly community, such internal squabbles would not happen at all. These scandalous cases and disputes, attributable in large part to the regulars' meddling, were themselves a hindrance to 'conversion', in the most far-reaching Catholic sense of the word. 'A good preist prisoner in London', wrote William Case (the marquis of Winchester's chaplain), 'told mee ... that the Catholiks are noted to bee [the] most litigeous, most exorbitant and most deboist of all other people here in London. And when hee hath laboured the conversion of some Protestants, they object these disorders, and that there is not menes to remedy them.'[61] As Case phrased it in a letter to Smith in May 1632, the regulars 'practise boldly the sending of children

---

60   AAW, A XXI, no. 49, p. 174.
61   Questier, *NCC*, p. 219.

to the church to be baptised; they marry young folks without consent of parents to the ruin of their families. They set people together by the eares in goeing to law, when they would willinglie end it by peacable compromises.'[62] This could be taken as a kind of social counterpart of their wider political corruption of the missionary endeavour, that is, by subordinating spiritual issues to temporal ones. Case added that Smith's opponents were trying to discredit him by linking him with the enemies of the imperialists in the current military confrontations in continental Europe:

> ... they calumniat you by saying that you are a French man, the cardinalls [that is, Richelieu's] creature, a stirring man, a stubborne man etc. They calumniat the cardinall by saying that hee is a fautor of haeretiks, nay as badd or worse than Sweden. They calumniat the pope by saying that hee hath beene colde in resisting haeretiks, and that hee hath thought it necessary for the howse of Austria to bee shockt.[63]

At one level, this was all rather petty. It was certainly typical of the clerical infighting which had been so public and prominent during the archpriest dispute thirty years before. But at another level, it served as a vehicle for a debate about the place of Catholicism in a society the national Church of which was not in communion with Rome but was, on some readings, not now necessarily inimical to a closer relationship with the Church defined by communion with Rome. In other words, the claim made here was that the exercise of Catholic episcopal authority would not cause divisions among the truly godly but instead would prevent them; it was an essential underpinning for the ideal division-less and harmonious community to which all good Catholics in England should aspire. It was the loose life and spleen of (some of) the regular clergy, not the enforcement of the bishop's authority, which not only set Catholics against each other but also gave public scandal and turned people away from the Catholic Church back towards the Church of England, a perverted mirror-image in fact of the 'conversion of England', which was the proper function of the Catholic clergy. Bishop Smith's friends glossed his interventions in the lives of English Catholics under the labels of order and decency. The 'fruict' of both his and William Bishop's episcopal 'endeavours' was listed in July 1627 under twelve separate heads. Stress was laid on the fact that 'the hierarchy hath bin sett up in an orderly and dew manner, by making vicar generalls, archdeacons, rurall deanes and other officers belonging therunto', and (impliedly as a result) 'ecclesiasticall

---

62   AAW, A XXVI, no. 69, p. 193.

63   Questier, *NCC*, p. 47.

discipline, which was utterly here decaied, doth begin hereby to florish againe.' The effects of that discipline were then listed: disorderly priests had been 'corrected and reclaimed from their bad courses'; others who had subscribed to the godless 1606 oath of allegiance had been made to recant; many of the laity had received the sacrament of confirmation, and had generally been nourished in a 'true devotion and obedience to the Sea Apostolicke'. Smith had not only 'determined' the 'feasts and fasts proper to our country', and started to collate a Catholic martyrology but had also 'by his authority ... doun many good offices to reconcile divers discontented wives and husbands, who lived ordinarily before a sunder'.[64]

At this point, we may appear to be getting rather far away from the intellectual history of Sussex, and in fact from Sussex and from intellectual history generally. But these cases which we have briefly reviewed were the practical outcome of a range of contemporary debates about diverse sorts of authority, papal, royal and episcopal. The supporters of Richard Smith did look for support to theologians in, for example, the University of Paris, and there clearly was a kind of intellectual Counter-Reformation underpinning for even the most trivial of these controversies. Or, rather, these bickerings are vivid reminders of the consequences of the ecclesiological differences between Catholics at this point, and for much of the seventeenth century, as to how they should define their relationship both with the British State and the national Church, as well as with the court and Church of Rome.

So, finally, why should we be bothered about the difficulties experienced by this fraction of the national Church, a fraction which has been largely written out of the period? There has, after all, been a consensus among scholars, following the line taken by John Bossy, that Catholicism became essentially sectarian and entirely separatist in the seventeenth century. But the point is that, here, what we have is the setting-out of a number of different ways in which Catholics could align themselves with the purposes of the State and of a regime which now, even if not exactly tolerant, was doing its best to extract itself from foreign alliances and engagements of exactly the kind which had generated the more violent, uncontrollable and (arguably) obtuse expressions of anti-popery. In the later 1620s, as the approbation controversy was in full swing, and Smith and his enemies were battling it out to represent themselves to a wider public as acceptable to the Caroline State, the crown's efforts to create a consensus for the prosecution of what now looked like a disastrous war were simply not working.

---

[64]　AAW, A XX, no. 102, p. 355. See also AAW, A XXI, no. 58 (Thomas White's Latinisation of these points for presentation in Rome).

The attempts by revisionist scholarship to explain the dysfunction of the early Caroline parliaments as the product of misunderstanding and personal and policy blunders on the part of the court and the king really should not divert our attention from the fact that there were major ideological issues at stake here. If the Parliament were to fail as a mechanism for securing the necessary means to carry out royal policy, then those who had their doubts about certain contemporary and, as they saw it, quasi-republican renderings of the relationship between crown and Parliament would start, as they did, to construct a different ideological and practical basis for the exercise of royal authority.[65] In these circumstances, the court might itself look for support from those, including Catholics of various stripes, who did not have a voice in the parliamentary arena.

This is, in some sense, what happened during the 1630s. Clearly, the 'personal rule' was not the crypto-popish conspiracy of the kind that Charles's critics imagined, nor was the king inclined to accommodate and incorporate Catholics in the way that some of them certainly wished. But, as the approbation controversy suggests, as much in Sussex as anywhere else, Catholics in the early Caroline Church were not only fighting their own battles over how their 'community' should be regulated but, in doing so, were also struggling to position themselves so as to exploit what many contemporaries perceived as a likely turn against some of the more obvious political implications of Calvinism and the crown's and its agents' attempts to deal with the loose ends of the Elizabethan settlement of religion, all in the context of a new peace policy and a deep, and perhaps justifiable, distrust of pan-European Protestantism and the apparent damage done to the English Church by those whom some called 'puritans'.

---

[65]   For contemporary Protestant renderings of the function of Parliament, see, for example, P. Lake, 'Anti-popery: the Structure of a Prejudice', in *Conflict in Early Stuart England*, R. Cust and A. Hughes, eds (London: Longman, 1989), pp. 72–106, esp. at p. 91.

Chapter 8

Richard Woodman, Sussex Protestantism and the Construction of Martyrdom

Paul Quinn

Richard Woodman (c. 1525–57) was executed in Lewes on 22 June 1557. Woodman was burnt, along with nine other Protestants, on a day of extraordinary violence. Woodman, an iron maker from Buxted who ran a successful forge or furnace in Warbleton in east Sussex,[1] is the most prominent member of a group of Marian Protestants problematically identified as 'the Sussex martyrs'.[2] This construction of a martyrological subset among the victims of Mary I's religious

---

[1]   See Tim Cornish, 'Richard Woodman – Ironmaster and Martyr', in *Wealden Iron*, Bulletin no. 27, second series (2007), pp. 11–17, at pp. 11–12 for the question as to whether Woodman owned a forge or a furnace. For Woodman's biography, see Thomas S. Freeman, 'Woodman, Richard', *ODNB* (2004); online edn, January 2008 <http://www.oxforddnb.com/view>. Mark Antony Lower extrapolated that Woodman's annual income was £56, see Lower, *The Worthies of Sussex* (Lewes, 1865), p. 139. This is based upon Woodman's statement: 'My father and he [Woodman's brother] had as much of my goods in their hands as I might have fifty-six pounds for by the year clear', see John Foxe, *The Unabridged Acts and Monuments Online* or *TAMO* (1570 edition) (HRI Online Publications, Sheffield, 2011) <http//www.johnfoxe.org> accessed 18 August 2013. Freeman's *ODNB* entry suggests that Woodman employed a hundred people. If these figures are correct, then Woodman was not an inconsiderable personality. Woodman's second arrest may have been influenced by economic and familial factors as much as by religious considerations.

[2]   See A.S. Gratwick and Christopher Whittick, 'The Loseley list of "Sussex Martyrs"', in *Sussex Archaeological Collections* (hereinafter *SAC*), 13 (1995): 225–40, at pp. 225–6 on the construction of 'the Sussex martyrs' as a separate group, distinct from other English counties. The number of Sussex martyrs is unclear, as is whether the term means people executed in Sussex regardless of origin or if the title includes people from other locations executed in Sussex or people from Sussex executed elsewhere. Foxe seems to list 34 martyrs from Sussex or executed in the county. Malcolm Kitch argues for 41, suggesting that Roger Manning's total of 27 'is clearly too low', see Kitch, 'The Reformation in Sussex', *Studies in Church History*: 94, n. 76. The Sussex Martyrs Commemoration Council argue for 36 martyrs; see <www.escis.org.uk/Entry/View/Sussex_Martyrs_Commemoration_Council/14942> accessed 23 July 2013. That figure is based on residence in the county. The appendix to *Mary Tudor: Old and New Perspectives*, Susan Doran and Thomas S. Freeman, eds (London: Palgrave, 2011) lists 28 names which could, by virtue of residence or place of execution, be classed as 'Sussex martyrs', pp. 225–71.

policies is essentially the product of a nineteenth-century reading of John Foxe's *Acts and Monuments*.[3]

Foxe did not categorise the martyrs of Sussex as a single group, but the collective discussion of Sussex Protestantism which produced the idea of the Sussex martyrs is based upon an over-reliance on Foxe, whose account of the Sussex martyrs contains significant gaps; this is the result of an absence of material relating to the vast majority of those executed in Sussex,[4] and because Foxe manipulated the material which he was able to acquire in order to suggest that Protestantism – in England, and by extension, in Sussex – was doctrinally homogeneous. This chapter will argue that this doctrinal homogeneity aided the establishment of the cult of the Sussex martyrs, but it also resulted in an overly simplified vision of Protestantism in early modern Sussex, one which neglected other important factors including intra-Protestant debate, cross-county relationships, and varieties of Protestant belief in Sussex. It also ignores the complicated relationship between Sussex's Protestant and Roman Catholic communities.

The cult of the Sussex martyrs is a product of John Foxe's desire to portray all those who died as a result of the attempt to restore Roman Catholicism as being orthodox according to the Elizabethan religious settlement. This chapter will argue that Foxe's accounts of the martyrs in Sussex was dictated by his editorial decision to present a coherent Protestant identity, one which removed any evidence of heterodox thought or intra-Protestant controversy. The exclusion of evidence of doctrinal debate or disagreement resulted in a skewed vision of Sussex Protestantism, one which led Foxe's nineteenth-century readers to see the county as doctrinally uniform.[5]

As this chapter will argue, the assumption of orthodox Protestant belief among the Sussex martyrs is dependent upon Foxe's accounts of the arrests and confessions of three Sussex martyrs – Derick Carver, a brewer from Brighton who

---

[3]   Gratwick and Whittick, 'The Loseley list', pp. 225–5; Whittick, 'Lower, Mark Antony', *ODNB* (2004). I am grateful to Christopher Whittick for providing me with this information in conversation at the outset of the research for this chapter.

[4]   Foxe had difficulty obtaining material from within Chichester Diocese; see the commentary accompanying the account of the Mayfield burnings (23 September 1556) which views the continuing absence of the names of two of the martyrs in the 1576 edition of *Acts and Monuments* as evidence of Foxe's problems in researching martyrdom in Sussex. See John Foxe, *TAMO* (1576 edition) (HRI Online Publications, Sheffield, 2011) <http//www.johnfoxe.org> accessed 12 January 2013.

[5]   Gratwick and Whittick suggest 'Because Foxe had a vested interest in concealing such theological aberrations and homogenising his martyrs, we may have failed to appreciate how important it was to the survivors, the early Elizabethans, to establish just what kind of heretics the victims were': 'The Loseley List', p. 229.

was burnt in Lewes on 22 July 1555, Stephen Gratwick, also from Brighton, who was executed in Southwark on 28 May 1557,[6] and Richard Woodman. Of these narratives, Woodman's is the longest by a considerable margin. The Woodman narrative features in all four editions of *Acts and Monuments* published during Foxe's lifetime and is, the reader is informed, predominantly an autobiographical account written by Woodman before his execution. Woodman's text evidently came into Foxe's possession between the publication of the first and second editions of *Acts and Monuments* (1563 and 1570).[7] The new information resulted in an expansion of the Woodman narrative in the second and subsequent editions of Foxe's martyrology.[8] Woodman's six interrogations before a range of Catholic clerics including Christopherson of Chichester, Edmund Bonner, Alban Langdale, John Story and Nicholas Harpsfield,[9] reveal Woodman to be an orthodox Edwardian Protestant who challenged the Catholic prelates on a wide range of theological issues including the Mass, clerical marriage, the number of sacraments, free will and ecclesiastical hierarchy, particularly in relation to the examination of those accused of heresy.[10] In the absence of information about the vast majority of those executed in Sussex between 1555 and 1557,[11] Woodman's

---

[6]   Doran and Freeman state that the place of execution was somewhere in Suffolk, see *Mary Tudor*, p. 252.

[7]   The Woodman narrative is an example of Foxe incorporating new material of a personal nature which he received following the publication of the first edition of *Acts and Monuments*: see Elizabeth Evenden and Thomas S. Freeman, *Religion and the Book in Early Modern England: the making of John Foxe's 'Book of Martyrs'* (Cambridge: Cambridge University Press, 2011), pp. 143–9.

[8]   The online edition of *Acts and Monuments* provides evidence of the development of the Woodman narrative. The old AMS eight-volume edition of *Acts and Monuments* (New York: AMS Press Inc., 1965) only includes the version of the Woodman narrative from the 1570 edition of Foxe. This is the more detailed version but the failure to acknowledge, or to be aware of, the shorter version found in the 1563 edition results in the omission of an examination of the development of the Woodman section of the text. The section on Woodman is found on pp. 332–77 of vol. 8 of the AMS edition. All further references to the Woodman narrative will be taken from this edition, with reference to the online edition of the 1570 edition, John Foxe, *TAMO* (1570 edition) (HRI Online Publications, Sheffield, 2011) <http//www.johnfoxe.org>.

[9]   Nicholas Harpsfield was appointed as Woodman's ordinary by Reginald Pole for the sixth and final examination on 16 June 1557. Harpsfield is not identified by name in the account; he may be the 'Fat Priest' or the 'Priest', see Foxe, *A&M*, pp. 372–3. Freeman identifies Harpsfield, see 'Woodman, Richard', *DNB*. The interrogation is found at John Foxe, *TAMO* (1570 edition).

[10]   Harpsfield's appointment as Woodman's ordinary was partly a response to Woodman's argument on 25 May and 15 June 1557 that John White, Bishop of Winchester, had no right to examine him as he was not Woodman's ordinary; see *A&M*, pp. 365, 367; John Foxe, *TAMO* (1570 edition).

[11]   The executions in Lewes on 22 June 1557 were the last to take place in Sussex during Mary's reign. The suppression of English Protestantism continued until 1558.

Protestantism becomes – by association – the orthodoxy of all the Sussex martyrs. However, as this chapter will suggest, reading Sussex Protestantism through Foxe's accounts of Woodman and Carver is problematic, leading to a misunderstanding as to the nature of belief among Sussex's Marian Protestant population.

This chapter will argue that Foxe's editorial processes may have resulted in a distorted portrayal of Woodman and his relationship with other Protestants in Sussex and in the south-east of England. Woodman was almost certainly involved in the doctrinal clash between Protestants which took place in the King's Bench during 1554–55.[12] These prison debates, which C.J. Clement describes as a continuation of Edwardian-era controversies between competing Protestant belief systems,[13] were a series of often vitriolic encounters between rival Protestants on the fundamental question of predestination and Free Will. Ostensibly prompted by Free Willer protests about the Predestinarians' attitudes towards gaming and other sports and pastimes, the King's Bench debates revealed deep splits among the Protestant prisoners. This led to a situation which Clement describes as 'a dispute between those influenced by the old English biblical traditions and those who had embraced the new Reformation movement from the Continent'.[14] The majority of Sussex prisoners were Predestinarians, although some, like John Trewe, were in doctrinal accord with the Kentish Free Willers. Woodman would have been a Predestinarian if he was involved in the debates while a prisoner in the King's Bench.

The Woodman narrative, as it appears in *Acts and Monuments*, is silent as to any possible involvement by Woodman in the debates. However, this does not preclude the possibility that the original text of Woodman's narrative included acknowledgement of the intra-Protestant controversies. References to the arguments between Predestinarians and Free Willers which were a feature of the account of John Careless were removed from the second and subsequent editions of *Acts and Monuments*.[15] A similar excision may have occurred in relation to the Woodman narrative.

---

[12]   Freeman, 'Woodman, Richard', *DNB*; C.J. Clement, *Religious Radicalism in England 1535–1565* (Cumbria: The Paternoster Press, 1997), pp. 264–89; D. Andrew Penny, *Freewill or Predestination: the battle over saving Grace in mid-Tudor England* (Suffolk: Royal Historical Society Studies/The Boydell Press, 1990), pp. 153–4.

[13]   Clement, *Religious Radicalism*, pp. 261–3.

[14]   Ibid., p. 264.

[15]   Evenden and Freeman, *Religion and the Book in Early Modern England*, p. 165. Again, anyone dependent upon the AMS edition of Foxe would be unaware of Foxe's excision of reference to the debates between Predestinarians and Free Willers. The online edition of Foxe allows a

D. Andrew Penny argues that the revelation of 'considerable variance over the finer points of Reformation theology' is unsurprising, given the collection of 'heretics and malcontents' gathered in King's Bench.[16] However, for Foxe, this dispute was problematic as it contradicted his vision of a unified Protestantism threatened by Roman Catholic attempts to enforce Papist practices and belief. Any such references to the debates in the Woodman narrative would have to be excised as part of Foxe's removal of evidence of problematic dissension or radical doctrinal beliefs within England's Protestant population.[17] Such an excision of problematic theology certainly occurred when Foxe produced his account of Carver.[18]

The absence from *Acts and Monuments* of any acknowledgement of the King's Bench debates, either in relation to Woodman or as a general point about Reform under Mary I, results in a misleading picture of Protestantism in Marian England, and in Sussex in particular. As this chapter will demonstrate, Woodman's arrests and interrogations illuminate the complex interplay of social, political, religious, historical and geographical factors at work in Sussex during the early modern period. This complexity is ignored or removed from the historical record by Foxe, resulting in Woodman and Sussex Protestantism being subsumed within a fantasy portrait of unified, suffering Protestantism beset by a tyrannical Romish central government. This editorial and ideological decision has clear historiographical consequences, evident in the nineteenth-century appropriations of the Sussex martyrs and the continued, overly simplified portrayal of Protestantism in Sussex which is based upon a partisan reading of a suspect text.

The Cult of the Sussex Martyrs: Appropriation and Misreading

The nineteenth-century cult of the Sussex martyrs was based upon a reading of Foxe's account of Marian Protestantism; as such, the Sussex martyrs were, and continue to be, incorrectly celebrated as a single body with uniform beliefs. However, the idea of a homogenous sixteenth-century county Protestantism

---

reader to observe Foxe's deletion of this doctrinally problematic event from his record of Marian era Protestantism.

[16]   Penny, *Freewill or Predestination*, p. 113. For Penny's discussion of the King's Bench debates, see pp. 113–24.

[17]   Evenden and Freeman, *Religion and the Book in Early Modern England*, pp. 164–5.

[18]   Foxe's excision of Carver's assertion that baptism was only an external sign with little grace is discussed below; see Clement, *Religious Radicalism*, p. 288.

was politically expedient for the creators of the construct of the county martyrs. For the proponents of the cult, it was the deaths of the Sussex Protestants at the hands of the Marian Catholic authorities which were of paramount importance. This is because, as Christopher Whittick and A.S. Gratwick have argued, the cult of the Sussex martyrs was instigated against the backdrop of the restoration of the Roman Catholic hierarchy in England and the high-profile conversions to Rome of members of the Oxford Movement, including Newman and Manning.[19] The conversion of the latter had a specific local resonance for nineteenth-century Sussex Protestantism.[20] When faced with a resurgent Roman Catholicism in England, bolstered by an increased Irish Catholic population, Mark Antony Lower – the nineteenth-century antiquary, co-founder of the Sussex Archaeological Society, and Low Church evangelical – turned to a local manifestation of historic Roman Catholic tyranny in order to warn against the apparent acceptance of Popery. In order to recall the dire actions of Catholicism in England, Lower inaugurated the cult of the Sussex martyrs after the publication of his 1851 book *The Sussex Martyrs*.[21] Lower was also influenced by his friend James Henry Hurdis, the engraver and co-founder of the Sussex Archaeological Society. Hurdis produced an engraving of Frederick Colvin's picture of the Lewes burnings of 22 June 1557 – that is, an engraving of a number of the martyrs which may have included Woodman.[22] This print 'became a virtual icon in the dissenting homes of the county'.[23] Recall of the burnings of Woodman and the other Protestants executed at Lewes in 1557, and the other burnings in Sussex during the reign of Mary, thus served as a symbol of dissent and also a means of reminding the population of Sussex of past Roman Catholic violence and enforced doctrinal conformity.

However, in focusing upon the shared fate of the Sussex martyrs, Lower and Hurdis – and later figures including the members of the Sussex Martyrs Commemoration Council – imposed a uniformity upon Sussex Protestantism which ignored doctrinal differences and which failed to acknowledge other ways of analysing the Sussex martyrs beyond broad geographical location and manner of death. In seeking to make the Sussex martyrs simply victims of Roman Catholicism in order to make a contemporary religio-political point, Lower and Hurdis performed a similar act of homogenisation as that committed

---

[19] I am indebted to Christopher Whittick for this suggestion and for providing background material on Lower; see Gratwick and Whittick, 'The Loseley list', pp. 225–6.

[20] Ibid.

[21] John H. Farrant, 'Lower, Mark Antony', *ODNB* (2004).

[22] Woodman may be the figure at the centre of the picture.

[23] Christopher Whittick, 'Hurdis, James Henry', *ODNB* (2004).

by Foxe. The Sussex martyrs as recorded in *Acts and Monuments* were made to be doctrinally acceptable to a late sixteenth-century readership; Lower and other commemorative authors were so dependant upon Foxe that they repeated his formulation, with emphasis on the method of execution demonstrating Roman Catholicism's cruelty and tyranny. But this construction of 'county martyrdom' ignores cross-county associations, significant clusters of martyrdom centred upon individual villages and intra-Protestant debate and dissension. In the 150 years since the publication of Lower's *The Sussex Martyrs* there has been significant work by historians which has resulted in a more nuanced understanding of religion and location during the English Reformation which has impacted upon the conception of the Reformation in Sussex;[24] however, it is still the case that 'popular' recollection of the Sussex martyrs is dependent upon the essentially Foxean version promulgated by Lower. The martyrs' memorials established at various sites in Sussex from the mid-nineteenth century are lasting reminders of the Sussex martyrs but they only record basic details – the martyrs' names, the fact that they were Protestant (without any reference to any variant in doctrinal belief) and that they were burnt during the reign of Mary I. The memorials act as a means of preserving an overly simplified narrative of Protestantism in Marian Sussex and in the wider nation. As with Lower's work, the memorials offer a streamlined version of Foxe's construction of the martyrs, one in which the religion of the victims – without any complicating acknowledgement or awareness of intra-Protestant controversy – and the religion of their persecutors are the key facts. This repetition of 'Foxe-lite' continues today.[25]

---

[24]   See, for example, Catharine Pullein, *Rotherfield: the story of some Wealden Manors* (Tunbridge Wells: Courier Printing and Publishing, 1928); John A.F. Thomson, *The Later Lollards 1414–1520* (Oxford: Oxford University Press, 1965) – each chapter of Thomson's study considers a different English county; Peter Clark, *English Provincial Society from the Reformation to the Revolution: Religion, Politics and Society in Kent 1500–1640* (Brighton: Harvester Press, 1977); John F. Davis, *Heresy and Reformation in the South-East of England, 1520–1559* (London: Royal Historical Society, 1983); Michael Questier, *Catholicism and Community in early modern England: Politics, aristocratic patronage and religion, c. 1550–1640* (Cambridge: Cambridge University Press, 2006). This chapter would have been impossible without reference to *Sussex Archaeological Collections*, which demonstrate the ongoing importance of local studies. J.J. Goring's work has been invaluable for the writing of this chapter, as has the work of Christopher Whittick.

[25]   See, for example, the website <www.lewesbonfirecelebrations.com> which could be mistaken for an official website of the Lewes Bonfire Societies but which is in fact an impressive amateur website which includes a narrative of the Sussex martyrs. However, the source for this section is Foxe; as such, this account of the martyrs concentrates on the method of execution employed by the Marian authorities and the fact that the martyrs died for 'Protestantism'. As with Lower and the martyrs' memorials, the complex relationship between Protestants and their

Sussex Protestantism

Foxe's account of Woodman and Carver sought to ensure both men were in doctrinal accord with the Elizabethan readership of *Acts and Monuments*. This portrayal of doctrinal agreement assisted Foxe's nineteenth-century readers in constructing the Sussex martyrs as a coherent group with uniform doctrinal beliefs. As Foxe only included three detailed confessions of faith by people martyred in Sussex – or in the case of Gratwick, someone from Sussex martyred elsewhere – these later readings of doctrinal conformity are primarily based upon the confessions of Carver, Woodman and Gratwick from which an extrapolation is made regarding the Protestantism of the other Sussex martyrs and the county as a whole. Although *Acts and Monuments* presents Woodman as doctrinally orthodox, it is not entirely clear that Carver's brand of Protestantism would have been acceptable to the Elizabethan Church. Foxe excluded details of Carver's baptismal beliefs which were incompatible with the official orthodoxy of the Elizabethan Church. As such, Foxe left a distorted account which then led to a misreading of both Carver and Sussex Protestantism.

In the account of Carver's confession which appeared in the first edition of *Acts and Monuments*, his Protestantism was described in the broadest possible terms. He rejected transubstantiation, denied any salvatory claims regarding the Mass in Latin and dismissed Church ceremony; he affirmed the benefits of auricular confession but rejected the profitability of absolution; he stated the faith taught in the Marian Church is 'not agreeable to God's word' and praised a number of the martyrs including Hooper and Rogers before admitting to possessing an English Bible and Psalter which were read at his house in Brighton and which he continued to read in Newgate.[26] Although the dismissal of Church ceremony may have prompted some questions in Elizabethan England, the confession is as orthodox as Woodman's. However, Miles Hogarde, writing a year after Carver's execution, preserved a version of the confession which included evidence of the Brighton brewer's beliefs regarding baptism: "'It is but an externe signe and worketh litle grace'".[27] This declaration is absent from Foxe's version of the confession, presumably because Carver's conception of baptism was very different from that of the Elizabethan Church. Carver's baptismal beliefs are evidence of the continuation among Protestants

---

fellow-religious, and between some of the martyrs and their Catholic adversaries, is ignored in favour of a model of Marian Sussex formulated from a dichotomy between suffering Protestantism and persecuting Roman Catholicism.

[26]   John Foxe, *TAMO* (1563 edition).

[27]   Hogarde, quoted by Clement in *Religious Radicalism in England*, p. 288.

of unresolved doctrinal disputes during the Marian period. Carver's ideas about baptism may also indicate influence from continental Protestantism or, as Clement suggests, contact with surviving – or resurgent – Lollard thought regarding baptism.[28] Foxe's exclusion of Carver's concept of baptism obscures the intra-Protestant controversy about the sacrament; it also avoids any question regarding historical or continental influences on the development of Protestant thought in Sussex.

Thomas S. Freeman has suggested that Carver was a radical and possibly a Free Willer;[29] there is no evidence of this in the account of Carver found in *Acts and Monuments* but, as with the excision of any acknowledgement of the King's Bench debates, any reference to Protestant anti-Predestinarianism would have been removed by Foxe in order to ensure the appearance of doctrinal conformity between the Marian martyrs and Foxe's Elizabethan readers. If Freeman is right, Foxe obscured Carver's heterodoxy; as with the excision of his statement about baptism, this editorial process resulted in a misreading of Carver and suggested, incorrectly, Protestant uniformity in Sussex. Even if Freeman is incorrect about Carver being a Free Willer,[30] the removal of the contentious view of baptism demonstrates Foxe's drive to eliminate any reference to Non-conformist doctrine and division among the Marian martyrs. Baptism and predestination were crucial areas of debate and disagreement among Protestants; discussion of the latter is excluded in Foxe's accounts of the Sussex martyrs, while the former only appears in doctrinally acceptable formulations. This removal of evidence of dissension among Protestantism occurs despite the importance of baptism and predestination to both Carver and Woodman, and wider Sussex Protestantism.

One of the few surviving documents written in Woodman's own hand is a confession of faith dated 1552.[31] Freeman and M.T. Pearce both argue that this date is incorrect and that the confession was written in 1555 as a means of rebutting Free Willer accusations that Woodman held Anabaptist and Catholic

---

[28] Clement sees links with William Raylond's 1527 declaration that "'baptism in water was but a token of repentance ... when a man cometh to years of discretion ... then she shall receive the baptism of the Holy Spirit'", see ibid., p. 289.

[29] See Freeman's detailed appendix on all the Marian martyrs at <http://www.johnfoxe.org/freeman-marion.pdf> accessed 10 April 2014.

[30] Clement argues that Carver, Launder and Iveson 'each clearly identified themselves with John Bradford', the leader of the Predestinarians in King's Bench, see *Religious Radicalism*, p. 289. However, Clement's source for this claim is E.T Stoneman, *Sussex Martyrs of the Reformation* (Burgess Hill: Sussex Martyrs Commemorative Council, 1967), which is a text dependent upon Foxe's account of Marian Sussex.

[31] The original version of Woodman's narrative in *Acts and Monuments* is lost.

opinions.[32] In the document, Woodman affirms his belief in the Trinity and infant baptism, rejects the pope as Anti-Christ, attacks the Anabaptists and accepts Cranmer's teaching on the sacrament.[33] It is a statement of orthodox Edwardian Protestantism and a declaration of faith acceptable to Elizabethan Protestants. If the 1555 date is correct, the statement of faith operates in two ways: it represents a Protestant assertion of belief in the face of the restoration of Roman Catholicism, and it is the product of the inter-Protestant rivalry figured in the clash between Reformed ideas in the King's Bench during the period of Woodman's initial imprisonment. In that context, the most significant section of the confession – the one which gives credence to the idea that Woodman took part in the King's Bench debates – is the discussion of baptism.

In the confession, Woodman stated 'to christen yonge children ys moste godly and agreinge to ye word of god'.[34] This is a clear anti-Anabaptist statement which refutes the accusation of Anabaptist sentiments. Woodman continued, declaring: 'Also I believe yt yf ye childe be baptysed in ye name of god ye father, ye sonne and ye holy ghoste ... that then it is truly and sufficientlie baptysed (be ye mynster never so wicked in lyfe or learnynge)'.[35] For Woodman, sufficiency of baptism extended to those children baptised by 'papisticall mynisters ... not withstanding that ye minister be a popish heretyke'.[36] This is a refutation of the position adopted by many of the Sussex and Kent Free Willers imprisoned in King's Bench who rejected the idea of legitimate baptism within the Roman Catholic Church and were abused by the Predestinarians as "'abominable heretics'" because they refused to acknowledge the legitimacy of Roman Catholic baptism.[37]

Carver's censored opinion on baptism, the view expressed by Woodman in his confession, and the position taken by the Free Willers – including the Sussex radical John Trewe, whose accounts of the events in King's Bench provide

---

[32]   M.T. Pearce, *Between Known Men and Visible Saints: A Study in Sixteenth Century Dissent* (London: Associated University Presses, 1994), p. 79; Freeman, 'Woodman, Richard', *DNB*. The confession was signed by John Philpot, a leading Predestinarian in King's Bench. Philpot's execution coincided with Woodman's release from Bonner's coalhouse: see John Foxe, *TAMO* (1570 edition). The confession was used by Burrage to refute Joseph Ivimey's claim that Woodman was an Anabaptist; see Burrage, *The Early English Dissenters* (Cambridge: Cambridge University Press, 1912), vol. 1, pp. 53–4. Burrage was responding to J. Ivimey, *History of the English Baptists* (1811), vol. 1, pp. 97–8.

[33]   Freeman, 'Woodman, Richard', *DNB*.

[34]   Woodman, quoted by Burrage in *The Early English Dissenters*, vol. 1, p. 54.

[35]   Ibid.

[36]   Ibid.

[37]   Clement, *Religious Radicalism in England*, p. 267.

much of the evidence of the clash between the opposing Protestant factions – demonstrate the plurality of beliefs within Sussex Protestantism during the reign of Mary. In this context, baptism acts as a means of Protestantism delineating the orthodox from the unorthodox. This use of baptism as a method of establishing Protestant – that is, Edwardian and Elizabethan – orthodoxy is discernible in Woodman's interrogations by the Roman Catholic authorities recorded in *Acts and Monuments*. During Woodman's third interrogation, Langdale accused him of baptising children, including his own child, before alleging that Woodman refused to have his child baptised, thus signalling his rejection of the sacrament.[38] Woodman denied the contradictory charges of rejecting baptism and of administering the sacrament. As such, he avoided the charge of Anabaptism and affirmed priestly administration of the sacraments. This affirmation of infant baptism by an ordained minister separated Woodman from radical Protestants like Trewe, while the subsequent debate with Langdale about baptism demonstrated the difference in the Roman Catholic position and that of orthodox English Protestantism.[39]

The opinions expressed by Woodman, Carver and Trewe regarding baptism demonstrate the variation in belief among Sussex Protestants. What unified the individual figures who became 'the Sussex martyrs' was a broad rejection of Roman Catholic doctrine and the manner of their deaths. It is his burning at the hands of Roman Catholics, his redacted confession of faith, and his geographical association with an orthodox figure like Woodman, which makes Carver orthodox. In the absence – either because the material was not available to Foxe, or because he suppressed difficult facts – of full accounts of the confessional backgrounds of the vast majority of the Sussex martyrs that geographical association becomes crucial. It is also highly misleading.

The King's Bench debates are the most obvious example of the split within Sussex Protestantism. The understanding of baptism found in Woodman's confession is in stark contrast to the position held by John Trewe and the other Free Willers, including Thomas Abington and Thomas Rede, who were burnt at Lewes in June 1556, and who signed a statement of belief issued by Trewe in January 1556.[40] Trewe's record of events in King's Bench also provides evidence of the personal animosity between the Predestinarians and the Free Willers; this material is also suggestive of Woodman's involvement in the debates. In a letter written by Trewe in which he criticised the Predestinarian doctrine of

---

[38]   Foxe, *A&M*, p.355; John Foxe, *TAMO* (1570 edition).
[39]   John Foxe, *TAMO* (1570 edition).
[40]   Gratwick and Whittick, 'The Loseley List', p. 228.

reprobation, a very local and potentially very pointed analogy was employed. The letter includes the familiar Free Willer objection that predestination makes God "'author of all the sin ... for he that maketh a thing only to do evil is the cause of the evil'". Trewe expanded upon this by referring to an important economic activity in the eastern half of Sussex:

> We have in Sussex very many iron mills, which in wasting wood do much hurt; and yet the fault is not in the mills but only in the beginners and makers of them; they cannot go without coals, that is made of wood; no more can the reprobate live (as they affirm) without committing of actual sin.[41]

Woodman, of course, was a very successful iron maker. It is likely that Trewe's association of the Sussex iron industry with theological evil was inspired by one of his Predestinarian opponents – Woodman is the most likely candidate for Trewe's opprobrium.[42] All the available evidence suggests that Woodman would have been involved in the prison debates: Woodman's six interrogations as recorded in *Acts and Monuments* do not indicate any acceptance of Free Will; his confession – signed by leaders of the Predestinarian faction in King's Bench – explicitly affirmed the contested position on baptism denounced by Trewe. The vision of Woodman that is found in *Acts and Monuments* – erudite, and able to marshal an argument based on Biblical principles –indicates someone equipped to argue a doctrinal point in public debate. Woodman's almost certain role in the debates would explain Trewe's reference to the iron industry, rather than Clement's suggestion that Trewe was an 'early conservationist ... a practical man who took a real interest in the mechanics of the iron mills'. Clement is correct when he suggests that Trewe 'would have had little in common with ... Woodman';[43] this lack of commonality was not simply 'socio-economic'[44] – although Trewe's reference to the iron industry does serve as an important reminder of the interplay of religion, politics and economics in the east of Sussex – but also a matter of fundamental belief. This split between Sussex and Kentish Protestantism, and within Sussex's Reformed community, undermines the construction of the Sussex martyrs and demonstrates the degree to which Foxe's emphasis on broad religious

---

[41]   Trew, quoted by Clement in *Religious Radicalism*, p. 284.

[42]   There is also the fascinating possibility that Trewe was the son of the founder of the Robertsbridge foundry; see Gratwick and Whittick, 'The Loseley List', p. 230. That opens up a potential psychological reading of Trewe's use of Sussex iron works in a theological debate.

[43]   Clement, *Religious Radicalism*, p. 284.

[44]   Ibid., p. 284.

agreement ignores a far more interesting and complex history of Protestantism in Marian Sussex.

Sussex's location left it peculiarly exposed to European Protestantism and residual or resurgent pre-Reformation Protestantism – this is particularly evident in the east of the county with its trading links with Protestant areas of northern Europe and its Wealden border with Kent. Clement's argument that the King's Bench debates were a continuation of Edwardian disagreements between continental-influenced Reform and earlier, English proto-Protestantism is an important consideration when examining the Protestant experience in Marian Sussex. Once we move beyond the Foxean-inspired uniform model of Protestantism, we find communities and individuals who demonstrate the influence of continental Protestantism, who provide evidence of the survival of Protestant thought in Sussex from at least the 1530s and who fundamentally challenge the notion of hegemonic Protestant doctrine.

Carver, the Flemish refugee, is the most obvious example of the potential engagement between Sussex and European Protestantism. Moreover, if Clement is correct about a possible connection between Carver's conception of baptism and William Raylond's 1527 declaration that "'baptism in water was but a token of repentance ... when a man cometh to years of discretion ... then he shall receive the baptism of the Holy Spirit'",[45] then we can also potentially associate Carver with residual Lollardy. Carver's problematic conception of baptism, and Freeman's suggestion that he was a Free Willer, should also prompt a reconsideration of the doctrinal beliefs of John Launder and Thomas Iveson, who were arrested with Carver at his conventicle in Brighton. The question must be asked whether the two men from Godstone would attend a conventicle with a Free Willer if they were Predestinarians. If Launder and Iveson were Free Willers, they would have very little in common with Woodman, particularly if the latter had been involved in the King's Bench disputes. And yet Launder, Iveson and Carver are grouped together indiscriminately with Woodman and the other 'Sussex martyrs'. If Carver, Launder and Iveson were Free Willers, then they could just as easily be discussed in relation to Trewe, Abingdon and Rede and their Kentish counterparts. Sussex could also be discussed in relation to Surrey, given that both Launder and Iveson were from Godstone; however, the focus on 'Sussex martyrdom' precludes a cross-county discussion. This is a great mistake: although the King's Bench controversies demonstrate the role of regional disagreements among England's Reformers, the border with Kent also exposed parts of eastern Sussex to forms of Protestantism which were present in

---

[45]   Ibid., p. 289.

the neighbouring county. If Lollardy was an influence on Sussex Protestantism, that Lollard-thought almost certainly came from Kent or from the Weald.

There is very little evidence of Lollardy in Sussex during the fifteenth century. Only one person, Thomas Bageley, appears to have been burnt as a Lollard;[46] the most famous example of heresy in the county prior to the 1530s was Reginald Pecock, Bishop of Chichester, whose theological writings resulted in him being arraigned for heresy in 1457.[47] It is hard to detect the historic presence of Lollardy in Sussex, yet Goring suggests, those in Rye who reacted to the Henrician reforms sounded 'more like Lollards than Lutherans', providing evidence of the effect on the far east of Sussex of 'an older brand of heresy'.[48] Goring argues for 'the presence of pockets of heresy in the High Weald of Kent and Sussex' for over a century before Henry VIII's break with Rome.[49] For Goring, the connection with Kent and the location of the pockets of 'heresy' in east Sussex are key factors in the survival of Lollard belief in the Sussex.[50] The earliest Kentish Lollard stronghold had been in the Weald, and by the early sixteenth century, Kent remained one of the most important locations of Lollardy in England.[51] Goring argues 'Lollards tended to congregate near diocesan boundaries across which they could flee to safety';[52] Woodman's six weeks in the woods is a version of this established pattern of flight and concealment.[53]

The proximity of Rye to the Weald was crucial in exposing the denizens of the town to earlier forms of native Protestantism.[54] Rye is a product of a combination of European Protestantism and native Reform. Europe had already had a

---

[46]   *Victoria History of Sussex*, vol. 1, p. 15 <www.victoriacountyhistory.ac.uk>. Bageley was executed in 1432.

[47]   Ibid.; John Fines, 'Bishop Reginald Pecock and the Lollards', in *Studies in Sussex Church History*, E.M. Kitch, ed., 1981: 57–75.

[48]   Goring, 'Reformation and reaction in Sussex, 1534–1559', *SAC*, 134 (1996): 141–54, at p. 145. For the existence of pre-Reformation Protestantism in Sussex, see also Christopher Haigh, 'The recent historiography of the English Reformation', in *The English Reformation Revised*, Haigh, ed. (Cambridge: Cambridge University Press, 1987), p. 26; R.B. Manning, *Religion and Society in Elizabethan Sussex* (Leicester: Leicester University Press, 1969), pp. 37–8.

[49]   Goring, 'Reformation and reaction', p. 145.

[50]   For the importance of Kent and the connections with Sussex, see Chapter 7 of John A.F. Thomson, *The Later Lollards* (Oxford: Oxford University Press, 1967).

[51]   Clark, *English Provincial Society*, p. 30

[52]   Goring, 'Reformation and reaction', p. 145.

[53]   Woodman's escape to France and Flanders and his three-week stay in northern Europe suggest the possibility of connections with European Protestantism, Foxe, *A&M*, p. 336. John Foxe, *TAMO* (1570 edition).

[54]   G. Mayhew, *Tudor Rye* (Falmer: Centre for Continuing Education, University of Sussex, 1987), pp. 55, 60–62, 67–72.

substantial affect upon religious practice in Rye during the 1520s and 1530s,[55] and there is clear evidence of Protestantism in Rye as early as 1533. Thomas Whit was accused of heresy based on a number of books found in his home. Whit claimed the books belonged to a Norwich merchant, whose name he did not know, who had left the books at Whit's house eighteen months earlier. Whit claimed he had not read the books and that he did not know they contained heretical material. In the absence of any other evidence, Whit was allowed to purge himself and was released.[56] The Norwich trade connection provides a link with areas of the England noted for early manifestations of Reform, but the most important native area of influence for Rye was almost certainly the Weald.

If we consider the concentration of villages in the eastern half of Sussex which produced the martyrs – Ardingly, West Hoathly, East Grinstead, Withyham, Rotherfield,[57] Buxted, Heathfield, Warbleton, Hellingly and Alfriston[58] – along with the coastal towns of Brighton, Eastbourne and Rye, we can see the importance of the proximity of the Weald. If we examine other documents from the Marian period, including those which detail excommunications, we find the same locations appearing. A list of ten people excommunicated in Sussex in March 1556 reveals the homes of the excommunicates to include Eastbourne, Hailsham, Rotherfield, Ticehurst, West Hoathly and East Hoathly.[59] There is

---

[55] Ibid., pp. 55, 60–1. The pre-1530 foreign influence on religion in Rye should force a reconsideration of D.M. Palliser's suggestion that Sussex remained unaffected by Protestant ideas from the Continent prior to 1530: D.M. Palliser, 'Popular reactions to the Reformation during the years of uncertainty 1530–70', in *The English Reformation Revised*, Christopher Haigh, ed. (Cambridge: Cambridge University Press, 1987), p. 95.

[56] C.E. Welch, 'Three Sussex heresy trials', *SAC*, 95 (1957): 57–70, at p. 64.

[57] Rotherfield was named by the Privy Council as somewhere 'out of order, especially in matters of religion', Letter to Lord Abergaveny, 24 August 1554, in *Acts of the Privy Council 1554–6* (London: Stationery Office, 1892), p. 376.

[58] Alfriston demonstrates some of the problems with *Acts and Monuments*. Richard Hooke of Alfriston, '"a child of devilish iniquity ... an obstinate and confirmed heretic"' was excommunicated in October 1555 and was handed over to the secular authorities to be '"punished and broken"'. Salzman suggests that there is no record of Hooke having been executed under Mary I: L.F. Salzman, 'Sussex Excommunicates', *SAC*, 82 (1941): 124–40, at p. 140. However, Foxe does record the execution of a Richard Hook in Chichester 'about the same season' as the burning of John Bradford (July 1555): John Foxe, *TAMO* (1563 edition). Freeman suggests a date of death of August 1556 <http://www.johnfoxe.org/freeman-marion.pdf>. Doran's and Freeman's appendix demonstrates that Hooke could not have been executed until after his condemnation in October 1555, suggesting that Foxe's record of a Richard Hooke being executed in Chester sometime in 1556 actually refers to Hooke's execution in Chichester in the summer of 1556: *Mary Tudor*, Doran and Freeman, eds, no. 34, p. 267, see also Gratwick and Whittick, 'The Loseley List', p. 232.

[59] Salzman, 'Sussex Excommunicates', p. 140.

no evidence that any of the ten people named on the list of excommunicates were executed;[60] they seem to have simply disappeared, perhaps into the Weald or perhaps they were protected by their neighbours. Again, the locations identified in the list reveals a clear concentration in the east of the county, close to the Weald, but also, in some cases, close to the coast. Those local connections and concentrations of communities of Protestants all offer valuable ways of examining Reform in the county at a micro level rather than an overly-simple county-wide study, one interested only in the martyrs' broad professions of faith and their deaths, and one which ignores the variety of beliefs, and influences upon doctrine, found within Sussex Protestantism.[61]

Alexander Hosmer, martyred with Woodman in Lewes, was from Rotherfield.[62] His father Richard Hosmer's will of 1540 includes the wish that his soul should have '"habitation among the holy saints in heaven"'. Goring suggests that this type of phrasing would have come naturally to 'those who believed, as did the Lollards, that they belonged to a select company of saints on earth'.[63] Although Graham Mayhew's examination of Sussex Wills has demonstrated the reduction in traditional preambles – with references to the Blessed Virgin and the Saints replaced by affirmations of the testator entrusting to be saved by the merit of Christ's death[64] – Roger Hosmer's will may be read not as evidence of the growth of 'new' Lutheran thought, rather of the continuation in East Sussex of Lollard theology.[65] If Alexander Hosmer shared his father's beliefs, it indicates the variety of Protestantisms which were represented at Lewes in July 1557.

East Grinstead suggests the value of a localised study of Reform, similar to Pullein's study of Rotherfield, one which demonstrates potentially suggestive county connections which can be established between small Sussex communities. East Grinstead was home to four of the Sussex martyrs and site of the burning of three of them: Henry Adlington, Anne (Mother) Tree, Thomas Dungate and John Foreman. Henry Adlington, burnt at Stratford le Bow on 27 June 1556,

---

[60]   Ibid. Pullein argues that the William Ashdown of Rotherfield who appears on the excommunication list was John Ashdown whose wife was executed at Lewes with Woodman and who Lower records as having been subsequently executed: see Pullein, *Rotherfield*, p. 269; Lower, *The Worthies of Sussex*, p. 16. See also Gratwick and Whittick, 'The Loseley List', p. 240.

[61]   Pullein's study of Rotherfield demonstrates the value in such a local study, see *Rotherfield*, pp. 265–75.

[62]   Doran and Freeman suggest that Hosmer, Maynard and a Wood were from Ashridge in Kent, see appendix to *Mary Tudor*.

[63]   Goring, 'Reform and reaction', p. 149.

[64]   Ibid., p. 150

[65]   See Goring's comment, 'it is likely that in the Weald of Sussex ... some of the Marian martyrs came from families with a long tradition of Lollardy': 'Reform and reactions', p. 149.

was arrested while visiting Stephen Gratwick while the latter was in prison. Gratwick was from Brighton and may have known Carver. Freeman suggests that Gratwick was a former Free Willer.[66] The connection with Gratwick may allow us to speculate about the orthodoxy of Adlington's Protestantism and from that to question the type of Protestantism in East Grinstead. It is possible that Anne Tree, executed on 18 July 1556, had been radicalised by someone from the first generation of English Reform. Goring suggests that Thomas Hoth, the former precentor of the Augustinian New Priory in Hastings, ministered in East Grinstead.[67] Hoth had been charged in May 1533 with rejecting purgatory, tithes and payment on the four offering days, and of supporting clerical marriage, a vernacular translation of the New Testament, and justification by faith. Welch suggests that Hoth's confession was influenced by Cambridge Protestantism;[68] as with Whit in Rye, there is the suggestion of the importing of Protestant ideas into Sussex.

If Goring is correct about Hoth's career after his heresy charge, a direct link can be drawn between East Grinstead in the 1550s and Reformist intent of the 1530s, demonstrating the historical survival in Sussex of early Henrician Protestantism. However, if this is the case, no reference survives in the account of Mother Tree and her two fellow martyrs, Dungate and Foreman. As for Hoth, it is possible that he is the Thomas Athoth who is named in a list of martyrs within Chichester Diocese that Foxe includes in the 1570 and 1576 editions of *Acts and Monuments*.[69] Gratwick and Whittick suggest that 'Athoth' is a mistake for Thomas Whood, who was executed at Lewes on 20 June 1556.[70] If Hoth, Athoth and Whood are the same person, it suggests a peripatetic ministry for Hoth/Athoth/Whood over the course of two decades, allowing for a degree of doctrinal influence over Sussex's burgeoning Protestant population.

The question of historic influence and previous appearances before ecclesiastical courts is also relevant in the case of Margery Morris who was burnt with Woodman and her son in 1557. Morris had been in trouble in 1551 for two years' non-attendance at Communion;[71] her husband John was charged in 1552

---

[66]   Freeman <http://www.johnfoxe.org/freeman-marion.pdf>.

[67]   Goring, 'Reform and reaction', p. 149. Goring does not provide any dates, nor does he elaborate on the term 'radicalised' in relation to Anne Tree. The charge against Tree in 1556 was failure to attend church: see, *Mary Tudor*, Doran and Freeman, eds, p. 249.

[68]   Welch, 'Three Sussex heresy trials', pp. 61–2.

[69]   John Foxe, *TAMO* (1570 edition).

[70]   Gratwick and Whittick, 'The Loseley List', p. 232.

[71]   Goring, 'Reformation and reaction', p. 149. Roger Davey gives the date of this charge as 1552: see 'Three Lewes Martyrs of 1557' in *SAC*, 138 (2000): 231–4, at p. 232. Goring may be

with refusal to pay his tithes.[72] The Morris family were radical Protestants. Margery's failure to receive the sacrament – 'even in its purified post-1548 form'[73] – indicates someone separated from the Edwardian Church, a member of a family who can be described as 'holding radical sacramentarian views akin to those of the Lollards'.[74] In Margery Morris's pseudo-Lollardy, there is the suggestion of a radical historic version of Protestantism in Marian Sussex, a proponent of which was burnt alongside the orthodox figure of Woodman. Of course, there is no mention in *Acts and Monuments* of Margery Morris's problems with the Edwardian Church and her probable heterodox beliefs regarding the Eucharist. Rather, she achieves orthodoxy through her death, and through her proximity to Woodman. As such, Woodman provides orthodoxy by proxy and his narrative in *Acts and Monuments* performs an important narrative and rhetorical function, demonstrating at a local level the veracity of Foxe's ideological and narrative design.

Woodman: Writing Martyrdom

Although the Woodman narrative can be read so as to provide a model of Protestant orthodoxy,[75] one which was overlaid onto other, less obviously

referring to April 1552 when Margery Morris was excommunicated as a result of her failure to carry out the penance imposed for non-attendance in 1551, see Davey, ibid.

[72]   Goring, 'Reformation and reaction', p. 149; Davey, 'Three Lewes Martyrs', p. 232.

[73]   Goring, 'Reformation and reaction', pp. 149–50.

[74]   Ibid., p. 150. Sacramentarian views are also discernible in Sussex during the 1530s. John Hoggesflesh of Lewes appeared before Sherbourne in October 1534 accused among other things of receiving the Host without priestly confession and denial of the Real Presence. Hoggesflesh was examined on 23 July and appealed to Scripture in order to prove his opinions. In an example of how uncertain religious belief had become in England, Sherbourne wrote to Cranmer regarding Hoggesflesh's 'heresies'. Cranmer may have consulted Cromwell and Henry VIII before finally condemning Hoggesflesh on 8 November. Norfolk also wrote to Sherbourne concerning the Hoggesflesh case, see Welch, 'Three Sussex heresy trials', p. 66.

[75]   Woodman was co-opted in the seventeenth century by figures in opposition to the Protestant Church establishment: William Prynne's 1637 text *A Quench-Coal* includes a large section of Woodman's account of his second examination. Prynne utilised Woodman's prolonged rejection of the altar in order to provide historical justification for his own opposition to Archbishop Laud's campaign of church reform which included the repositioning of the communion table, a move denounced as a restoration of the altar, see *The Quench-Coal or the brief disquistion and enquiry in what place of the Church or chancel the Lord's table might be situated* (London, 1637), pp. 129–32. Woodman was also used by William Penn in his 1673 refutation of John Faldo's claims that Quakerism was un-Christian: see *The invalidity of John Faldo's vindication of his book*

orthodox Protestants executed in Sussex during the reign of Mary, the account of Woodman's arrests and execution also demonstrates both the construction of a martyrdom text and the complex nature of Reform at a local level. Woodman's narrative reveals an erudite figure, one whose mastery of scripture is such that he is able to defeat the sophistic arguments of his Roman Catholic examiners. Andrew Pettegree states:

> ... who could doubt that some people, such as ... Richard Woodman ... were the authentic voice of English Protestantism? The hand of God was visible to all ... in the patient untutored eloquence of these simple folk as they laid out their beliefs before petulant and exasperated inquisitors.[76]

A reader of the Woodman narrative may question how 'untutored' and 'simple' Woodman was; the purported autobiographical text which Foxe reproduces in *Acts and Monuments* contains stylistic features which either suggest that Woodman was a sophisticated writer making use of deliberate biblical allusion, or that Foxe's role as editor extended beyond simply imposing the standard presentational features of *Acts and Monuments* upon Woodman's text. In keeping with the rest of Foxe's history, all of the examinations are printed as dialogues between Woodman and his interrogators. There is also some evidence that the version of Woodman's narrative which appeared in the 1563 edition of *Acts and Monuments* was a partial version of the iteration which appears in 1570, resulting in Foxe making slight alterations in order to integrate the 'new' material.[77] If

---

called *Quakerism no Christianity: Being a rejoinder in Defence of answer entitled Quakerism a new nick name for Old Christianity* (London, 1673), p. 341. Although Prynne's incorporation of part of the Woodman narrative from Foxe may demonstrate that Prynne's mode of Protestantism was closer to the Protestant orthodoxy of the Edwardian Church, it is more difficult to reconcile Woodman's Protestantism with Penn's Non-conformity.

[76]   Andrew Pettegree, *Marian Protestantism: Six Studies* (Aldershot: Scolar Press, 1996), p. 115.

[77]   The Woodman narrative in the 1563 edition of *Acts and Monuments* opens with the copy of a letter sent by Woodman to a local Protestant woman called Roberts. This is followed by a subtitle that reads 'The examination of Richard Woodman before the bishop of Chichester as it was reported his own handwriting'. This account opens with the line 'Furthermore, you shall understand that I was sent from the Sheriff's to London on the 12th day of April in the year of our Lord God 1557', before detailing the first interrogation before Christopherson, Story and Cooke. The adverb 'Furthermore' has nothing to do with the preceding letter to Mrs Roberts and suggests something is missing. The version of Woodman's narrative as it appears in the 1570 edition of *Acts and Monuments* moves the Roberts letter to the end of the section on Woodman, opens with longer prefatory material by Foxe and includes an expanded narrative which details Woodman's

these stylistic and syntactical changes are the extent of Foxe's editorial processes, then Woodman cast himself as a Christ-like figure through use of pointed biblical quotation. Woodman informs the reader they 'shall perceive how the scriptures be partly fulfilled on me,'[78] before declaring 'woe unto him by whom I am betrayed: it had been good for that man that he had never been born'.[79] It is the first of a number of occasions at which Woodman compares himself to, or co-opts the words of, Christ.[80] He is even betrayed by someone he knows, and dragged away in the middle of the night. The affect is to enhance Woodman's status as martyr by making him a version of a biblical mode of suffering.[81]

That Woodman was of some note within sections of the Protestant community in the eastern half of Sussex is established during his first examination when he is informed that 'All the heretics in the county hang on ... [you] as the people in times past upon St. Augustine or St. Ambrose'.[82] The letter to a fellow Protestant, Mrs. Roberts, which appears in the narrative, also indicates a figure whose advice and opinions were sought. It may be that Woodman preached to local communities;[83] this possibility caused concern for the Catholic authorities, hence the question about Woodman preaching at a fair which was put by Christopherson during his first examination.[84] Although J.W Martin is probably correct that Woodman organised no known congregation,[85] the evidence would seem to suggest that Woodman did fulfil some type of pastoral or ministerial

---

initial arrest and imprisonment in 1554, his release, avoidance of further capture, his three weeks in northern Europe, his six weeks in the woods near his home and his final recapture. This section ends with Woodman being taken from the Gages' house at Firle and would lead naturally to the existing line 'Furthermore you shall understand that I was sent from the Sheriff's to London'. However, the line in the 1570 edition reads '*First* you shall understand that I was sent from the Sheriff's to London'. The replacement of 'furthermore' with 'first' looks like an editorial mistake. See John Foxe, *TAMO* (1570 edition).

[78]   Foxe, *A&M*, p. 334. John Foxe, *TAMO* (1570 edition).

[79]   Ibid., p. 338.

[80]   Ibid., pp. 339, 47.

[81]   The account of John Rough's interrogation by Bonner sees Rough transformed into a version of the Suffering Servant from Isaiah 50: see Paul Quinn, 'John Rough's beard and Isaiah', *Notes and Queries*, 56 (2009): 552–3. The account of John Rough is expanded in the 1570 edition of *Acts and Monuments*, the reference to Bonner's tearing at Rough's beard appears for the first time in this edition; see Foxe, *A&M*, pp. 339, 47. John Foxe, *TAMO* (1570 edition).

[82]   Foxe, *A&M*, p. 345. John Foxe, *TAMO* (1570 edition).

[83]   Freeman states that Woodman became an itinerant preacher after his release from prison in 1555/6, see 'Woodman, Richard', *DNB*.

[84]   Foxe, *A&M*, pp. 342–3. John Foxe, *TAMO* (1570 edition).

[85]   J.W. Martin, *Religious Radicals in Tudor England* (London and Ronceverte: The Hambledon Press, 1989), p. 128.

function. Woodman is clear that he did not perform the tasks of an ordained minster,[86] but that does not preclude his role as preacher or spiritual adviser. When Woodman recounted his flight to the woods, he informed his reader that he took with him his Bible, his pen and his ink.[87] Text is at the centre of the Woodman narrative and the narrative itself can function as a continuation of Woodman's role in guiding the community of Sussex Protestants with who he was in doctrinal accord.

However, Woodman's initial arrest in June 1554 was not a result of preaching, nor was he arrested on anti-heresy legislation. Rather, Woodman fell foul of an Act passed during the first Parliament of Mary's reign, the Act 'Against offenders of preachers and other ministers of the Church' (1 Mary c. 3).[88] The Act was designed to avoid incidents like the disruption of the first public Roman Catholic sermon of Mary's reign in which the preacher, Gilbert Bourne, was heckled and had a knife thrown at him.[89] Woodman had reproved 'a preacher in the pulpit in the parish of Warbleton,[90] this lead to his apprehension and his appearance before Sussex's Justices of the Peace – John Ashburnham, Tonston, Culpepper and Roberts.[91] Woodman's own account details his appearance before two quarter sessions which resulted in his imprisonment; these periods of incarceration were followed by two further appearances before the sessions, two examinations by George Day, Bishop of Chichester, and five interrogations by the commissioners before being sent to London in the custody of Bishop Bonner. Woodman then

---

[86] See the discussion of baptism above.

[87] Foxe, *A&M*, p. 336. John Foxe, *TAMO* (1570 edition).

[88] Eamon Duffy, *Fires of Faith: Catholic England under Mary Tudor* (New Haven, CT and London: Yale University Press, 2010), p. 86; Freeman, 'Woodman, Richard', *DNB*.

[89] Duffy, *Fires of Faith*, p. 86.

[90] Foxe, *A&M*, p. 334. John Foxe, *TAMO* (1570 edition). Foxe states that the preacher was George Fairbank, a man who, during the reign of Edward 'often persuaded the people not to credit any other doctrine but that, which he then preached, taught and set forth'. On the accession of Mary, Fairbank, 'turning head to tail', denounced his previous positions and accepted the restoration of Roman Catholicism, despite the fact that he had married: Foxe, *A&M*, p. 333. John Foxe, *TAMO* (1570 edition). The major drawback to Foxe's narrative is that Fairbank had left Warbleton in 1552: see Goring, 'Reform and reaction', p. 150, where an analysis of formulations in Wills indicates that Fairbank was vicar of Tarring Neville from 1552 onwards. The Church of England clergy database lists George Fairbank as rector of Tarring Neville from September 1552 to March 1561, with George Farybaux as curate of Warbleton in 1551. The rectors of Warbleton in 1554 were Aristotle Webb and Thomas Browne: see <www.theclergydatabase.org.uk/jsp/persons/index.jsp>.

[91] Foxe *A&M*, p. 333. John Foxe, *TAMO* (1570 edition). Michael Questier has identified Culpepper as Alexander Culpepper who would subsequently marry into the Montague family: *Catholicism and Community*, p. 163.

spent eighteen months in the King's Bench, followed by eight weeks in Bonner's coalhouse before being released in December 1555.[92] This period in the King's Bench coincided with the debates between the Predestinarians and the Free Willers but the narrative is silent as to this controversy.

The Woodman narrative states that after his release 'the Papists said that I [Woodman] has consented to them'.[93] To counter this accusation of apostasy, Woodman 'went from parish to parish, and talked with them to the number of 13. or 14. and that of the chiefest in all the country'.[94] The result of this preaching tour was a complaint to the Lord Chamberlain and the accusation from Sir John Gage that Woodman had baptised children and performed marriages. The narrative refutes these charges, declaring them to be a means 'to bring me into their hands again'.[95] Prefiguring the later discussion with Christopherson about baptism, Woodman denies performing rites that – within both the Roman Catholic and the Elizabethan Church – were the preserve of ordained ministers. Woodman once again established his own Edwardian/Elizabethan orthodoxy which would set him apart from other, more radical Sussex Protestants during the reign of Mary.

Woodman's public defence of his continuing Protestantism was the cause of the warrant which was issued in 1556; Woodman successfully evaded arrest for several weeks, including six weeks concealed in the woods near his home, three weeks in France and Flanders, and then a period of time at home making use of a hiding space constructed in the roof.[96] It was from here that Woodman attempted to escape in March 1557 when Sir Edward Gage, the Sheriff of Sussex, arrived to search the house.[97] Gage appeared at the house as a result of having received information as to Woodman's whereabouts from Woodman's father or brother; the pretext for the act of betrayal was not religious scruples, rather a business disagreement between Richard Woodman and members of his family.[98] Woodman's assertion of Edwardian orthodoxy, and his ministry to

---

[92]   Foxe, *A&M*, p. 334. John Foxe, *TAMO* (1570 edition). Woodman dates his release with reference to the burning of John Philpot (18 December). Freeman's *ODNB* entry gives Woodman's date of release as November 1555. Freeman's account of Woodman's first arrest and examination by various figures in the Marian legal and ecclesiastical hierarchy is less convoluted than the version which appears in *Acts and Monuments*.

[93]   Fox, *A&M*, p. 334. John Foxe, *TAMO* (1570 edition).

[94]   Ibid.

[95]   Ibid.

[96]   Ibid., p. 336.

[97]   Ibid., pp. 336–7.

[98]   Ibid., p. 336. See also Gratwick and Whittick, 'The Loseley List', pp. 225–40.

other Sussex Protestants, fatally interconnected with familial, financial and local industrial concerns.

This financial motivation leading to an arrest under the auspices of anti-heresy legislation may have been a repetition of the events surrounding Woodman's earlier arrest in 1554; John Ashburnham, one of the sheriffs who arrested Woodman after his public criticism of the preacher in Warbleton may have been involved in the iron industry – the Ashburnhams were certainly key members of the Wealden iron industry by 1574.[99] If John Ashburnham was an ironmaster, he may have used the pretext of Woodman's complaints as a means to remove a local rival.

The role played by Ashburnham in the first arrest and Gage in the second recalls the combination of national policy and local governance at work in the arrest of many of the Marian martyrs. The enforcement of the central government's policy of the re-imposition of Roman Catholic doctrine and restoration of orthodoxy was undertaken by the local ecclesiastical and secular hierarchy. In Sussex, several of those responsible for the arrests of Woodman were members of the Roman Catholic families who dominated county politics and who would continue to occupy important roles until the 1580s; as such, the figures who were responsible for the arrests and punishments of Sussex Protestants as part of the imposition of Marian religious policies were the same figures who prevented Bishop Curteys's attempt to impose conformity upon the county in the 1570s.[100] Chief among those involved in the Woodman case were the Brownes and the Gages. A client of the Browne family, Culpepper, was present at the first arrest of Woodman. The Browne connection continued during the examinations after Woodman's second arrest. Woodman's third examination (12 May 1557) took place at Montague House in Southwark, while the fifth (15 June 1557) occurred at Browne's parish church in Southwark.[101] Alban Langdale, Vicar of Buxted and later chaplain to Browne, took part in the third and fifth examinations. Langdale

---

[99]   The lack of a complete list of Wealden Ironmasters during the Tudor period is a major drawback to identifying who was an ironmaster. The only surviving lists which 'have any claim to completeness' date from 1574, see J.J. Goring, 'Wealden Ironmasters in the Age of Elizabeth', in *Wealth and Power in Tudor England*, E.W. Ives, R.J. Knecht and J.J. Scarisbrick, eds (London: The Athlone Press, 1978), pp. 204–27, at p. 205. For the Ashburnham family's place in the industry, see pp. 211, 215–16, 219.

[100]   Manning, *Religion and Society in Elizabethan Sussex*, pp 64–90, 113–25.

[101]   Questier, *Catholicism and Community*, p. 163. Montague House would become a suspect site during the reigns of Elizabeth I and James I with searches made for priests concealed in the building and allegations of suspicious activities prior to the discovery of the Gunpowder Plot: see ibid., pp. 281–2.

had been a disputant against Cranmer, Latimer and Ridley in Oxford in 1554.[102] The Gage family were particularly involved in the Woodman case. Edward Gage arrested Woodman in 1556, Woodman was held at the Gage house in Firle for three weeks and James Gage, Edward's brother, was also present at Woodman's third examination. Although the Gages have been described as 'zealous' in 'identifying and presenting recalcitrant elements in Sussex for examination,'[103] that determination to expunge heresy from the county did not extend to all members of the Sussex hierarchy, either secular or ecclesiastical.

Reading the account of Woodman's examinations, it is clear that Christopherson, Bishop of Chichester, was not actively seeking Woodman's death, rather Woodman was offered various verbal and doctrinal escape routes.[104] Woodman and Christopher had dinner together after the first examination and Christopher declared 'pray God I may do you some good'.[105] Christopherson appears to have attempted to avoid any judgement at all, arguing that he did not posses 'full authority' as he had not yet been ordained at that point.[106] Lower went so far as to correct the impression of Christopherson in Thomas Fuller's *Worthies of Sussex* in which Christopherson was described as 'Junior Bonner'.[107] Although Christopherson was correct when he stated that he did not have ecclesiastical jurisdiction over Woodman until he was ordained bishop, it is possible that we can detect a lack of enthusiasm for the task of correcting the Sussex iron master. There is evidence from the mid-sixteenth century of recalcitrance on the part of the ecclesiastical authorities of Sussex in the enforcement of religious orthodoxy. Richard Sherbourne left the implementation of the Henrician Reforms to William Howe, who was equally unenthusiastic about the changes mandated by Henry VIII and Cromwell; Richard Sampson was suspected of being opposed to religious change and was imprisoned by Cromwell; George Day refused to enforce the Reforms and was deprived and imprisoned in 1550. In August 1554, Sussex's JPs were ordered to be 'more diligent in punishing "such evil, disordered

---

[102]   Kitch, 'The Chichester Cathedral Chapter at the time of the Reformation', *SAC*, 117 (1978): 277–92, at p. 289; Questier, *Catholicism and Community*, p. 163.

[103]   Gratwick and Whittick, 'The Loseley List', p. 230. John Trewe made a complaint against Edward Gage in 1559, alleging that Gage had pilloried him at Hailsham and Lewes during the reign of Mary and had cut off his ears; see 'The Loseley List', p. 228.

[104]   See, in particular, Woodman's first examination (14 April 1557); Duffy, *Fires of Faith*, pp. 144–6.

[105]   Foxe, *A&M*, p. 345. John Foxe, *TAMO* (1570 edition).

[106]   Ibid., pp. 343, 372. See also Freeman, 'Woodman, Richard', *DNB*.

[107]   Lower, *Worthies of Sussex*, p. 147. Fuller's book had the same title.

persons as use to rail upon the mysteries of Christ's religion'".[108] Christopherson's reluctance to correct and punish Woodman may stem from the same essentially conservative approach as his predecessors at Chichester. A reluctance to burn Woodman may have stemmed from the lack of burnings in Sussex during the Lollard suppressions in the fifteenth century.

It is certainly the case that Christopherson did not decide Woodman's fate. Rather, Woodman was ultimately the victim of familiar Foxean villains – Nicholas Harpsfield, John Story and Edmund Bonner.[109] At the moment of condemnation, Woodman became subsumed beneath the uniform martyr-narrative in *Acts and Monuments*. He assures the readership of his Protestant orthodoxy by denying the most contentious areas of Roman Catholic doctrine and his Protestantism is affirmed by his burning. He is opposed to, and condemned by, the 'blood thirsty' Bonner who was 'like to have blood to drink in hell'.[110] He suffers the shared fate of the majority of Foxe's martyrs. He becomes a victim of national policy. Woodman's orthodoxy is read against the model found in the rest of *Acts and Monuments*; in the same way, Foxe's later readers read Sussex Protestantism through Woodman and through an extrapolation of the other county martyrs based on Woodman's narrative and Foxe's censored account of Carver. In so doing, they ignored or obscured the historical nature of elements of Sussex Protestantism; they failed to address the problematic relationship between early English Non-conformity, Edwardian Protestantism, and continental Reformed thought, and they omitted analysis of the complex interconnection of religion, family and commerce in Sussex. This misreading is the result of Foxe's appropriation of the Woodman narrative, which was transformed into a fantasy vision of local Protestantism, sacrificed for later, national hegemony.

---

[108] Goring, 'Reform and reaction', p. 148.

[109] Alban's name can be added to this list of national persecutors. Although he was a regional ecclesiastical figure, his role in the Oxford debates – and his opposition to Cranmer, Latimer and Ridley – gave Langdale a national prominence. This may account for the portrayal of his active hostility towards Woodman which we find in *Acts and Monuments*.

[110] Foxe, *A&M*, p. 334. John Foxe, *TAMO* (1570 edition).

Chapter 9

'The Happy Preserver of his Brother's Posterity': From Monumental Text to Sculptural Figure in Early Modern Sussex

Nigel Llewellyn

Figure 9.1   Monument to John Ashburnham (d. 1671) and his wives, erected c. 1673(?), Ashburnham; © Author.

Figure 9.2   Monument to William Ashburnham (d. 1679) and his wife
               Jane, Countess of Marlborough (d. 1672), erected c. 1674(?),
               Ashburnham; © Author.

Now in remote farmland, in the seventeenth century, the Ashburnham estate lay
in East Sussex's iron-industrial region.[1] In the early 1670s, William Ashburnham –
the family were named for the place – erected two substantial funeral monuments
here, which despite their proximity in time, are different from one another in ways
that demand explanation (see Figures 9.1 and 9.2).[2]

---

[1]   H. Cleere and D. Crossley, *The Iron Industry of the Weald*, 2nd edn, J. Hodgkinson, ed.,
Cardiff: Merton Priory Press, 1995.

[2]   Commentators on Ashburnham have largely ignored the close dating of these two
monuments and there have been few comments on the John Ashburnham tomb. What observers
have commented on – usually adversely – is the baroque quality of the William Ashburnham
tomb. I gave an account of two other wall monuments, found to be co-terminal (from the 1570s)
which show remarkably different stylistic characteristics, but where style does not appear to have
been an issue for the patron, see 'Accident or Design? John Gildon's funeral monuments and
Italianate taste in Elizabethan England', in *England and the Continental Renaissance: Essays in
Honour of J.B. Trapp*, E. Chaney and P. Mack, eds, Woodbridge: Boydell, 1990, pp. 143–52.

The first, a wall-tomb for William's brother, John and John's two wives, was conservative in form and purpose, while the monument to William's late wife, took the unprecedented form of a tableau. This second monument was perhaps the first in England that sought to exploit the emotional potential of a free-standing, gesturing figure. This chapter explains the contrasting aims of the Ashburnham monuments and explores how the design of the second one challenged the existing forms and discursive possibilities for the genre as it had developed in East Sussex since the Reformation.

In common with many English counties, seventeenth-century commemorative art in Sussex comprises almost entirely tombs erected by and for social elites. There are substantial wall monuments – like those at Ashburnham – as well as smaller murals, engraved brasses and ledger-stones, all of which record and proclaim virtues and achievements, plot careers and proclaim lineages – some invented – of individuals and families. As they construct narratives and identities, attract attention, make claims, establish positions, negotiate tensions between individuals and the state, clans, relatives, enemies and rivals, and record emotional responses to bereavement, these works of art use a complex interwoven set of four languages: architectural framing, sculpture, heraldry and the inscribed word.[3]

Although monuments meet a universal need, local particularities play an important role: Sussex tombs had specific Sussex contexts. London, the great centre for monument-making, was no great distance but in this period, Sussex was no 'home' county, being isolated by its non-transportable roads, 'a fruitful county, though very dirty for the travellers therein'.[4] It also had a coastal border with an enemy state, France. Furthermore, Sussex protected local pockets of ideological opposition on questions of religion and royal authority: such conflicts were sometimes referred in monumental inscriptions.[5] Indeed, tombs were used to communicate their subjects' positions on religious change, political allegiance, clan rivalry and sectarian difference. Although the inscriptions on tombs were public statements and often in Latin, only readable by the literate minority, they were capable of startling personal intimacies. Monumental inscriptions were highly formalised in their structure and orthography and communicated complex information about ritual and

---

[3]   For a full exposition of this approach to monuments see Nigel Llewellyn, *Funeral Monuments in post-Reformation England* (Cambridge: Cambridge University Press, 2000), *passim*.

[4]   Thomas Fuller quoted in Kim Leslie and Brian Short, *An Historical Atlas of Sussex* (Chichester: Phillimore, 1999), p. 69

[5]   Malcolm Kitch, ed., *Studies in Sussex Church History*, London, 1981.

social differentiation. Yet when written on ledger-stones, set into the church floor, such texts were often trodden underfoot.

This chapter argues that in the 1670s there was a telling shift from the verbal – expressed in different thematic paradigms – to the figural.[6] Some tombs addressed matters of state and were used as public signs of loyalty to the prince, while others addressed questions of devotional orthodoxy. These were some of the many important didactic roles demanded of post-Reformation monuments. Sussex's important set of patrician or quasi-patrician monuments, including the remarkable and contrasting Ashburnham tombs of the mid-1670s, also expressed over-arching anxieties about dynastic continuity.

Loyalty to the Prince

We start at Battle where the sense of social change that accompanied the dissolution of the abbey in 1538 must have been portentous.[7] The fear that the secularisation and domestication of the abbot's monastic quarters would disrupt the social order of the small town at its gates, may have encouraged the new lord, Sir Anthony Browne (c. 1500–48) – not a radical thinker by any means – to maintain continuity by fitting out a courthouse, both a useful public facility and a symbol of authority. But Browne also built himself a monument on the north side of the abbey church sanctuary (see Figure 9.3).[8]

The monument took the traditional form of a free-standing tomb-chest bearing recumbent effigies of Browne and of his recently dead wife. Its progressive Renaissance decoration is rare in Henrician England and has received some art-historical attention; however, it is the detailed portrayal of Browne's armour and heraldic escutcheons emblazoned along the long sides of the tomb-chest that would have caught the eye of a Tudor onlooker. The literate minority may well have paused over the prominent monumental inscription, incised in English on the chamfered top edge, which emphasises Browne's loyalty to his prince and

  [6] The ideas argued here were generated in the context of 'Court, Country, City: Art in Britain 1660–1735, a research project funded by the Arts and Humanities Research Council and located at the University of York and Tate and led by Professor Mark Hallett. The material on East Sussex monuments was gathered in an earlier AHRC-funded project, for which see Nigel Llewellyn, *East Sussex Church Monuments 1530–1830* (hereinafter *ESCM*) Chichester: Sussex Records Society, vol. 93, 2011). Grateful acknowledgement is duly made to the AHRC for its support.
  [7] Maurice Howard, *The Early Tudor Country House* (London: Hamlyn, 1987), p. 204.
  [8] Exactly where remains unclear, see Llewellyn, *ESCM*, pp. 26–7 and plate 12.

Figure 9.3   Monument to Sir Anthony Browne (d. 1548) and his wife Alice
Gage (d. 1540), Battle; © Author.

confirms his high status in the immediate orbit of the king. Since there is no
mention of Edward VI, this text must have been composed between 1540 when
Browne's wife, Alice Gage, died and early 1547, when Henry himself died. It starts:
'... Sir Anthony Browne, Knight of the Garter, Master of the King's Majesty's
Horse and one of the honourable Privy Council of our most dread sovereign
Lord and victorious prince King Henry the Eighth ... '[spelling modernised].

Its ending – 'On whose soul and all Christians, Jesus have mercy' – gives
vernacular expression to orthodox, devotional sentiments by assuming that the
souls of the dead lay still within reach of the living. It reflects Browne's determined
conservatism, expressed here at a time when the political balances across Henry's
realm were becoming ever more fragile and the young King Edward and his
radically inclined circle were about to take England in quite new directions. As
later antiquaries noted, texts like this offered later iconoclasts an excuse to molest
or destroy an inscription or even a whole tomb.[9] Browne had erected this tomb

---

[9]   John Weever, *Ancient Funerall Monuments*, London, 1631, pp. 50 ff; Llewellyn, *Funeral
Monuments*, p. 258; on the general issue, Phillip Lindley, *Tomb Destruction and Scholarship.
Medieval Monuments in Early Modern England* (Donington: Shaun Tyas Publishing, 2007).

himself and as he prayed alongside his effigy, he might have reflected on the dangers of using monuments for too overt propagandising, intended as they were to stand in perpetuity against the vagaries of change. Indeed, monumental texts could age and inadvertently expose dynastic descendants to question or even ruin. The risks attendant on the astonishing inscription written about Thomas Eade on his ledger at Chiddingly, 150 years later, by which time the Hanoverians were secure on the English throne, must have daunted his immediate descendants:

> The body of **Mr Thomas Eade** lies here.
> A faithful shepherd that did not pow'rs fear;
> But kept old Truth, and would not let her go,
> Nor turn out of the way for Friend or foe.
> Who was suspended in the Dutchman's days,
> Because he would not walk in their Strang ways
> *Daemona non armis sed morte subegit Iesus*
> As Christ by death is Rampant foes trodd on
> So must all those who doe expect a crown.
> He died 1717, Aged about 80 Years.[10]

Monumental inscriptions indicate how religious tensions like those at Battle – and evidently at Chiddingly – continued to resonate in post-Reformation Sussex. Tomb-patrons used monuments to state their loyalty, but as the Tudors became more firmly established and were succeeded by the Stuarts, needs changed. The remarkable series at Isfield, erected c. 1530–c. 1630, illustrate this pattern of change. The founder of the family fortunes was John Shurley (d. 1527), who had five children from two marriages and built a house at Isfield and a family chapel in the church. Leaving room for tombs to his successors, Shurley built an ambitious monument using expensive Dorset stone.[11] He was intent on establishing a dynasty and found that putting up monuments was a valuable means towards that end. He equipped his chapel with a squinch so that the family could sit in prestigious isolation in their 'pew' amongst the ancestral tombs, but still able to see the high altar during the Mass. In his will, Shurley requested a brass effigy and heraldry and his epitaph proudly lists his relatively minor court offices: Clerk of the Kitchen to Henry VII and Cofferer to Henry VIII (see Figure 9.4).

---

10   Llewellyn, *ESCM*, no. 56P.
11   Ibid., no. 145A.

Figure 9.4   Monument to John Shurley (d. 1527), erected c. 1530, Isfield;
              © Author.

Over many years, Shurley's descendants followed his lead and more monuments were built, one to his third son and heir, Edward Shurley (d. 1558) and his spouse, Joan Fenner and another to John's grandson, Thomas Shurley (d. 1579) and to Thomas's wife (died young in April 1571). By the 1570s, the religious and political context had changed markedly, Anglicanism was established, though still resented in many parts of Sussex. But by now, the Shurleys had been at Isfield for as long as almost anyone could remember and the changed political circumstances caused a shift in commemorative policy, not a devaluation of monuments themselves but a new approach towards monumental inscriptions.

The text on Edward's monument links clearly to the dynastic founder by naming his father's wives and their progeny and by referring to John as the king's Cofferer. By contrast, Thomas Shurley's inscription is almost entirely about local Sussex intermarriages, with the Laughton Pelhams and the Buckhurst Sackvilles. This is the pattern that is retained in the fourth and final Shurley monument, to

Figure 9.5   Monument to Sir John Shurley (d. 1631) and his wives, erected
              c. 1635, Isfield; © Author.

Sir John (died 1631) and his two wives, Jane, a Wiston Shurley, and Dorothy
Goring of Danny, which was the great house at Hurstpierpoint about ten miles
(and ten narrow parishes) due west of Isfield. No expense was spared in this
final Shurley commission, which exhausted the remaining available space in the
chapel (see Figure 9.5).

A top-flight London maker – William Wright – was employed, although
had he sent an assistant down to Sussex to check the site or had he been better
briefed by the patron, he would surely have faced Sir John's nine children
towards the high altar of the tiny church rather than towards the family
pew.[12] The drafting of the inscription must have been left to a family friend by
Shurley's widow. Its final couplets stress Sir John's fame, magnanimity, justice
and stout performance in good causes and Dorothy's own female virtues –

---

[12]   For the attribution to Wright, see Adam White, *A Biographical Dictionary of London
Tomb Sculptors c.1560–1660* (London: Walpole Society, vol. 61, 1999), p. 147.

Figure 9.6   Monument to Sir John Gage (d. 1556), erected 1595, (West) Firle; © Author.

charity, generosity, sympathy, piety and devotion. What the Shurley series suggests is that although loyalty to the ruling dynasty (or prevailing polity) is a major issue in the earlier sixteenth century and could be communicated by text, by heraldry and by reference to continuity of dynasty and estate, by the later seventeenth, it was an issue that was increasingly taken for granted. The monument to Anne Shurley's father, Sir Nicholas Pelham (d. 1559), substantial parts of which survive at St Michael's, Lewes, makes much of his heroic defence of Seaford against the French but remains silent about his troubled political career.[13]

The question of loyalty, so challenging under Elizabeth and then again in the mid-seventeenth century, is the key to understanding the Gage monuments at West Firle. These are the best documented of all Elizabethan

---

[13]   Llewellyn, *ESCM*, no. 160D; Pelham was on dangerously poor terms with the Duke of Northumberland in the early 1550s.

Figure 9.7   Monument to Sir Edward Gage (d. 1556), erected 1595,
              (West) Firle; © Author.

tombs in Sussex and they result from a unified campaign of tomb-patronage, undertaken by John Gage (d. 1598) in 1595, the date recorded on his own monument. Three monuments survive plus some loose brasses: first, a free-standing tomb to the patron's grandfather, Sir John (d. 1556) and his wife Philippa, followed by two pendant wall-tombs commemorating first, the patron's father, Sir Edward (d. 1569) and his wife Elizabeth and second, the patron himself, John Gage and his two wives, another Elizabeth and Margaret (see Figures 9.6, 9.7 and 9.8).[14]

The additional collections of brasses, which commemorate two of John Gage's brothers and have lost their original settings were probably on the former south wall of the family chapel, a space now occupied by an organ.[15] Before this, the arrangement adopted at Firle was probably close to that at Isfield. The inscriptions, together with the surviving documents, reveal the motives and personality of John Gage, who was a tomb-patron driven by a mixed set of significant forces. Most powerful amongst them was his

---

[14]   Ibid., nos 281D–F.
[15]   Ibid., nos 281B–C.

Figure 9.8   Monument to John Gage (d. 1598), erected 1595,
               (West) Firle; © Author.

interest in restoring his family's reputation, tainted by the stigma of recusant
Catholicism that had hung over the politically loyal Gages throughout
Elizabeth's long reign. Furthermore, in 1595, Gage had just lost his second
wife: he was old and childless, and was contemplating mortality. Indeed, he
died three years later.

The Firle tombs establish an honourable memory for Gage and for his
ancestors displaying their monumental bodies without any stigma of recusancy
or disloyalty. Indeed, familial and personal honour is alluded to in the annotated
estimate and contract drawings for these tombs, which include careful
instructions to the tomb-maker, Garret Johnson. Gage's wives were to be depicted
modestly, attired in French hoods coming low over the forehead, and gowns not
fitted but loose, closed in front and covering part of their feet. Furthermore, in a
formula that was becoming increasingly rare, Latin is used in both the inscribed
biographical details and scriptural quotations, chosen because it could address
the educated political elite and perhaps (at Firle) because it was the language of
the unreformed Roman liturgy. The Gage inscriptions stress social status, blood
lineage and public office and the monuments employ a classical architectural

framework, rich and well-worked materials and decorous ornament. However, the Firle tombs do not make much use of figuration: Sir John Gage's carved stone effigies are static, recumbent forms and all the others are engraved on flat brass plates.[16]

True Sons of the Church of England

Anglicanism's effective and continuing authority over the spiritual life of Sussex was, of course, tested many times and the seventeenth-century monuments make some clear references to the conflicting political and religious positions that were taken even within families. At Ringmer, where the Springett family was prominent, the monuments record the tensions that burst into open hostility during the Civil War. After 1660, it became acceptable once again for monumental inscriptions to allude to some of the differences that had determined the previous twenty years of Sussex history. Sir Herbert Springett (d. January 1661, aged 49) had been excluded under the Commonwealth as an MP for New Shoreham – from whence Charles II had embarked for France in 1651 – but with the Restoration had enjoyed – albeit briefly – the return of monarchical government. His ledger-stone in the sanctuary floor at Ringmer declares his late Stuart, Tory position: 'Here lyeth interred the body of Sir Herbert Springett who was a true son of the Church of England and for his love and loyalty to his king and country his death was lamented by all that knew him'.[17] Although probably widespread, the lamentation for Springett's death may not have been universal: a few feet away and overlooked by the mural monument of their father, also Herbert,[18] is the monument to Sir Herbert's twin brother, Sir William,[19] which celebrates his career as a colonel in the service of Parliament, who died of an unspecified 'sicknes" at the siege of

---

[16]   Another Gage monument, which needs to be bracketed with the Firle tombs and is surely part of a co-ordinated family project, is at Framfield a few miles to the north, is also dated 1595 and commemorates Edward Gage, his wife and children (Llewellyn, *ESCM*, no. 110I). This branch of the Gages was settled at Bentley by 1539. As at Firle, the Gage tomb at Framfield uses alabaster framing and engraved brasses typical of the Johnson workshop, but its scale is much smaller than anything surviving at Firle: perhaps the Framfield tomb gives a clue about the form of the lost Firle monuments commemorating the families of John Gage's siblings, from which only the brasses survive.

[17]   Spelling modernised; Llewellyn, *ESCM*, no. 212V.

[18]   Ibid., no. 212FF.

[19]   Ibid., no. 212GG.

Figure 9.9   Monument to Sir William Springett (d. 1643), Ringmer;
© Author.

Arundel, the castle having been taken by Waller from a small royalist garrison in
December 1642, retaken for the king a year later and won back in January 1644
(see Figure 9.9).

William Springett's tomb was erected by his widowed wife, Ann Fagge,
who had her husband portrayed bust-length, gazing calmly out at the spectator
from an oval recess, his status as a fallen hero of timeless virtue alluded to by the
all'antica robes pinned across his shoulder. The portrait bust makes no gesture
or action to give 'testimony of her deare affection to him'. Figuration here is still
subservient to text.

It was the continuation of these Civil War tensions and memories that made
Ringmer an attractive commemorative site for firm statements of loyalty. The
monument to Sir Herbert Whalley (d. 1689),[20] also set up in the Springett
chapel, commemorates a young man, who donated to the church painted panels

---

[20]   Ibid., no. 212Z.

Figure 9.10   Monument to Thomas Delves (d. 1669) and Ann Delves
(d. 1686/7), erected c. 1670, St Clement's, Hastings; © Author.

with the Ten Commandments to flank the Communion Table 'in token of his
zeal for the Church of England'. Similar sentiments to these are engraved on the
now deeply pitted surface of a ledger at Westmeston church recording Richard
Chaloner (d. 1661), '[who] lived an orthodox Christian, feared God, honoured
the King, obeyed the Church and walked the full round of charities'.[21] Pride in
personal loyalty is expressed in a conventional small mural monument erected in
the south aisle of St Clement's, Hastings, the centre of that ancient town's civic
commemorative tradition (see Figure 9.10).

The career of Thomas Delves (d. 1669) peaked when 'he had the Honor of
being one of the Barons of this Ancient Towne ... who carried the Canepy over
King Charles ye second at his coronation'. Indeed, Hastings fiercely protected its
precedence amongst the barons of the Cinque Ports.[22] Delves's monument appears

---

[21]   Ibid., no. 294A.

[22]   C. Dawson reference, see ibid., no. 1250; the staves used by the canopy holders appear to
have been made on each occasion and perhaps presented to the bearers: an object marked ' ... part

Figure 9.11   Ledger-stone for Colonel Herbert Morley (d. 1667), with later brasses, Glynde; © Author.

to have been erected after 1682 by his brother, a City of London alderman. An entirely orthodox late seventeenth-century mural design, it is only the inscribed text that gives voice to Delves's preferment. There are no figural references.

Other monuments from the revolutionary period document the genuine dilemmas faced by individuals and communities. A ledger at Rotherfield to Thomas Theele (d. 1658, aged 70), uses Latin discreetly to offer a flavour of these: 'He was always approached for advice and help by friends through the most difficult of times [and] maintained undiminished his loyalty to god and king'.[23] Another ledger, relocated in the rebuilt church at Glynde, is even more discrete, failing entirely to mention that Colonel Herbert Morley (d. 1667) had been a staunch Parliamentarian (see Figure 9.11).[24]

---

of one of the eight staves ... by which the canopy was borne by the Barons of the Cinque Ports ... 1821' appears as no. 295, plate 181 in the CINOA International Art Treasures Exhibition at the V&A Museum, London in 1962.

[23]   Llewellyn, *ESCM*, no. 216C.

[24]   Ibid., no. 114J.

Figure 9.12   Monument to Sir Thomas Parker (d. 1663) and Sir Robert Parker (d. 1691), Willingdon; © Author.

Two later monuments show prominent landed families negotiating the waves of political convulsion that ended with the flight of James II and the invasion of William III in 1688/89. A standing monument at Willingdon, now a suburb of Eastbourne, again shuns effigies and deploys plenty of heraldry and a huge decorative urn, a symbolic container of the deceased's ashes (see Figure 9.12).

It commemorates Sir Thomas Parker (1595–1663), MP for Seaford in the Long Parliament (1640–48) and his grandson, Sir Robert Parker (1655–91), sometime MP for Hastings, JP and Deputy-Lieutenant, who was outlawed for treason in 1690, arrested on his return from France in 1691, immediately pardoned, only to die the following November.[25] The monument appears to have been erected well after this, and the magnificent inscribed nomenclature on the front gives precedence to the ancestor rather than to the immediate deceased; it is a commemorative formula that represents the triumph of expedience.

---

[25]   Ibid., no. 297A.

Figure 9.13   Monument to Sir George Courthope, erected before (?) his death in 1685, Ticehurst; © Author.

At Ticehurst, similarly careful wording conveys to posterity the loyalty to the Stuarts and the closeness to the royal person of Sir George Courthope (d. 1685), who in the late 1670s both wrote his memoirs and built monuments for himself and his late father, the first Sir George (d. 1642). Since some of the same wording appears in both Sir George's autobiography and in the inscription on his tomb, it is clear that Courthope was his own epigrapher (see Figure 9.13).

By the 1720s, and despite the arrival of the Hanoverians in 1714, the monument to the third Sir George (erected by the fourth) makes no reference to political allegiance or loyalty to the throne.[26] None of the three Courthope monuments, erected over a thirty-year period, use any kind of figuration to communicate the complex sentiments of affection, bereavement, duty, loyalty and service that their tombs express verbally.

---

[26]   Ibid., nos 258E, F and G.

Figure 9.14   Monument to John Thetcher, erected after his death in 1649,
Westham; © Author.

Devotional Orthodoxy

As we saw, in the mid-1540s, Sir Anthony Browne was unabashed in asking for
passers-by to pray for his soul. The same message is communicated via the brass
on the back wall of the Richard Covert monument at Slaugham – '*cuius anime
propicietur deus amen*' – and again on brasses at Lindfield to Stephen and Parnell
Board,[27] which also displays a skull, the standard image of the memento mori. These
accord conventionally with pre-Reformation devotional practice but the public
statement on John Thetcher's monument at Westham (he died 1649) accords but
weakly with his private wish to restore the old religion (see Figure 9.14).[28]

The monument states: '... Iohn Thetcher Esq desended of the antient and
noble familie of the Thetchers of Priesthawes in Sussex and the last of that name
and familie hee dyed without isshew ...' By contrast, his will was addressed

27   Ibid., nos 234D and 164J.
28   Ibid., no. 292W.

Figure 9.15   Monument to Ninian Burrell, erected after his death in 1628,
Cuckfield; © Author.

to 'The Old Brethren', a style of title by then banned in law and disregarded
in the court of probate. Thetcher's demand that his bequest to the church
was conditional on the restoration of Roman Catholicism, the re-erection
of the altar stone and the saying of masses for his soul had to be ignored.
It is not known how the money he left to bring *émigré* Catholic youths from
France to study in England was spent and the monument does little to catch
attention except to deploy a memento mori skull at the spectator's eye level.
The monument to Thomas Theele (d. 1658) at Rye makes no obvious reference
to his Catholic sympathies except perhaps in its quoting of scripture in Latin,[29]
and it is hard to understand how permission was granted for Theele to be
commemorated in the parish church given his and his wife's notoriety in a
town that was famously and intolerantly Protestant in its sympathies. Well into
the 1670s, we continue to find inscriptions with the Latin abbreviation 'OPA'

---

[29]   Matthew 7:8 and ibid., no. 221A.

('*orate pro anime*'), for example, the mural monument for Dame Katherine Courtenay (d. 1672) at Worth.[30]

Alongside such traces of adherence to the old religion, the monuments of seventeenth-century East Sussex are touched by a new emphasis on the didactic, invariably conveyed not by pictorial content but by inscribed text. The Burrells at Cuckfield have one of the most distinguished series of ancestral monuments in the county, with at least fourteen family tombs in the south aisle. One of these illustrates the rule that where an early demise disallowed an emphasis on achievement, stress could be laid on a virtuous life and a good death. The elegant London-made tomb erected for Ninian Burrell (d. 1628) (see Figure 9.15) claims to quote the young lawyer's own death-bed utterances, but there is no glimpse of Burrell's death-bed on his tomb.

Similarly, we read that Elizabeth Parker at Willingdon, at an advanced age and 'in a quiet minde, lifting up her hands to hea[ven] say[d] O lord receave my soul'.[31] This was entirely characteristic of a woman who, we are told, spent with 'great plenty & bountie in hospitallatee, she was wise, temperate, milde and gentell in behaviour, very charitable, pious and devout ... for goodness her life and death deserve perpetuall memorie'. However, both Parker and Burrell are both shown alive, kneeling in prayer within a niche, in his case theatrically revealed by angels.

Women who died young could also have virtues worth emulating. Margaret Jefferay (d. 1620 at Chiddingly) was prudent, pious and beautiful, and Sarah Brabon (d. 1626 at Udimore) was 'pious, prudent, peaceful' and 'praiseful' in the life she led, 'fitting a Sarah and a sacred's wife' (the 'sacred' being her husband John Brabon, the incumbent).[32] The monument to Obedience Nevitt (1619) at Burwash, now on the wall of the inner porch, is almost entirely taken up by the text that tells us that she was a daughter of this parish and: ' ... her name and nature did accord / obedient was shee to her lord' – a Gentleman of London – 'and to his hests shee did attend / with diligence until her end ... '.[33]

By comparison, the exemplary qualities of these women's male counterparts were expressed in homilies about academic attainment and personal belief. John Wythins (d. 1615) is shown in his robes as a fellow of Brasenose and Dean (or incumbent) of Battle but also as the promoter of the traditional sentiments of the memento mori: '*nec mihi vita brevis nec mihi longa fuit*' (see Figure 9.16).[34]

30   Ibid., no. 306P.
31   Ibid., nos 72P and 297F.
32   Ibid., nos 56D and 265F.
33   Ibid., no. 45Q.
34   Ibid., no. 20J.

Figure 9.16   Monumental brass for John Wythins (d. 1615), Battle; © Author.

The author of the physician Thomas Twynne's inscription at Lewes (after 1613) – another brass, though much more modest – was almost certainly his son Brian, a man of advanced antiquarian interests, who concentrates on his father's weighty contribution to medical knowledge and active practice in the locality. Along the same lines, the inscription for James Graves at Eastbourne (d. 1647) lauds his learning and especially his skill as a preacher: '*viri docti, concionatoris eximii ... et hius ecclesisiae olim sacerdotis qui cum concionatorio suo munere.*'[35]

The shift from public statement of public interest to monuments that are personal, esoteric and inward-looking, more concerned with feelings than with public image, is a key dynamic in this essay and parallels the shift from the verbal to the figural. Two clerical monuments are so challenging in terms of comprehension and impact that they operate on the level of personal revelation

---

[35]   Ibid., no. 93JJ; for another learned rector, see George Hall at Berwick, died 1668 (no. 25A).

Figure 9.17   Monument to Guy Carleton, erected after his death in 1628, Cuckfield; © Author.

rather than as public-facing didactic texts. In the north-east chapel at Cuckfield, well away from the Burrell tombs, is a mural monument of a kind virtually unique in Sussex and very rare in England (see Figure 9.17).[36]

Erected in the late 1620s by, or at the request of, George Carleton, Bishop of Chichester, in the church of which his son-in-law was incumbent, its main commemorative subject is the bishop's third son, Guy (1602–28). It comprises a rectangular black marble tablet within an alabaster surround with heraldic escutcheons top and bottom. The tablet acts as an engraved field for inscription, caption and symbolic imagery of a highly emblematic and arcane sort, with symbols of eternity and hope, biblical citations, angels pointing to the correct path, all-seeing eyes and a flaming heart. The prime mover of this mysterious piece must have been the priest at Cuckfield, the appropriately named George Vicar, who was a scholar and who wrote verse,

---

[36]   Ibid., no. 72G.

Figure 9.18   Monument to Richard Randes (d. 1640), Hartfield; © Author.

designed a title-page and published a book written by his protector, the same Bishop Carleton, entitled *The madness of Astrologie.*

The final monument in this group dates from a few years later but once again centres on an inscribed panel; but this time the framing is more eye-catching, more ambitious than at Cuckfield.[37] It was erected for Richard Randes (or Rondes, d. 1640), at Hartfield (see Figure 9.18) and has polished black Corinthian columns flanking an alabaster frame with decorative scrollwork to the sides and above, the whole structure supported on corbels ornamented by a trio of winged cherubs.

Randes held degrees from both ancient English universities. The tomb has no effigy but the lack of subject figuration is compensated for by the astonishing power of the long Latin inscription, strongly moralising, didactic and – quite unusually – remarkably self-deprecating. The monument raises the question of audience and purpose: how many visitors in this remote

---

[37]   Ibid., no. 1231.

Figure 9.19   Monument to Thomas Selwyn and his wife, erected after his death
             in 1614, Friston; © Author.

spot could have grasped its message, how many would even have noticed
it, however striking its frame? Perhaps these issues of human spectatorship
are simply by-the-by, since Randes intended his inscription to address the
Almighty perpetually and directly?

Dynasty Building

The uncertain fate of Richard Randes's soul was more than matched by early-
modern concerns about the fate of dynasties. Many East Sussex monuments
sought to establish and enhance the family's reputation and counter the buffeting
received at the hands of ill judgement, ill fortune and chance. The remedial value
of monuments in the face of chance is suggested by the tomb to Sir John Pelham
(d. 1580) and his son Oliver (d. 1584), which was first erected in London and
later translated to the family's new estate at Stanmer.[38] Dynasties were loyal to
particular burial sites. Well after their seat had moved to Stanmer and despite
the antiquarian gesture of relocating their ancestor there, the Pelhams continued

---

[38]   Ibid., no. 244A.

Figure 9.20 Monument to William Thomas (d. 1639), erected after the death of his wife in 1625, West Dean (near Eastbourne); © Author.

to be buried at Laughton, just as the Coverts were buried at Slaugham. Jane Covert (d. 1587), daughter of John and twice married, was nevertheless buried and commemorated at Slaugham by her nephew and executor William.[39] Under the property laws of patriarchal primogeniture, moments of crises came when the male line was under threat or had expired and, at such points, monuments could be deployed to set up perpetual correctives. At Friston, an isolated place on the chalk cliffs near Beachy Head, the monumental inscription to Thomas Selwyn (d. 1614) and Elizabeth his wife (see Figure 9.19) stresses the antiquity of the Selwyns in the context of the deaths in infancy of their three male children, leaving only their six daughters, three of whom were married at the time the text was written. The three boys are included in the form of chrisom-clad babes but the overall message is clear: the fate of the lineage now lies in the hands of the Selwyns' female offspring.[40]

---

[39] Ibid., no. 234E–F.
[40] Ibid., no. 112B.

At nearby West Dean, two Thomas family tombs are also directed at ancestral continuity but here in the context of a newly established dynasty.[41] The monument to William Thomas himself (d. 1640) was erected after the death of his wife Anne Michelborne in 1625 (see Figure 9.20).

Thomas was from nearby Lewes, where he was a clerk of the peace; he became lord of West Dean in about 1611 but seems to have retained his Lewes connections and residence into the 1630s. Remarkably, the main inscription on the Thomas tomb cites only the six daughters; no mention is made of his male heirs, although the dynasty continued to flourish with the grandson, Sir William Thomas, Bt, becoming lord of Folkington by the end of the century.[42] One of the six daughters commemorated on William Thomas's monument was Susan, who married George Tirrey of Gray's Inn but quickly died (in 1637), a premature loss commemorated in her monument also at West Dean.[43] Old William, who was still alive and was the patron of the church, must surely have been involved in setting this monument up for his daughter – less grand than his own but nevertheless a fine work – and indeed it is his name that appears early in the long Latin inscription, before even that of Susan's husband.

What we find at Ashburnham in the 1670s, and at Withyham – a day's ride to the north-west across the High Weald – is aristocratic patrons starting to commission an entirely new kind of monument, one designed to express feelings as well as to confirm status and lineage, monuments that use life-sized figures, dramatically posed, to communicate emotion. To understand how this came about, we have to take into account the aristocratic culture of the Coverts, Gages and Pelhams that associated the functions and issues of burial and commemoration with the ancient centres of family power and lineage. Dedicated ancient places gave those families status through continuity, ownership and by association with lineage. The remarkable seventeenth-century church at Ashburnham, with its impressive painted reredos, pulpit, gallery, box pews, iron railings and funeral monuments, all of the highest importance, belonged to the household at Ashburnham House, immediately alongside. It was built 1662–65 in a revived 'Perpendicular', a rare and intriguing stylistic choice for the mid-1660s and evidence of an acute awareness of style decorum and commemorative history on the part of the patrons, who clearly directed the makers of both church and monuments with care, precision and urgency. The key figure – the builder of the house and of the church (but not of the

---

[41]　Ibid., no. 280D.

[42]　And, then of Streat, see ibid., no. 250B.

[43]　Ibid., no. 280C.

monuments) – was John Ashburnham (1603–71), Groom of the Bedchamber to Charles I, a courtier with direct access to the royal person. Fined under the Commonwealth, John Ashburnham was restored to prosperity under Charles II.[44]

The Ashburnham family pew offers a direct view of the two monuments that were set up in the north chapel in the early 1670s. After his death in 1671, John Ashburnham's tomb was built against the north wall (see Figure 9.1). It is an enormous construction, 2.67 metres wide, 1.28 metres at its maximum depth and just over 5 metres in height, higher than anything comparable for the Coverts or the Selwyns. The tomb chest alone is 2.52 metres from end to end, demonstrating the more-than-life size of the three recumbent effigies set on its top, carved in white marble, their hands clasped in prayer and their feet oriented to the east in a pose that was already redolent of considerable antiquity when it was employed on this monument. These effigies represent John lying between his two wives, one of them shrouded denoting that she was already long dead.

On the front of the chest are low relief and miniature kneeling representations of John Ashburnham's children, shown as mourners. His four sons kneel opposite their four sisters, the attention of all eight centred on a single prayer-desk. Above and behind the carved figures, on the back wall and carried prominently on polished black columns, is an immensely long monumental inscription engraved on a slate tablet. This text confirms a consistent theme in John Ashburnham's letters, that he was dedicated to the restoration of the estate squandered by his father. Writing to a relative in 1662, John reflected to a cousin that he had the

> ... greatest confidence imaginable that God will deliver most of these lands into my hands, and that I shall return and live there, have the comfort of you and your wife to dwell with me, and lay my bones amongst those of my Ancestors ... It is time for me and my brother to have these thoughts about us ... .[45]

---

[44]   Although the church was rebuilt, the family understood the old and new buildings to create a continuous space (H. Avray Tipping, 'Ashburnham Place, Sussex. A seat of the Earl of Ashburnham ... ', *Country Life* XXXIX, 1916; see also Christopher Hussey, 'Ashburnham of Ashburnham ... ', *Country Life* LXIII (1953): 1158, 1246 and 1334). A later John Ashburnham, created Baron Ashburnham in 1689, referred to the north chapel in the church in 1703 as 'an ancient chapel belonging to my family'. Indeed, extending beneath chancel and both north and south chapels, the first John Ashburnham had constructed a family vault, which by the late nineteenth century was reported as containing forty family coffins.

[45]   Quoted by Hussey, 'Ashburnham of Ashburnham ... ', p. 1159; his father had been buried at St Andrew, Holborn.

Over this text is heraldry in the form of an achievement-of-arms and an arched superstructure with a splendid scrolled pediment in a progressive baroque style unmatched elsewhere on the tomb. The monument has benefited from the continuity of the Ashburnhams at Ashburnham and from the fact that their descendants did not see fit to embark on radical modernisation or fashionable improvements. Everything was simply left more or less as it was.

John Ashburnham (d. 15 June 1671, aged 68), was the first son of the first member of the family to have moved into the centre of national life. The family were in residence from at least the late twelfth century (they were of 'stupendous antiquity', said Thomas Fuller) until 1953, when the succession ran out, the estate was sold and the main block of the great house was demolished. The earlier calamitous situation, addressed at such length in John Ashburnham's inscription, was caused by his father, Sir John (1570/71–1620), who was knighted early in the reign of James I, a man of fashion and a wastrel, who died a debtor in the Fleet Prison. It was young John's task to restore the family fortunes, the achievement referred to by the monumental inscription.

This restoration of fortune took many years, during which time the younger John Ashburnham was himself becoming prominent at court using the influence of his mother's family, not his disgraced father's. She was Elizabeth (1577/78–1651, died aged 75), the daughter of Sir Thomas Beaumont of Staughton, Leicestershire and – more crucially –related to King Charles' favourite George Villiers, Duke of Buckingham. Such was young John Ashburnham's rise that by November 1628 he had been sworn in as a Groom of the Bedchamber, although he seems rarely to have served in that capacity. At about this time he married Frances Holland of Westburton, West Sussex (died aged 37 and shown shrouded on her husband's monument). They quickly started to produce the eight children shown on the tomb.[46]

Through the 1630s, young John exploited his court contacts, built his wealth and influence and, by 1633, was rich enough to petition the crown to regain control of the Ashburnham estate that had had to be mortgaged off under his father. The judicial process took many years. He remained active on behalf of the king through the Civil War period but by 1644, he had had to give up his parliamentary seat (Hastings) and he was imprisoned on New Year's Day, 1648. By that date, the four sons and four daughters who appear as mourners at the foot of his monument had all been born. On the death of his first wife, he swiftly remarried Elizabeth Kenn (1593–1663), widowed in 1649 of Ashburnham's fellow Royalist John Poulett, 1st Baron Poulett, acquiring

---

[46] Eight survived; the exact number of births appears to be unknown.

additional estates through that marriage.[47] Given his links to Charles Stuart, it is unsurprising that John Ashburnham continued to be penalised, imprisoned and fined through the 1650s, although he does not appear to have been too harshly treated under the Commonwealth, which is perhaps why there were persistent rumours that he had betrayed his royal master. Indeed, he was only made a squire at the Stuart Restoration in 1660, although John, by now in his late fifties, did regain his estates with their attendant wealth, in those days a question of industry not agriculture, which was focused on the ore mined locally, the iron-casting process fired by means of the ample local supplies of timber. John Ashburnham became an MP again in 1661, although he was expelled from Parliament in 1667 for accepting bribes from French merchants, and died on 15 June 1671.

The authorship of the John Ashburnham monument is not proven or documented. Both of John's wives were dead before the inscription was written, which produces a *terminus post quem* for that tomb of 1663 (when Elizabeth died); furthermore, we can draw some important conclusions from the tomb's style. First, in its composition and in some details such as Ashburnham's sixteenth-century armour, it parodies a monument of some sixty years earlier, works such as the tomb of the last of the Shurleys considered above, but without the contrasting black-and-white colour scheme. Secondly, the sensibility of the 1670s is just apparent in the fabric-like forms hanging from the circular scroll-ends in the pediment and in the design of the brackets beneath the flanking columns. The great early twentieth-century expert on the subject, Mrs Arundel Esdaile, regarded the John Ashburnham monument as made by Thomas Burman (1619–74), who was trained by Edward Marshall, and was himself the master of the great troubled genius of early English baroque carving, John Bushnell, of whom, more anon.[48]

The second wall monument at Ashburnham stands against the west wall of the north chapel, at right angles to John's tomb and is dedicated to the memory of his brother William and William's wife Jane, Countess of Marlborough. It is dated 1675 and was put up after Jane's burial in 1672. William Ashburnham outlived her by seven years (d. 1679). This second monument looks eastwards directly at the high altar of the church and its scale exceeds even the first Ashburnham tomb at 4.34 metres in width and 5.2 metres in height. The tomb-chest alone is 2.33 metres long. Again, its condition is generally very good

---

[47] Her rank is symbolised by the coronet worn by her effigy.
[48] Margaret Whinney, *Sculpture in England 1530–1830*, 1964, rev. edn by John Physick (Harmondsworth: Penguin, 1988), p. 95.

although there is some damage which possibly may have been done even before it reached the church in the mid-1670s.

On a white marble tomb-chest, topped by a polished black ledger-stone, lies the semi-recumbent effigy of the countess, referred to with that title, though long widowed. To our right kneels William wearing robes and Roman armour and making a gesture of supplication. The monumental backdrop to these figures is dominated by grey marble. Behind and above is a *baldacchino*, topped by an achievement-of-arms. There are more arms on the back wall, being arranged by cherubim, one of whom crowns the countess with an appropriate coronet. On the face of the tomb chest is a monumental inscription in a decorated panel and to left and right, on four pedestals there are trophies and attributes of passing nobility – a coronet, plumed helmet, shield and burnt-out lamp.

Two aspects of this monument illustrate my thesis: the inscription is remarkable for its highly personal tone as are the pose and gestures of the two main figures. The inscription is written in the voice of William himself. It recounts that he and Jane were married for 44 years, without issue, but in a state of ardent affection. Her father was John, Lord Butler and her first husband, for seven years, was James, Earl of Marlborough, Lord High Treasurer. As we have seen, William (1604/5–79), was the second son of Sir John Ashburnham and just two years younger than his brother John, the subject of the first monument. William was a soldier: he fought in the Low Countries and was active on the English-Scottish border in the late 1630s. As did his brother John, William suffered politically and financially during the Commonwealth but was restored to prosperity in the 1660s, pursuing a wide range of commercial interests, including mining and colonial ventures in Africa. He also invested in a London theatre and, in 1671, with his brother, in the revived Mortlake tapestry factory. He died in his 75th year on 9 December 1679.

The baroque design of this work by John Bushnell (1636–1701) has sometimes been condemned as a transgression of decorum.[49] The bereaved husband, in loose classical draping, has climbed on to the sarcophagus to approach the reclining figure of his wife, who is propped up on a pile of day-bed cushions, carried by stray scrolls while a cherub places a wreath of immortality on her head. The carver, Bushnell, is an extraordinary figure. After an apprenticeship in London he travelled abroad, to Rome, Venice (by 1663) and elsewhere. Indeed, the Ashburnham tomb shows the influence of the Venetian

---

[49]   Ibid.; Whinney treats Bushnell sympathetically; for the Ashburnham tomb, see pp. 97–100.

works of the Flemish artist Josse de Corte (1627–79), who sculpted for the most distinguished late seventeenth-century Venetian architects, Sardi and Longhena.[50] Perhaps the supplicant kneeling figure of William Ashburnham is an echo in Bushnell's mind of de Corte's sculpted personification of 'Venetia' at the Salute, which has the Doge's '*corno*' on a cushion nearby her, as with Jane's coronet at Ashburnham.[51] Back in London at the end of the 1660s and flush with his Italian successes, Bushnell set up a practice, became increasingly successful and moved to progressively larger workshop premises. His character was depressive, probably addictive, occasionally demented, eccentric, highly litigious, vain and capricious. Amongst his schemes was a tavern constructed inside a vast Trojan Horse, for Hyde Park Corner; not surprisingly, this project failed dramatically. Bushnell died poor and mad. His William Ashburnham tomb is highly eclectic. It replays the device of the four flanking pedestals, used by Bushnell on his Lord Mordaunt monument at Fulham Church and the heraldry is, generally, in the English manner. But there are also flying cherubs in the Italian and Dutch traditions and an impassioned husband in the French style. The sculpture of the Countess of Marlborough appears to have impressed the Sussex well-to-do: its form is closely followed in the effigy that Lady May had made for herself from Bushnell for use at Mid-Lavant in 1676, described by Dallaway as 'capricious but the portrait exact and the execution good'.[52]

What is remarkable – and here a comparison must be made with the monuments of dynasties such as the Shurleys, Gages and Coverts – is that having overseen his late brother's monument, with its decorous acknowledgement of his heroic role as restorer of the family fortune, William should choose to indulge his sentiments through monumental sculpture of such a different kind. The circumstances of his wife's death were such that after 44 years, we cannot here be dealing just with a broken heart. The inscription on William Ashburnham's monument does make great play of affection and loss and of William's duty to his brother's memory with a strong suggestion that he had already been the one to become the 'happy Preserver of his Brothers Posterity':

[Jane was] a young, beautifull & rich widow/ When this William ... married her, and after / Lived almost five and forty yeares most happily with her; she was a very

---

[50]   K.A. Esdaile, 'John Bushness', *Walpole Society* XV (1927): 21, and idem, 'Additional Notes on Bushnell', *Walpole Society* XXI (1933): 105.

[51]   Andrew Hopkins, *Santa Maria della Salute. Architecture and Ceremony in Baroque Venice* (Cambridge: Cambridge University Press, 2000), pp. 75 ff., figs 35, 39.

[52]   Hussey, 'Ashburnham of Ashburnham ... ', who cites Dallaway; F.G. Aldsworth in *Sussex Archaeological Collections* CXX (1980): 231.

Figure 9.21   Monument to Thomas Sackville, erected after his death in 1675,
Withyham; © Author.

great lover and (through / Gods mercy) a great blessing to this family, which is hoped
will ever remember it with honouring her memory. / This William Ashburnham her
husband lived after her to a great age, & gloried in nothing in this World / But this
his Wife, and the almost unparalleled love and intire friendship that for / Above fifty
yeares was betweene his Deare Elder Brother John Ashburnham and himselfe / He
was ... a happy Preserver of his Brothers Posterity ... .

Never the titular head of the family but regarded by his older brother as
co-responsible for the restoration of the family fortune, when it came to
commemorating his late wife, William was released from formal restraint as a
tomb patron to commission sculpture to express his grief. His lineage was not
the issue, he was not the titular head of the family, which was John Ashburnham's
eldest son and, of course, William had no title of his own, being merely the
consort of the daughter of a baron and the widow of an earl. William's roles
were as the distraught lover and the grateful younger brother. His tomb was
not the stage for a painful rehearsal of the recovery of the family finances: that
performance he had already undertaken in John's monument.

Different and quite extraordinary outpourings of emotion are suggested by a near team-mate of the William Ashburnham monument; this is Cibber's monument, erected at Withyham to mark the loss of a young man described as perfect in every particular and a work checked for quality on behalf of the patron by Peter Lely, the King's Painter[53] (see Figure 9.21).

It is Cibber's monument at Withyham that demonstrates that Bushnell's Ashburnham tomb, although a rare phenomenon, is also part of a trend, albeit modest, but a trend nevertheless. Free-standing, in the centre of the family chapel, a tomb-chest is raised on a plinth and on it reclines the semi-recumbent figure of Thomas Sackville (d. 1675), the thirteenth child and the seventh son of the Earl of Dorset, a work set in train before the earl's own death in 1677 and set up by Cibber in the following year. Thomas contemplates a skull while his mother and father kneel on either side, like parents gazing into a cradle. As the inscription says, their 'drowned eyes' are visible in their sculpted faces, not merely alluded to in the modest incised text. At Withyham, as at Ashburnham, a family chapel has become the site for the public display of private grief and the power of figuration in sculpture has been released from the constraints of text. This is a transformative moment not only for Sussex but in the history of British art.

---

[53]   Llewellyn, *ESCM*, no. 302J, and see Whinney, *Sculpture in England 1530–1830*, p. 112 and plate 72.

Afterword

Not the Last Word: Scraps of History

Duncan Salkeld

An afterword can be many things but never the last word. It is, however, always an opportunity to reflect on the chapters that precede it, and that is pretty much what this one will do. Attention has lately centred on early modern 'material culture' and the various ways in which its people, objects, artefacts and events (together with their conditions, causes, triggers and consequences) interacted in a complex, multiform and changing world.[1] Coinciding with this development has been an archival turn towards re-reading controversies, disputes and competing interests in the period via relatively neglected or unfamiliar documentary sources. This pioneering collection of essays adds to these developments. It builds on the work of former scholarship to develop an incisive study of early modern Sussex. Each chapter recognises the ideological situatedness of historical agents and artefacts caught up in the cross-currents of wider political or religious conflict. Covering a rich array of topics, including records of royal progresses, intense clerical disputes, a cathedral institution, provincial painting, martyrdom, funerary monuments and dispersed books, these essays avoid any tendency towards grand narrative. Varied as they are, one aspect that they share is a self-conscious awareness that they too are not the last word. Others will build on the new ground they have established. Much, of course, will continue to remain hidden. While this volume tells us a great deal that we did not know before about early modern Sussex, it also points up the virtuous constraints of all that we do not (yet) know. Those who follow it up are likely to note its contributors' caution in sifting likelihood from certainty, the plausible from the possible, and the more probable from the less.

These chapters focus on complexities at work in a locality struggling with powerful national and international forces. Those pressures were, of course,

---

[1]   See, for example, Lena Cowen Orlin, ed., *Material London ca.1600* (Pittsburgh: University of Pennsylvania Press, 2000), Tara Hamling and Catherine Richardson, eds, *Everyday Objects: Medieval and Early Modern Material Culture and Its Meanings* (Farnham: Ashgate, 2010), and Catherine Richardson, *Shakespeare and Material Culture* (Oxford and New York: Oxford University Press, 2011).

divided mainly along religious lines – directed either towards stability, or to resistance and change. They show the Reformation's effects on the ground and in process rather than as an abstract series of legislative Acts, edicts and proclamations culled from history books. Roads and by-ways connected market towns to cities, hamlets to villages, hovels to farmhouses, serving quite literally as ingresses and exits for doctrinal commitment and dissent. Ideas, as Philip Howard's prison graffiti in the Tower still shows today, were physically felt. Diocese and parish provided the principal forms of social organisation. Labour was broadly rural, generational and static. Minor local disputes could be settled via the gentry or more formally by local church or assize courts, or the petty sessions. Tensions arising from religious allegiance were deep-rooted and less easily resolved. While several of these chapters highlight that important tension, early modern life in Sussex was also subject to less ideological vicissitudes of disease, disability and family mortality, all of which could displace an inhabitant and force her or him to head for larger towns or cities in search of a living. In the background to these chapters is a sense of people on the move, from Elizabeth I making her stately progresses to Sussex in 1573 and 1591, to contentious figures such as Thomas Drant and Anthony Copley travelling around Sussex, or of books in transit, the library of Bishop Henry King broken up and carted off after Waller's troops took Chichester in 1643.

As Caroline Adams notably points out, not everyone welcomed Queen Elizabeth to England's green and woody provinces. Adams's chapter on Elizabeth's progresses to Sussex in 1573 and 1591 gives fascinating detail regarding where she stayed and the people she met; Nonsuch Palace in Surrey, her starting point, stood 15 miles south-west of Westminster and the Thames, and so within practicable reach of Cowdray, Chichester and Stansted. In Chichester, she seems to have lodged at what later became the 'Royal Arms' or 'Punch House Inn', now an upmarket retail outlet for women's clothing with rentable flats above. Eight years before her visit in 1591, it seems that Henry Percy, 8th Earl of Northumberland at Petworth House, sought to avoid the costs of a proposed royal visit by insisting local roads were so poor and hilly that her royal highness was unlikely to enjoy the journey. A hint of ambiguity seems to hide in his excuse: 'neither can ther be in this cuntrey any wayes devised to avoid those ould wayes.' For years, Northumberland had maintained an uneasy balance of outward loyalty to the crown and private support for Mary Queen of Scots. It was perhaps this allegiance that led to his murder in the Tower in 1585.

Two figures who represent polar opposites of late sixteenth-century religious contention were Thomas Drant and Anthony Copley. Drant was an outsider, brought into Sussex by Bishop Richard Curteys of Chichester to impose conformity in the county. He was educated, a writer practised in Skeltonics and interested in poetics and translation, with well-placed associations in the Sidney-Spenser circle. But he was also cantankerous, a man of rough edges who quickly made enemies, and did not seem to mind it. Writing of his literary endeavours, R.W. McConchie has concluded, 'Drant's contribution as poets began to experiment and seek new forms was significant, and awaits fuller appreciation.'[2] Mat Dimmock and Andrew Hadfield's chapter in this volume goes a good way towards developing that appreciation. It also usefully counterposes the case of Anthony Copley, a recusant Sussex insider, related to Cecil, Walsingham and even the queen. Copley was, like Drant, a writer influenced by Spenser, the allegorical form a seemingly apt vehicle for his latent (and sometimes manifest) Catholic loyalties. What Dimmock and Hadfield show with particular colour is the way Sussex, having a wide coastline open to the Continent and harbouring Catholic families around its towns and villages, became a 'key battleground' for early modern hearts and minds.

In the north and south transepts of Chichester Cathedral, the casual visitor is struck by two enormous panel paintings fixed upon the ancient walls. These are part of the artistic *oeuvre* of Lambert Barnard, painter by appointment to Robert Sherborn, Bishop of Chichester 1508–36. Barnard might have been influenced by continental trends, but he was singular in execution. The south transept painting is perhaps his most remarkable, showing St Wilfrid's petition to Caedwalla for land to build the abbey at Selsey as a prelude to Sherborn's suit to Henry VIII to confirm that gift. The narrative is proleptic, its left-to-right futurity confirmed by portraits of successive English monarchs set in roundels, establishing not only the incumbent Sherborn as St Wilfrid's rightful successor, but also King Henry as a true Saxon heir. Out of this picture stares a figure in a white cap, looking at us – Barnard himself, it seems (Fig. 3.6). What this picture could never say, of course, is that St Wilfrid was a faithful servant of Rome. The panel in the north transept, as Karen Coke explains, presents a series of portrait heads of the bishops of Selsey and Chichester, from Wilfrid to Sherborn. Today, the (overpainted) piece comes across almost as a visual joke. Barnard of course did not know what St Wilfrid or the other bishops looked like, saving Sherborn, so he painted every roundel with pretty much the same face, a visage, so it seems, not unlike the figure in the white cap on the south transept panel. Coke's chapter

---

    [2]   R.W. McConchie, 'Drant, Thomas (*c.*1540–1578)', *Oxford Dictionary of National Biography* (Oxford: Oxford University Press, 2004); online edn, January 2008 <http://www.oxforddnb.com/view/article/8034>.

is richly informative and makes a substantial contribution to our knowledge of the early modern visual arts outside London. It points to a relationship of collaboration between patron and painter, and a recognition that when religious text and meaning were in such controversy, continuities in ecclesiastical history could play an important role. It is perhaps precisely because they did *not* depict biblical scenes that these astonishing works of art survived both the English Reformation and the Civil War.

Lancelot Andrews became Bishop of Chichester just before the Gunpowder Plot in 1605, serving for four years, before moving on to Ely, and then Winchester. In his will of 1626, he left over a thousand pounds to his old university, Pembroke Hall at Cambridge, plus a silver cup he had commissioned in imitation of that owned by the college's founder, Marie de St Pol. Amid several other bequests, he left a fairly modest sum of ten pounds 'to the poore of Chichester'. The will makes abundantly clear that, in later life, the 'Master, fellowes and Schollers and theire successors' of Pembroke were closest to Andrews's heart.[3] As the appendix to Andrew Foster's absorbing chapter shows, virtually all the ecclesisasts associated with Chichester Cathedral were alumni of Oxford or Cambridge. In effect, the cathedral served as a hub for a continually regenerating intellectual network. Foster shows that Chichester retained a substantial number of clergy, possibly the sixth largest in England, several of whom had links to the lawyers' colleges and communities in London. Unconnected to the cathedral, a number of the Sussex yeomanry, or upper 'middling sort', found their way into these communities via entry to the inns of court. Andrews himself was a member of Gray's Inn, as were Thomas Walwyn of Arundel, Samuel Virgo of Chichester, William Newton of Lewes, Edward Burton of Bourne, Anthony Fowle of Rotherfield, Herbert Pelham of Michelham, Henry Brown of Cowdray (son of Viscount Montagu), Ralph Cooper of Slinfold and Oliver Cheney of Walberton.[4] Foster's distinctive and probing chapter comes close to taking us inside the workings of an early modern institution, one that was well-positioned to sustain cultural and intellectual activity in the region.

Paul Quinn centres attention on the so-called Sussex Protestant martyrs who went to the stake at Lewes late in the reign of Mary Tudor. Quinn argues that John Foxe, whose *Acts and Monuments* (1563) so shaped the later puritan outlook, tidied up serious dissensions that simmered between Sussex Protestants, smoothing over convictions that divided Predestinarians from

---

[3]   The National Archive (TNA) PROB 11/150/49.

[4]   See Joseph Foster, *The Register of Admissions to Gray's Inn 1521–1889* (London: Hansard, 1889).

others who might broadly be described as Free Willers. Quinn's focus on the case of Richard Woodman points to a more nuanced religious position than one might expect. Woodman accepted Protestant doctrine regarding the Trinity or the pope as Anti-Christ, but endorsed infant baptism even if that baptism had been performed by 'papisticall mynisters ... not withstanding that ye minister be a popish heretyke'. His particular brand of faith, broadly Edwardian, emerged out of the 'inter-Protestant rivalry' that fuelled disputes about Reformed ideas among dissenter prisoners in the King's Bench. Quinn's thought-provoking chapter on pluralism and faction among English Protestant communities finely complements that by Michael Questier a little later in the volume.

Mary Arundel is perhaps better known as Mary Howard, daughter of the twelfth Earl of Arundel, younger sister of the writer Jane Lumley, and mother of Philip Howard, who died so miserably in the Tower in 1595. She excelled at languages and produced four impressive collections of *sententiae*, translated into Latin from Greek and English sources. As Elizabeth McCutcheon lucidly explains, the garnering of aphoristic and proverbial phrases was a popular mode of learning in the mid-sixteenth century, a product of the Erasmian injunction to foster 'copiousness', or richness in note-taking and recorded observation. Mary Arundel's literary productions illustrate the importance and value women attached to their own education at the time, and their willingness to participate in what was predominantly a male world of letters. McCutcheon's detailed chapter demonstrates that her manuscripts were not merely notebooks for jottings and miscellanea. They evidence focused study of serious works, including Thomas Elyot's *The Image of Governance* (1541), which engaged with matters of politics, ethics and action. Mary Arundel clearly saw the relevance of this work to her family's own position: she signalled in a dedicatory letter to her father that the story of Alexander Severus pointed up a number of pitfalls facing those in authority. We gain an impression of an explorative, inquisitive, sensible and learned mind, a woman whose preference for terse, firmly stated, epigrammatic thought is evident in her method of rationally organising material according to antithetical categories. Yet perhaps the most remarkable aspect of this literary woman's story is that at her death in 1557, she was only 16.

While McCutcheon explores the writerly interests within a major Sussex Catholic family, Michael Questier turns his attention to the community to which they belonged, and finds a good deal of 'bitching', 'dissing' and 'bust-up' going on; indeed, 'enough to send many people up the wall'. This lively chapter brings Questier's expertise to bear on tensions among the Catholic clergy of Sussex, after they were forced (in 1625) to accept the jurisdiction of a Roman bishop, Richard Smith, in all matters of conduct and dispute, including marital breaches of contract. Catholic clergy were now compelled to seek and accept Smith's 'approbation' in order to continue in their benefices. The acrimony arising from this imposition points up a number of fault-lines for religious controversy in the period. It seems that Romanist elements saw in James's foreign policy the opportunity of regulating a parallel Church within England alongside the Anglican conformity. But this project was frustrated by intense rancour generated by arguments over clerical authority and a priest's right to carry out sacramental duties. Questier points out that Smith had powerful backers, not just in Rome but also in England, especially in his patron Anthony Brown, Viscount Montague of Cowdray. But despite this, bitter resentment expressed by some led to the extraordinary irony of 'regulars' regarding Smith and his ilk, by implication the pope himself, as 'Anti-Christ'. What this eye-opening chapter illustrates is a rare view of recusant allegiances from the inside. Quinn pointed to divided conviction among Protestants. It turns out, Questier maintains, that English Catholicism in the seventeenth century was a good deal more fractious and less separatist than has hitherto been acknowledged.

Walk into any of the larger English churches of the sixteenth and seventeenth centuries and you are likely to encounter tombs with sculpted effigies resting silently upon them, devout hands clasped or crossed. Funerals could be elaborate events, involving processions, bell-ringing, specially appointed prayers, and the release of money or bread to the poor and needy. Nigel Llewellyn reads the designs, images and texts on funerary monuments in Sussex as pointing up a shift in signification, in the later seventeenth century, from the verbal or static to the imagistic or expressive. Texts on sixteenth-century tombs tended to highlight local networks of intermarriage and family loyalty. And, as Llewellyn points out, under Elizabeth, the question of loyalty permeated every aspect of English life, including its ending. Llewellyn's reading of funerary monuments brings out evocations of grief such as that instanced by the memorial to Jane, Countess of Marlborough, dated 1675. Its sculptor, John Bushnell, depicts the bereaved husband climbing upon her sarcophagus, a display that figures him in a performative role he preferred others to remember. Reading this chapter, one is inevitably reminded of Larkin's poem 'An Arundel Tomb'. The poem studies a tomb with effigies in Chichester Cathedral where an earl and countess lie beside each other frozen in stone, timeless, and hand-in-hand. Larkin observes that after all 'the lengths and breadths of time', their monument has faded to just a 'scrap of history', for 'only an attitude remains'. This attitude, for Larkin, would seem to 'prove true' our 'almost-instinct' that what will only 'survive of us is love'.

Foster's comments on Chichester Cathedral's library link usefully to work in this volume by Daniel Starza Smith, who presents new manuscript evidence about where Bishop Henry King acquired his books, who else owned or read them, and where they ended up after the 1642 siege of Chichester. King's collection seems to have numbered over a thousand books, including the popular *De incertitudine et vanitate* by Agrippa, but also rarer works by Erasmus and Vives. Some of his books had been owned by John Donne, a friend of King's. We do not know exactly why Waller set about ransacking the cathedral library, but it seems the books were sold off in London to raise money. Samuel Harsnett, Bishop of Chichester 1609–19, gave instruction in his will for his own books: 'I give to the Bayleffes & Incorporacon of the Towne of Colchester all my Librarie of Bookes Provided that they provide a decent Rowme to sett them up in that the Clergie of the Towne of Colchester & other divines may have free accesse for the readinge & studdyenge of them.'[5] Perhaps King might have made a similar bequest to Chichester, had history been kinder to him and his collection.

In sum, these chapters share a willingness to read early modern culture via archaeological, documentary and manuscript sources. What sets them apart from a Rankean quest after history as it 'really happened', is their acknowledgement of all those lacunae that open up possibilities but also narrow explanation. Historical analysis often comes down to a matter of weighing up and piecing together fragments, and then weighing them up again. The question for literary historians is not so much 'what matters?' but 'how and why do some things come to matter more than others?' Charles Taylor has shown that the concept of mattering itself is defined most starkly by the weight (or 'characterization') of reasons, motives, desires and value on either side of a difficult choice.[6] These chapters show in detail how the things that mattered in early modern Sussex connected with their wider material and spiritual culture. While it seems that many early modern lives were often little more than leaves blown in the wind, driven by contingency and chance, we know too that, politically, the dice were loaded. For all that history is shaped by accident, it is clear that religion was not the only force that divided early modern individuals and communities. Gendered forms of social prejudice and presumption also governed day-to-

---

5　TNA PROB 11/160/25.
6　Charles Taylor, *Human Agency and Language: Philosophical Papers*, Vol. 1 (Cambridge and New York: Cambridge University Press, 1984), pp. 34–5.

day economics, separating the advantaged from the disadvantaged. We might consider in this respect the little we know of two women who were also on the move, in transit between London and Chichester. Jane Fletcher was arrested in September 1601 for having been a single woman with child. At her hearing, she explained she had been residing with a Master King at a tavern in Lambeth, where she slept with 'one Captain Hayes' of Clerkenwell. Hayes would visit her twice a week, but only until he discovered she was pregnant. Thereafter, she was thrown out and found refuge in Westminster. A chamberlain at the inn seems to have arranged for her to give birth at a house in Southwark. He also secured her some small provision from Hayes, who finally paid her off with 'xxx^s'. Her child, she later learned, was dead, buried at St George's, Southwark. A man named 'Hall', her 'cuntryman', sent her down by carrier to Chichester, but, learning she had once been with child, he denounced her as a whore and had her turned out of her lodgings once more. The thirty shillings Hayes gave her she had spent 'in her sicknes since she was delivered of her childe'.[7] Two months later, Joan Birde, originally of Chichester, found herself in court explaining that she had come up from the country to seek 'service'. She ended up 'by chaunce' at Gracious Street, perhaps at the 'Bell' or 'Cross Keys' inns, and made enquiries but subsequently got lost while looking for lodging in Southwark. Stopping near a cook's shop, she encountered one Stephen Nicholas, a 'Frenchman', who offered her a room in his rents. He took her up 'three paier of staires' and locked her in, taking the key. Waiting till she was abed, he returned and raped her. The commotion brought up the master and mistress of the house who urgently called the watch. In the fray, Nicholas also stole her purse.[8] But there the narrative ends. We know no more about these women, nothing further of their prosecution or detention, or what happened to them afterwards. What we do learn is that a locality may serve as home only for a while, that privation might displace individuals into a traumatic future where they are vulnerable to chance encounters, hardship and exploitation. Following Larkin, we might say that these 'scraps of history' do indeed speak of 'instinct', and leave us with 'an attitude', but hardly one of love. What we do not know about any of these lives or events for now remains as a kind of after-impression, a silent imprint, an 'almost-instinct', a room for further guesses which future words, we must hope, will realise into something more.

---

[7]   Bridewell Court Minute Book (BCB), 4.258v.
[8]   Ibid., 4.278r.

Index

For Product Safety Concerns and Information please contact our EU
representative GPSR@taylorandfrancis.com
Taylor & Francis Verlag GmbH, Kaufingerstraße 24, 80331 München, Germany

www.ingramcontent.com/pod-product-compliance
Ingram Content Group UK Ltd.
Pitfield, Milton Keynes, MK11 3LW, UK
UKHW021619240425
457818UK00018B/636